UNDERBELLY

HOOPS

ADVENTURES IN THE CBA
A.K.A THE CRAZY BASKETBALL ASSOCIATION

CARSON CUNNINGHAM

Diversion Books
A Division of Diversion Publishing Corp.
80 Fifth Avenue, Suite 1101
New York, New York 10011
www.DiversionBooks.com

First Diversion Books edition January 2012.

ISBN: 978-1-938120-00-8

1 3 5 7 9 10 8 6 4 2

ACKNOWLEDGMENTS

To my wife Christy and our three children, Caroline, Case, and Catie Joy, thank you for the love and inspiration, the space to write and the tightness of home. Gratitude also goes out to Scott Waxman, Mary Cummings, and Diversion Books, for giving *Underbelly Hoops* a shot. And a big thank you to editor extraordinaire Eric "Superman" Furman. Your great childhood buddy agrees to edit *Underbelly Hoops*? Now that's buckets.

There are others who helped with this project, like Jeff Riggs, Beth Ina, and Marshall Phillips, Justin Smith, Carlito Labarda and Kip Meyer, and Randy Roberts, John Schulian, and Elliott Gorn. Thank you to all.

1

It was midmorning on day three of training camp and the Rockford Lightning's two point guard slots were still up for grabs. Practice would start in a few minutes, but first, Lightning head man Chris "Dales" Daleo, with his steely eyes, slicked-back graying hair, and slightly hunched-over shoulders wanted to offer us advice on how to survive the looming cuts. He called us to half-court, and we stood around the center circle. You could tell he was all jacked up. He tended to get excited before starting in on one of his speeches.

"First of all, have a clear head and listen to what is going on. If you're staying up all night trying to get laid and putting that wacky shit in your lungs, when you come out here it shows. Get the THC or whatever out of your system. I don't have time for that shit. I don't have time...there's no time, fuck," he said. "It's easy in Rockford. Shit, man, you don't even have to learn any plays. We have three plays. Three. All these coaches run these sets: x here, y there, z there. You stand there and watch the other guys do a pick-and-roll, fuck that. Here, I give you a chance. You want to score? Get a steal and score, go to the rack, make something happen! Fuck. I get coaches telling me, 'Oh shit, don't hire that guy, he can't remember a play. We have twelve plays and he can only remember half of them.' I don't give a fuck. Can he score? If I find out he can score, then fine, bring him in. He can't learn plays? I don't give a fuck.

"On defense, we're pressing and running the entire game, we're taking chances. You get burned gambling on a steal, fuck, I got no beefs. You get scored on for being passive, not stepping up, shit, then we've got a problem. It's organized chaos, man. We're taking teams out of their shit." He turned to address Renaldo Thomas, one of his assistant coaches. "Coach Thomas, how many plays did you guys have in your playbook in Gary? I mean, shit, there were tons of 'em."

"Oh man, yeah, we had a lot of plays," Thomas said, referring to an earlier stint with the Gary Steelheads.

Continuing, Dales asserted: "They learn all those plays, but against us, that shit goes out the window. We're running around trapping all over the place. They can't call all these ridiculous plays where this guy stands here, that guy there, and then this guy takes his time getting the ball to a teammate. Fuck that. We want to take them out of their shit, organized chaos, man. And then they must prepare for that, and that way we take them out of their shit further. Do you see?"

As goofy as it sounded, much of it rang true. Two years prior, for thirty-two games during the 2002-03 season, I'd started at point guard for Dales—the only white starting point guard in the CBA, at least for a little while. We went 22-10 in that stretch, and with a motley group of guys, many of whom had been given up on before. Before I got canned, we'd stood comfortably atop the standings, despite running just three, ridiculously simple plays. The main one was called "whirl." It consisted of one forward standing on one low block and the other forward standing on the other low block, while the guards carried out a dribble weave. That's it. We watched no tape. In fact, we did virtually no scouting of opponents of any kind. And on defense we trapped all over the court. Most basketball aficionados would tell you that none of it would work on the professional level, yet in averaging right around 130 points per game that season, the Lightning scored more on average than any professional team in North America and made the playoffs. Dales won the Continental Basketball Association (CBA) Coach of the Year award, his first season manning a professional sideline.

But I didn't get to experience the CBA playoffs that year because I'd had it out with Dales in a locker room in Grand Rapids thirty-two games in. That's how I ended up taking a Greyhound to Chicago and sleeping in a bus terminal, before making it back to Rockford, Illinois. There I got my stuff and then moved in with my parents in Indiana, before heading off for a gig in Estonia.

But in 2004 I was back at it, trying to play for Dales in the CBA. There were about eighteen of us vying for ten roster spots. Really, though, about five players arrived at camp as virtual locks to make the squad. The rest of us faced a high level of uncertainty. We'd either have a job in ten days or not.

2

In part, my return to the CBA can be viewed as an indictment of regular office jobs. I had spent part of the previous year trying to function in the normal working world, and it felt stifling. I missed the raw competition and the physicality of playing high-level hoops. It helped me feel alive, which I suppose you could consider an indictment of myself.

That year without basketball marked my first in about twenty years. I'd gone into the season with high hopes that I'd sign on with some squad, but when no legitimate contract offers rolled in, the involuntary retirement had resulted. And it was in the fall of that involuntary retirement that the actual job with a desk and benefits and regular hours came.

The idea of researching oil and pipeline companies had seemed interesting enough initially, but early on, maybe a few weeks in, sinking feelings engulfed me as I gazed around at people sitting in cubicles or watched folks eating small chocolates at the printer, talking about the new way they'd configured their desks or the arrival of new office supplies or some other mind-numbing thing. That type of stuff can just wallop you, if you let it.

Soon, I'd resolved to finish my basketball career on my own terms by playing one final season and going for a championship. Channeling the Alfred, Lord Tennyson from within, *Strong in will,* eager *To strive, to seek, to find, and not to yield,* I decided to seek a CBA title.

That was a key part of the argument I made to myself: winning a championship. I hadn't done so since sixth grade. When I was a senior playing at Andrean High School in Indiana, our team was ranked second in all of Hoosierland and our state championship hopes had been high, but in the first round of the Indiana state tournament—back when Hoosier Hysteria had no class divisions—

we lost to the ninth-ranked Gary West Side Cougars. On my college team at Purdue, when I was a junior point guard playing for the Hall of Fame coach, hair icon, and feisty Irishman Gene Keady, we came within a game of the Big Ten championship only to lose to our bitter rival Indiana in the final game of the regular season.

A few weeks after that loss, we sat in Albuquerque one game away from the Final Four, which was scheduled to be played in our home state's capital, Indianapolis. The one thing standing between us and the opportunity to cap decades devoted to hoops was the Wisconsin Badgers. In the second half of the game, we found ourselves tied with four minutes to go, and we could practically taste the victory. A win would not only crown Coach Keady's career, but would frame the college careers of the entire Boilermaker roster.

Take Jaraan Cornell, an Indiana legend who had helped his high school team win a state championship with a gargantuan three, and as a sophomore at Purdue, had ranked among the nation's deadliest three-point shooters before suffering a terrible ankle injury that not only ended that season but hurt his professional future. Could he help take us to the title as a senior and thereby make his legend stand up to the likes of Steve Alford and Rick Mount? Or consider walk-on Chad Kerkhof, an engineering whiz with a crooked jumper, who somehow didn't miss a shot in our first three games as we danced to the Elite Eight. Could his sheer grit help us get to the Final Four?

And there I was: a 1997 *Sporting News* All-American freshman out of Oregon State and former runner-up for PAC-10 freshman of the year to Mike Bibby, who—having let the losing and general lack of team maturity at Oregon State wear on me—had transferred to Purdue. Would the questions about why I'd transferred stop if we made it to the Final Four? Would folks stop wondering—would I stop wondering—if I'd cost myself a shot at the NBA by going to play for an old-school coach in the Big Ten rather than continuing to put up big numbers at Oregon State?

When I'd decided to transfer, I'd done so fully aware that the Final Four would be in Indianapolis in 2000. I thought that perhaps I could get there with the fellows at Purdue. And now we were in Albuquerque a game away. Only, as awesome as Purdue had been and as exciting as the prospect of getting to a Final Four in my home state was, I still didn't like the idea of having transferred. In fact, in the summer of 1997, a couple of months after having announced my decision to do so, I'd called Oregon State back to tell the coach that I'd had a change of heart. I felt like our young team at Oregon State could pull it together. Plus, Corvallis was chock full of good people, and it seemed like the whole state of Oregon had been cheering for me when I'd played there. But the coach had already signed another guard. Weeks earlier he'd tried to talk me into staying, and now he was telling me there were no more scholarships.

I thought about it for a day or two and called him again. I told him it didn't matter if there weren't any scholarships, I'd like to finish what we'd started anyway by walking-on to the team—the same team whose players had voted me as MVP. As nicely as he could, though, he told me that that ship had sailed. He probably figured that the standout point guard from Los Angeles that they'd signed to replace me would fit in better with Corey Benjamin, the other ballyhooed freshman during my one season in Corvallis and an eventual first-round pick of the Chicago Bulls.

But that wasn't worth dwelling on in Albuquerque in 2000 when a few short minutes separated the Boilermakers from seashells and balloons: a trip to the Final Four in our home state. And in those few minutes we all had opportunities. Future NBA-veteran Brian Cardinal threw me a great pass out of a double for a fifteen-footer at the elbow that I'd hit thousands of times. It felt good but it was just off. A missed free throw here, a missed jumper there, a tough make by the Badgers, and boom it was over. We lost by four. Near sports nirvana turned to crushing defeat that quickly.

I'd missed out on championships as a pro as well. During my first CBA season, with the Gary Steelheads in 2001-02, I languished on the bench even though we were bad. The following year I'd started on that strong, high-scoring Lightning team. At 22-10 it looked like we might very well have a shot. But then Dales and I had it out in Grand Rapids. That Lightning squad, led by former McDonald's All-Americans Ronnie Fields and Albert White, ended up losing in the CBA Finals.

I'd also played on two other continents—Australia and Europe (in Estonia)—but no title had resulted in either.

Basketball had taken me many places. I had hit a lefty scoop on the Wizard of Westwood's home floor and thrown an alley-oop in Madison Square Garden to Gary McQuay, a childhood friend and college roommate who later succumbed to leukemia. I'd helped the

Boilermakers beat Bobby Knight in Assembly Hall, Billy Donovan's Gators in Maui, and Izzo's Spartans in Mackey Arena.

Basketball had taken me to even greater places than these. For years, if I was down, basketball had been there to bring me back up. If I was lonely, it would make me feel less so, and when I was with friends, it gave us something to do for hours on end. We would play all types of games: five-on-five, twenty-one, three-two-one, dunk-off, Chicago, one-on-one, seasons, three-on-three. We'd travel the neighborhood on long summer days and play on the different types of baskets that Indiana towns seem to grow, whether it was a short hoop or a high hoop, a soft rim or a tight rim, it didn't matter. Shoot, at one park in my hometown of Ogden Dunes there was even a skinny rim.

Growing up with loving and hard-working parents, neither of whom played any high school sports, I caught the basketball fire as a kindergartner that has lit many a native Hoosier. Some kindergartners show up to school knowing how to read. I knew Georgetown's starting five. I'd try to do the moves that my older brother Kirk could do, and I'd watch college games with my dad, who loved sports even if he hadn't played them in high school.

Watching on television as a youngster, I was inspired not by Steve Alford or Bob Knight, but by the exploits of Gary McLain and Dwayne McCain of Villanova, Reggie Williams and Michael Jackson of Georgetown, and later, the great Sherman Douglas of Syracuse. Douglas spoke to me: the smoothness, the quickness and creativity, the alley-oop to Derrick Coleman.

The precision and fundamentals of the traditional Indiana game didn't interest me as much as the rhythms of the improvisational game, which was very much alive and well in Indiana too, if you sought it out. The innovation, spontaneity, and speed of players like Douglas, that's where the game thrived in my mind.

In 1987, as a ten-year old, I attended Indiana Assistant Coach Dan Dakich's day camp, a couple of months after the Hoosiers had beaten my beloved Orangemen for the national championship. Keith Smart, fresh off of his memorable championship-clinching baseline jumper, visited one day as a guest speaker. He spoke to us about what it took to make it to the top. Nervously I raised my hand. He called on me.

"How often do you have to practice to make it?"

"Everyday," he said.

I took him at his word. Told myself right then that I'd play every day. And I did. For the next twelve years I played at least an hour a day, and usually it was much longer than that. (I might've missed four days of hoops over those twelve years. One because of a nasty concussion, and it gnawed at me to miss a day even then).

If everyone in my family would be piling into the mini-van in the morning for a family vacation bound for Florida, facing a full day of driving, I'd need to know in advance when exactly we would depart. If my parents said 6:00 a.m., then I'd set the alarm for 4:30 to make sure I could get an hour of hooping in before hitting the road. In middle school, for extra work during the season—since practice and games didn't really count toward that hour-a-day—I'd get up early before school to shovel the basketball court on the side of my house and get some shots in. This wasn't work as much as it was simply what you did if you wanted to get good. It's how you learned things that you knew only true hoopers knew. Like that it helped to have two basketballs for your work-outs when you were deep into winter. One to play with, and one to leave in the laundry room, so that when the one you were playing with stopped bouncing well, you could trade it for the warm one inside.

And it wasn't work when, at the age of fourteen, I played hour after hour, day after day with my right hand in my pocket because a small part of my right elbow bone and accompanying cartilage had died from a lack of blood flow—thanks to throwing junk balls in Little League. It took eight months to get the elbow right because a string of doctors couldn't figure out what the problem was, and when one did determine the problem, it meant surgery. But waiting wasn't too much trouble because I had two arms. And who knew, maybe when I got to the PAC-10, they'd write articles about how I appeared to be ambidextrous.

It was sweet to see how much more dynamic my game could be with a high-functioning left-hand. By the end of that year, I could finish around the bucket with the left just as easily as with my right, perhaps more so. It was the type of thing that made you think, even though it was twisted and you didn't really believe it, that every serious player, at some time in their childhood, should break their strong arm .

When the basketball flow was real good, it could produce rhythms within my body that are hard to express, but seemed to relate to the very sense of being. I would feel a part of the ball, and the ball would seem in tune with the rim. Airborne and in traffic, facing away from the rim, I'd feel—deep within my bones—that the ball had a chance, if only I could somehow help it navigate a tight, yet circuitous route: gently loop around the defenders' outstretched hands, rise up to the backboard for an ever-so-slight kiss—with just the right amount of velocity and spin—and then on its way back down - voila, twinkle the twine. If so, two points would be mine, and better yet, so too would several moments of complete peace, of feeling as if—no matter what Yeats said—the center could hold.

At a young age in Indiana, you were liable to learn that these types of feelings could also be conjured with your teammates. It was heart-thumping to beat a team no one thought you could, and all because you'd moved the ball crisply, handled it niftily, and shot it well. When you didn't have the rock, you'd cut and screened. Tough, end-of-season wins were especially invigorating, something to be cherished, a motivator during the summer when you sharpened your game before starting the cycle all over again.

The ebb and flow of a basketball season, in fact, is woven into many a native Indianans' annual rhythms. It works well in Indiana to structure your days around basketball: work on your game with buddies outdoors in the summer and then in the winter live and die with your teammates through every game of the season, barely aware of the bitter cold, ever-hopeful that spring and the tournament—at your local Y or grade school—will usher in sunny days and a championship.

It was captivating to work on tough dribble moves—crosses, hesitations, double changes of direction—on elusiveness and illusion, on trick-shots. Honing my game could keep me on the court into the late hours of night and the early hours of morning. Policemen would receive calls about a kid on a public park in the rain at a ridiculous hour and they knew right away. My mom would encourage me not to let basketball define me, to think about pursuing other things with a similar passion, but I didn't listen very well to that.

Thank goodness she routinely forced me to read. This, I'm convinced, was what helped me earn strong enough marks in college, when I finally became a more focused student, to earn Academic All-American honors twice. And it helped me, in my first year out of college—in between Gary Steelhead practices and games—to start the coursework needed to earn a Ph.D. in history from Purdue.

But my passion for reading, or anything else for that matter, wasn't enough to get my appetite for high-level hoops out my system. In 2004, I felt like I needed to give it yet another go. Returning to the hardwood for the 2004-05 campaign would give me a final shot at a championship, and then I could walk away content. At least that's what I told myself.

All I needed was a team. I was hoping that my agent could find a solid gig even though he hadn't exactly been delivering, when, not long after I made my resolution to go out on top, Daleo called me. This was a bit surprising considering the way our last stint together had ended. He wanted to know if I had any interest in coaching in the CBA. I didn't know whether to take that as a compliment or not, seeing as how he'd treated our assistant during my first season playing for him. Plus, coaching wasn't on my mind as much as playing was. So instead, I told him about my interest in coming back to play. Happily, he sounded at least mildly receptive—or at least not too shocked—and he invited me to camp.

Why the CBA constituted my only option I do not know. Maybe my agent didn't know what he was doing. Maybe I wasn't that good. I can tell you there were guys playing all over Europe and the rest of the world who could not make a CBA team, and yet many of those guys got better offers overseas than I did. Sure, since most international leagues had quotas limiting their teams to two Americans, the bulk of international teams preferred to sign big Americans. But plenty of little guys get decent jobs abroad—I just didn't happen to be one of them. Ultimately, I didn't have to worry about that anymore, now that I'd heard from Daleo. He was giving me an opportunity and I was glad to take it.

After his call, my blood felt like it flowed a little more smoothly. For a while, a little while at least, the blows to my psyche that had come during my first couple CBA stints receded into the background. The paltry pay, including the five-dollar bonus I once received, did not matter, or the lack of job security, or the fact that Daleo made life miserable for people. Even the fact that the city of Rockford isn't exactly a destination point for young adults was of no real concern. And it didn't matter that not too many people really knew what the CBA was, let alone cared who won the CBA championship in any given year. For me, just playing and going out on my own terms mattered.

And who knows? Maybe I can ride this chance to a solid European contract, or even to the NBA.

3

It was on August 27, 2004 that I signed a contract with the Rockford Lightning to undertake what became my third and final season in the CBA. Seeing as I'd played for the Gary Steelheads in 2001-02 and then for the Lightning in 2002-03, this third signing marked a day to celebrate—and to rue. On one hand, of course, it meant that I could pursue my mission. On the other, it meant that I was teetering on the brink of a Crash Davis-like existence: becoming a CBA lifer.

The signing took place in front of a few local members of the media at the new Pepsi distributorship in Rockford—Pepsi counted as one of the Lightning's sponsors. Daleo loved to call these "press conferences." He arranged them all the time, virtually for anything. For this one, Rockford's local NBC, CBS, and ABC affiliates attended, and sure enough, a few hours later I showed up on Rockford's local news as the squad's first signing for the upcoming season. Apparently, it was a slow news day. "I'm excited to be back playing for Rockford. I'm looking forward to getting back to playing like we did during the 2002-03 season when we were the highest scoring professional team in North America," I said.

Later that evening I threw out the first pitch at the Rockford Riverhawks minor league baseball game. The Riverhawks played in the independent Frontier League, which is pretty low on the minor league baseball rung, or so I hear. It was all part of the hype surrounding my return.

Before that first pitch, the PA guy announced my name and I walked to the mound amid a smattering of cheers. As I stood on the hump, I paused for a moment to take in how cool it felt to be back. I hadn't played pro ball in over a year—my last stint having been in Tallin, Estonia—but now I was throwing out the first pitch at a Riverhawks game. I didn't know what the Frontier League was, but I was throwing out the first pitch and people were cheering.

My enthusiasm, though, was marred by self-reflection. On that mound, the insanity of playing in the CBA came back to me in a wave: the ridiculous road trips, the irrationality, the uncertainty. *What are you doing? People will cheer for anything if the conditions are right.*

The day before I took the mound, Dales and I had finalized the details of my contract. He tried to sign me for the same amount I'd gotten in 2002, $400 per week, but, hoping my veteran status would provide some leverage, I asked for $500. I realize the difference might sound immaterial, but you must understand that Daleo was remarkably cheap even by CBA standards. Not only were the odds of me getting a raise very low, but the mere act of asking for it carried some risk because Dales didn't take kindly to that type of thing.

Now, to be fair, the CBA demanded thriftiness since so many of its teams lost money, the Rockford Lightning in particular. During Daleo's tenure, Rockford lost roughly $400,000 a year. (Most of the Lightning budget went to a bad lease deal with the downtown MetroCentre, where the team played, and another sizable chunk went to worker's compensation insurance. Players' salaries cost about $120,000. Total team overhead amounted to approximately $800,000 to $900,000, compared with an estimated $500,000 in revenue).[1]

Yet despite these stark financial realities, Dales agreed to split the difference. I signed for $450 per week. (By comparison, the guy I lost to for PAC-10 Freshman of the Year, Mike Bibby, made $11.5 million that year.)

A little chagrinned that he had to come up with an extra $50 per check, Daleo declared it "the first time in history a player got a raise in the CBA after being fired."

Despite the raise, the TV interview, and the first pitch, my contract meant nothing. The union-less CBA guaranteed no contracts. Because of this, teams could afford to sign a bunch of people for training camp and then keep only ten for the regular season, without worrying about compensating those who got cut. Your contract kicked in only if you survived, and even then there were no guarantees. If you didn't produce, you could get sent home immediately—no two weeks' notice. Sustaining an injury that would require more than a brief time for recovery would very likely lead to an unceremonious axing, or a spot on the injured reserve (which some players actually considered fortunate, as opposed to getting fired, because getting put on the IR meant you could collect workers' compensation checks).

Within this ultra-competitive environment, the turnover rate could astound. It got weird. For instance, for the few of us who remained all year during the 2001-02 Gary Steelheads' season, during which the team went through some forty players, it began to seem a little frivolous to introduce ourselves to newcomers until they'd been around for more than a week or so.

Unpredictable as the situation was, there was something attractive about the relentless competition. The CBA was a tough place, but a place where merit-based performance in real time mattered and little else. That can be mighty invigorating.

Of course, with so much turnover, getting cut didn't mean you were a bum. Even people who would later standout in the NBA, such as Stephen Jackson and Earl Boykins, have been cut by CBA teams. And putting up good numbers didn't always help your cause either. Daleo used to tell us: "I don't care about your stats or your 'rep,' or any other bullshit. I'll cut your ass. If you don't fit well, or you don't listen, I'll cut your ass. Look at Quincy Wadley, leading the league in scoring, cut by the Dales. He was leading the league in scoring. It doesn't matter."

Yet if you could survive, you got great runs with some of the best basketball players in the world—some of whom, if not for a mistake earlier in life or a tough break, would've been in the NBA.

And when I say great runs, I mean great runs. As much as I might not have guessed it coming out of Purdue, the CBA offered more talent than major NCAA conferences. Plus it had experienced veterans. I learned quickly that professional players go hard—no matter what people might think. A professional game might not look as frenetic as a college game, but that's largely because it's hard to frazzle professionals. In the CBA, if you over-committed on defense, you got taken to the rack. If you over-helped or doubled ineffectively, offensive players didn't respond frantically. They'd been there before. And so, more often than not, they made an efficient pass to a player who had either made a smart cut or slid over to a logical area. Sure, with so many games, with such long trips between back-to-backers, there were times when it took a team a little longer than usual to catch a groove, but I came to learn that what some observers call a lack of hustle is oftentimes actually an efficiency of movement, good-old-fashioned economy.

Still, as good as the ball was, if you survived the ax but didn't get called up, and you weren't able to parlay your time into a nice contract overseas, then you might have been better off not making the CBA to begin with.

Rather maddeningly, while thousands of people tried to get into the CBA, once in, nobody really wanted to be there.

4

N ow, despite the fact that most people in the CBA wanted to get out, the league had been carrying on for decades. Originally called the Eastern League, what became known as the CBA formed on April 23, 1946, a month and a half before the NBA was founded. This made the CBA the oldest continual, if you use the term a bit loosely, professional basketball league in the world—up until 2009, when it went under.

It was in the 1970s that the league changed its name to the Continental Basketball Association, and by the time the new millennium neared, the CBA had somehow managed to survive the Cold War, economic recession, relative obscurity, and Vietnam, among other things. Over fifty-three years, nothing seemed capable of toppling it. But then, in 1999, Isiah Thomas showed up.

In October of that year, Thomas bought the CBA for $10 million and proceeded to run it into the ground in fewer than two years, nearly ending its streak of continuation. Considering what the league had weathered beforehand, this was an extraordinary development (and yet this didn't stop Thomas from publishing, the year his CBA tanked, *The Fundamentals: 8 Plays for Winning the Games of Business and Life*, or from working in high-level management positions and making millions in basketball since then).

In fairness to Thomas, a lot of people initially thought he would help revive the struggling league. The year before his arrival, the CBA, despite apparently enjoying record-setting attendance figures of 3,809 per game (CBA attendance figures are shadier than a Redwood), had seen its nine teams lose a combined $9 million. In fact, when Thomas made the purchase, one CBA owner told *Sports Illustrated,* "Isiah saved the league. Three teams stayed in business last year just because of rumors of this deal. If they had folded, no more CBA. You can't play with six."[2] (The CBA did, however, play with seven squads in 2003-04.)

Sports Illustrated went on to sing Isiah's praises, invoking biblical references as it proclaimed, "In the Old Testament, the Book of Isaiah is filled with messianic hope. In the front offices of the Continental Basketball Association, the book on Isiah Lord Thomas III is that he's something of a savior too."

When asked by *Sports Illustrated* how to account for his evolution from point guard to the "Profit Isiah" (I don't make this stuff up), Thomas, who's been known to refer to himself in the third person, or even occasionally, exercise use of the rare first-person plural (the royal we) said, "Isiah is a brand. It's a brand that's accepted internationally. But what the brand really [represents] is credibility, trust, loyalty. Now, if you can put a credible business behind that..." He went on to say such things as, "We want to be the Microsoft of basketball" and, presumably in all seriousness, to claim that he envisioned a CBA with *300* teams in "tier-2, tier-3 cities" that he called "emerging domestic sports markets."

Another part of Isiah's plan involved the formation of a strong central office (himself and a few cronies?) taking over all aspects of teams' activities, from player personnel moves to marketing.[3] The plan didn't work well. Perhaps part of the problem was the conference calls Isiah would make to general managers of CBA teams. During Isiah's reign, Diane Bosshard, who owned the La Crosse (WI) Bobcats along with her husband Bill, used to let her staff into her office to listen to these calls because she found them so over-the-top. Isiah would rant and scream and threaten to kick asses. "I wasn't supposed to let them listen, but I just had to let someone hear this," Diane told the *New York Daily News*. "It was just like, 'If I swear enough or if I act like I'm tough enough you're going to back down.'" The former GM of the CBA's Fort Wayne (IN) Fury, Rich Coffey, described Isiah as, "Just the rudest person that I have ever run into in my entire life."[4]

Players, meanwhile, bristled in response to Isiah's decision to set a ceiling on weekly wages, which meant that, rather than making up to three thousand a week as players had in the mid-1990s playing for teams like the Florida Beach Dogs, they were making less than half of that under Thomas's new rules (Either way it sounded like a darn near fortune to me in 2004.)

The optimistic *Sports Illustrated* article about Isiah's ownership of the CBA was printed in February 2000. Facing millions of dollars in debt, by February 2001 the CBA suspended play. It happened that quickly.

Compounding the frustrations of those who had believed in the league, it later emerged that in March 2000, just a month after the *SI* article ran, the NBA had offered to buy the CBA from Thomas for $11 million and a percentage of profits. Thomas had declined: he'd wanted more dough. So instead, the NBA started a development league, the NBDL, which survives and has since expanded. Indeed, it has gobbled up several of the former hallmark CBA franchises.

Post-Isiah, the CBA, drawing upon its stubborn-minded, against-all-odds ability to survive, much like the attitudes of so many of its players over the decades, managed to come back to life. Five former local owners bought back their franchises after play ceased, and for the rest of the 2001-02 season joined the International Basketball League (IBL). Then, shortly after that IBL season—right around the time I signed my first CBA contract—a conglomeration of teams, including the Gary Steelheads, formed the International Basketball Association (IBA). Within weeks the IBA renamed itself the CBA.

By this time word was rife within the newfangled CBA that the old guard CBA owners couldn't stand Isiah. Apparently you didn't even want to speak his name around them. The Isiah "brand" was off-limits.

The revamped CBA chose as its new commissioner Gary Hunter, who had directed athletic departments at a few different universities, worked as a lawyer and judge, and even served as executive vice-president of the Communications Satellite Corporation (COMSAT). Upon taking the top CBA post, he declared, "NBA all-stars, several of the greatest coaches in pro basketball history, and exciting family entertainment are the heart of the CBA's legacy. We are eager to bring new vitality and business discipline to this important contributor to American sports history. We are thrilled to be back."[5]

5

t was in early November 2004, with the revamped, post-Isiah CBA now a few years old, that I readied for a trip west on Interstate 90 across Chicago, bound for Rockford, to start my third and final CBA training camp.

Just as I'd finished packing my stuff, the phone rang. It was Daleo. All excited, he said: "One down, one down, SirValiant Brown missed his plane. He asked me if I could schedule a later flight. I told him don't worry about it.... He's done. SirValiant Brown, done. Forget about it. That leaves you, Andre McCollum, Teddy Dupay, and Stais Boseman, so that's it...four guards left. SirValiant Brown...down."

Then he hung up.

To me, SirValiant's absence from training camp was no small matter, particularly because Daleo loved to score and Brown was a scoring point guard—in 2000 at George Washington University he came within .02 points of becoming the first-ever freshman to lead Division I NCAA hoops in scoring. But even without Brown, the other three point guards who would be at the Lightning training camp, Dupay, Boseman, and McCollum, presented a mighty challenge. Since it was likely that Dales would, at most, keep just two point guards, at least two of these players stood in the way of my plan to end my basketball career on satisfying terms.

Following Daleo's call and my drive down Interstate 90, I walked into Rockford's Fairfield Inn, which had struck some kind of deal with the Lightning to house its players. Daleo met me in the lobby, armed with our daily per diem. He handed me my $20 and I went up to my room to get ready for that night's session. Some guys had attended a session earlier in the day, so I was a little behind. Compounding matters, ever since I'd thrown out the first pitch, Dales had been leaving messages on my cell phone telling me that he thought I looked fat. He'd be creative about it. He'd maybe tell me in a message that he was holding a workout in Rockford that he'd like me to attend or mention some other thing about the approaching season, and then, at the end, add, "But I don't know if we'll have jerseys to fit you."

In my room at the Fairfield, I put my stuff up and my tight-like leggings on -- to keep my knees warm -- and headed back down to the lobby to get into one of the two passenger vans that would transport us to Jefferson High School, where that first night's training session took place. On the drive over, I realized a trend had apparently taken root as guys' cell phones played the music of various rappers and hip-hoppers to signal a call. I didn't even know who the rappers were.

Is that 8-ball? Wu Tang? Those guys are probably old news. You're out of the loop, dude. How do you even program a cell phone?

I learned later that guys had special ringtones for certain ladies. One player had programmed a cut from a porno soundtrack to denote when a particularly accommodating woman called.

At that night's workout, Dales ran us through a couple of bootleg drills, and then we played a full game—in the CBA we didn't do a bunch of repetitive drills, we mostly played, and under rules that captured the spirit of basketball's fast-paced and creative past.

For the scrimmage games, Dales liked to mix up the player combinations. Some nights he would put mostly guards together to play against big guys. It could be anything. Before we got started on this first night, though, Daleo huddled us together. He told us to run hard and hit the gaps. "Rotations may not be great. I don't care, just run," he said.

Just before the center jump, Andre McCollum, who had basically just walked off a plane, leaned in and asked me to take it easy. I told him, "Man, in this system you can't take it easy, there's nothing you can do. It's crazy. The score will probably be something like 140-130."

I was wrong; the final score of the scrimmage was 173-160. Action reigned. We ran and trapped and threw up shots all over the place. It felt like recess. It was awesome. About the only critique you heard on the offensive end was Daleo shouting, "Take it to the rack!"

We played furiously, like you're supposed to, like I love to. Since basketball's inception, and even more so now, the game has called for bursts of controlled athleticism in confined space and has allowed individual creativity to flourish amid coordinated team action. Its essence rests with its ability to meld individual creativity with the well-oiled collective, gracefulness with power, thoughtfulness with dash. And my penchant for speed, my get-up-and-go, which had motivated

Dales to start me in 2002, is what I hoped would help me land a roster spot again.

And I'm telling you Dales loved to score. He loved to score so much that he liked the word itself and other words that alluded to it, like "buckets." My first year in Rockford, it seemed like Dales had opportunities to say "buckets" all the time. A guy hit a three, "Buckets." A guy connnected on a driving scoop in the lane, "Buckets." And in Dales's speeches, it was often made quite clear what he expected us to deliver at a high rate, "Buckets." It go so that, amongst us players, anything great could be buckets. Eatin' a fine meal, "This grub's buckets." Saw a great film, "That was buckets." Spotted a hottie in the stands, "She's buckets."

It didn't hurt, on this high-scoring night at Jefferson High, that the team I was on won the scrimmage. Dales paid attention to that kind of thing. We got up big in the early going behind the strong play of 6'9" 270-pound forward Jermaine Williams out of UNC-Charlotte, who Daleo credited with being "a beast." Near the end of the scrimmage, even though I was exhausted, I felt good. While I was taking a breather on a sideline, however, Daleo came over and started pushing his arms straight out from his chest as if he were bench-pressing. I had no idea what he was driving at, but he kept doing it, so I asked, "What does that mean?"

"You need to hit the weight room."

I just kind of nodded, thinking, *What is this dude talking about? He just spent the last several weeks leaving messages on my phone calling me fat. Now he's telling me to lift more weights to get bigger.Maybe he's angling for reasons to send me home.*

As for my competitors at the point guard spot on this first night of camp, Boseman utilized his size and strength on both ends of the floor, and Dupay shot solidly. But McCollum struggled a bit. Still, with his sturdy build, solid fundamentals, and European experience, it seemed as if he would get stronger as camp progressed. Surviving looked tough.

Back at the Fairfield, with our next session just eleven hours away, I shut it down quickly, hoping to conserve energy, especially since the following day only four hours would separate the morning session from our afternoon workout, and then the next day we'd do it all over again.

When the alarm went off, I woke up all sore—my legs in particular. I'd expected some soreness, even though I'd done individual workouts and scrimmaged in preparation for camp, but seeing as I had trained and that I was, at six feet tall, a reasonable 185 pounds, I didn't expect to be this sore. Initially, I ascribed it to age. I was only twenty-seven but I'd played a lot of hoops over the years and had undergone two surgeries on my right elbow, in addition to the work done on each of my knee's patellar tendons. Several days later, as the soreness became more and more pronounced, I started to figure it must've been from the darn creatine I'd started downing just before camp.[6] I put it on the creatine because I recalled reading somewhere that it could cause you to hold fluids and thereby make you susceptible to muscle soreness and pulls. (This theory has apparently since been debunked.) Regardless, I felt like my entire body had been tenderized.

6

By the third day of camp it was still tough to say who Dales would keep as the two point guards. It looked like the front-runners were Dupay and Boseman.

Dupay, a good-looking fellow with blue eyes and light brown hair, stood only 5'9," but in high school he'd been Florida's most ballyhooed basketball legend of all time. And in college his legend continued to grow when he helped lead the Florida Gators to the 2000 national championship game. (That season, as a Boilermaker, I'd played against Teddy in the Maui Classic. We beat the Gators there, but they'd gone on to make it to the NCAA title game in Indianapolis, while we lost that heartbreaker to Wisconsin.) Dupay could not only shoot, he could shoot legitimate jump shots from the NBA three-point line. This separated him from others. In Gainesville—throughout the state, really—women adored the boy-wonder-turned-college-star and grown men celebrated him. From the outside, it seemed as if he lived a fairy-tale existence.

With an absurd 3,744 career points, he finished his high school career at Mariner High as Florida's all-time leading scorer. As a senior he *averaged* 41.5 points. In his first game of that year stories circulated across the nation about how in nineteen minutes of action, he'd scored fifty-five points. In another game, with his team down fifteen to Ohio's Shaker Heights, Dupay scored twenty-nine points in just over four minutes. He once scored seventy points in a high school game. Many people at the time considered him destined for the NBA. The only question was when he intended to declare.

His jumper, they said, was like pure gold, just like his smile and easy-going nature. Fans enjoyed watching him shoot so much that, as much as Teddy didn't like it, sometimes they'd boo if one of his teammates took a shot. They hadn't come for that. Dupay had energy and a sense of adventure, like he could take on anything. People loved that his dad cooked him eggs in the morning and worked him out, and that Teddy's tattoo on his left shoulder was simply the Roman numeral III, a nod to his roots as the third Teddy Dupay in succession. That he could shoot threes like no one else in the history of Florida high school basketball only made the tattoo that much cooler.[7]

Every major college pursued him, including Duke. Yet to the delight of Floridians he chose Gainesville. As Florida coach Billy "The Kid" Donovan's first signee, Dupay has been credited with starting a domino effect that led almost immediately to a slew of other prep stars committing to the Gators. The list of those stars includes future NBA players Mike Miller, Udonis Haslem, and Matt Bonner, and, a short time later, the West Virginia high school phenom Brett Nelson, who was celebrated then as the next Jerry West. After his college career, in an interview with *ESPN the Magazine*, Dupay said, "I got the program started...If I didn't go there, no Mike, no Brett Nelson, no Matt Bonner, no Brent Wright, no Haslem. Coach is a great recruiter, but it might not have happened so quickly."[8]

But the Teddy Dupay saga took an unexpected turn a few weeks after Florida's run to the title game, when reports surfaced that the NCAA was investigating him for maintaining a relationship with a bookie. Little news emerged in the ensuing weeks, yet in a methodical, bureaucratic, and some might say secretive manner, the NCAA built its case. Finally, just before the start of what was to be Dupay's final collegiate season, news agencies reported that the NCAA had banned him from college basketball for associating with "known gamblers."

For a prep standout with no previous record and a successful orthopedic surgeon for a father, the charges made little sense. If he could he do it over, Dupay says he'd fight the charges more vigorously. But Dupay told me that Donovan, his assistants, and the NCAA kept him in the dark as the case dragged on through the summer. Feeling powerless, when the NCAA finally rendered its verdict, he said he figured, "The heck with it, I won't fight. I'll just start my professional career, fuck those guys."

In 2002, playing for a team of traveling "all-stars" who played preseason games versus top colleges, Dupay exploded for forty-five points against Rick Pitino's Louisville squad. He nailed an eye-popping eleven of fourteen three-pointers. At one point, Pitino had to put star guard Taquan Dean, who had been defending Dupay, on the bench because Pitino didn't want Dean's confidence busted. After the game, Pitino, a former NBA head coach, said, "I'm shocked Teddy Dupay is not in the NBA." By the 2004 Rockford Lightning camp though,

Dupay still hadn't made it to the League, and he admitted that he felt as if the gambling scandal followed him everywhere. "It ruined my life, bro," he said.

With the NCAA having suffered from a couple of headline-grabbing gambling probes in the 1990s, the allegations came at a particularly bad time for Teddy. Banning a guy like him sent a message of vigilance to the public and served as a warning to others, even if the NCAA was sanctioning holiday tournaments in Vegas.

Following his NCAA banishment, Dupay ended up in Venezuela playing for the Caracas Cocodrilos. That's what led *ESPN the Magazine* to send a reporter to Caracas to write a cover story about Dupay titled "The Exile."

As it happened, Teddy ended up trapped in Caracas for a bit in 2002 as thousands of Venezuelans took to the streets—some of them protesting, some of them supporting Hugo Chavez's socialist-minded regime. Teddy was in his eighteenth-floor condo in the central downtown section of Caracas when one of the anti-Chavez protests erupted in the street below. Just before it did, he had wondered why people in his building were banging pots and pans together. Eventually, he realized it was a signal, because he could see stuff burning in the street down below. Soon someone came to his door and told him to stay inside until things quieted down. In the ensuing days, people brought meals up to him.

A few days into being holed up—not unlike Chavez and his advisors, who at that point were overthrown—Dupay watched on television as Pedro Cormona was sworn in as the new President of the now-renamed Republic of Venezuela. Just days after that, still in his room, Dupay watched as Chavez, who had wrestled back power, addressed the nation.

Dupay eventually made it down from his condo, but he was still branded by tough breaks and personal demons. By the 2004 Lightning camp he had played in a number of different leagues, overseas and domestic. In 2003, in fact, it was Teddy that Dales had brought in to replace me. Dupay played well during that stint but a bad leg injury ended his season prematurely.

In 2004, Dupay figured his ability to make shots, the long ball especially, would fit well with Daleo's high-scoring style again. Upon signing with the Lightning, he told the press that he liked Daleo's system as well as the opportunity to play point guard. "My goal is to get to the NBA, and playing point guard will be my best chance to get there," he said.[9]

7

T eddy, of course, was not alone in his desire to get to the big show. Indeed, he had plenty of company. It was a law within the realm: All players in the CBA think they will make it to the NBA.

Some believed this more strongly than others. Virtually all first or second-year guys considered it very likely that they'd get there—and soon—while most veterans held less unreasonable expectations. But regardless of how many years someone had played in the CBA, all players thought it *should,* and very well could, happen.

In some ways it made sense to think that the CBA would provide a path to the League. For decades, it put the highest percentage of players into the NBA of all minor leagues. Each season anywhere from ten to twenty-five CBA players would receive an NBA call-up.

This might not seem like much, but it's worth keeping in mind that in 2004 the CBA only consisted of eight teams, meaning that, since there was a limit of ten active players per roster, at any given time only eighty players made up the league. With ten to twenty-five call-ups per season and only eighty players in total, this seemed to put your odds of getting called up at roughly 20 percent.

However, in addition to the all-important issue of actually being good enough to get called up, roster turnover pushed those odds considerably lower. The 2001-02 Gary Steelheads squad that I played on highlighted the turnover factor particularly well—over forty players suited up for Gary that year. Moreover, the penchant of NBA brass to call mostly on those who had already received a call-up before made the odds of getting a first-time call-up even lower. As a result, for most, the hopes of a call-up were unrealistic. We just didn't know it yet. The situation came to remind me of the scene in the film *The Shawshank Redemption* when Red (Morgan Freeman) tells Andy Dufresne (Tim Robbins), "Everyone in here is innocent, you know that?" If Red played in the CBA, he might've told Andy, "Everybody in here is going to the NBA, you know that?"

Still, the CBA did put the most minor leaguers in the NBA, and players and their agents recognized this. The main hope was for a ten-day contract, the standard call-up deal. A few fortunate folks signed a full-year or even multiyear deal straight out of the CBA, like Eddie Gill, but that was rare. The standard ten-day NBA call-up paid roughly $40,000, or about twice the amount that the highest paid players in the CBA received in a whole season. An initial ten-day could lead to a second, and then, if the team still wanted you, it would have to sign you for the remainder of the season, paying at least a prorated salary based on a minimum contract of about $510,000 per year. That minimum NBA full-year contract worked out to roughly thirty times a top-level CBA salary. For us, it approximated winning the lottery.

And just as lotteries attract ticket buyers, the prospect of a call-up, despite the fact that such an occurrence was unlikely, motivated hundreds upon hundreds of players each year to vie for a spot on a CBA roster. It is an odd phenomenon of human existence that winner-take-all markets in which the distribution of income is radically unequal are typically overcrowded. The economist Adam Smith realized this many years ago, writing, "The overweening conceit which the greater part of men have of their own abilities is an ancient evil remarked by the philosophers and moralists of all ages…The chance of gain is by every man more or less overvalued, and the chance of loss is by most men under-valued."[10] This applied to the CBA, and CBA teams would capitalize on this overweening conceit by hosting "free-agent camps" throughout the summer and fall. The camps generated much-needed cash each year because altogether over a thousand players from all over the country—the world, for that matter—would pay more than a hundred dollars apiece to participate in one of them. Players would drive for hours, catch flights—do whatever it took to give it a shot. What most of these attendees didn't seem to know, though, was that rarely did a player make it to the CBA from a "free-agent camp," especially if you actually paid the camp fee.

On average, probably only one or two of the players among those who paid the tryout-camp fee would get chosen to attend a team's two-week-long preseason training camp. And even then the odds were against them, since at training camp they'd be competing for a roster spot with eighteen or so other guys, all of whom had been invited straightaway. Furthermore, about five-to-seven of the invited players would arrive to camp virtually assured of making it. The odds, then, of making a final CBA roster through the "free-agent camp" route were ridiculously low.

Oddly enough, it was my performance at a free-agent camp in the summer of 2002—after my anarchic, unproductive season with the Gary Steelheads—that helped me get invited to my first Rockford training camp and in turn earn a spot on that record-setting 2002-03 Lightning team. (For the record, I didn't have to pay the camp fee.)

Now, while everyone in the CBA thought they could and should be in the NBA, no correlation usually existed between how likely a call-up for a particular person actually was and the strength of his belief in an imminent call-up. In fact, if anything, a law of inverse proportion seemed at work here. It read something like this: The less likely your odds of receiving a call-up, the stronger your belief in the likelihood of a call-up.

Early on, this powerful inverse illusion seized me. And by the time it fully occurred to me that I'd fallen victim to it, I suspected that a different condition affected me. I was addicted to professional basketball, which counted as yet another potential minor-league pitfall.

The addicts belonged to a group of veterans who had come to realize the unlikelihood of their being called up without being able to altogether abandon the hope that it might still happen to them. As a result, they chose to stay in the CBA. Sure, perhaps some veterans—still hopeful of reaching the NBA—also stayed in the CBA because they had failed drug tests during earlier runs in Europe, and some others might've stayed because they liked to play in the States during the winter months and then parlay their CBA stats into a job in Venezuela, the Dominican Republic, or the Philippines, where leagues run in the spring and summer. (This way, players could enjoy the benefits of living in America, even if it was Rockford or Gary, rather than enduring a nine- to ten-month season overseas in Europe, where everything is little: little beds, little water bottles, little meals.) It's the addicts, though—those not entirely unlike the old-timers in *Shawshank* who don't want to get to the outside—that made up perhaps the most peculiar lot. Those of us who fell into this category didn't necessarily want to keep playing in the CBA, we just didn't have a conception of what else we could or would want to do. Basketball constituted virtually all we knew.

Of course, I didn't tell myself that I fell into this category. I was on a championship mission.

8

As for McCollum and Boseman, the other two players vying for one of the two point guard spots, they presented a stiff challenge to me just as Dupay did. McCollum was a longer shot than Boseman to make it, despite a strong professional European resume. This was partly because Boseman was a better-known commodity to Dales, and partly because McCollum played a more traditional, steadier style than Daleo tended to prefer.

McCollum was a Division II standout at Cal State-Bakersfield before he parlayed this into a string of European gigs, including a stop in Israel, a country known for paying players well and on time and for featuring amenities about as close as you can get to those in America. Of course, it's a job that for some comes with a price—you live hoping you don't get on the wrong bus. But Andre said he felt fine in Israel, never feared for his safety. On the court, he was strong and stable and his smooth shot made him an attractive option for Dales, even if he didn't play fast and furiously.

While Dupay's range separated him from others and McCollum's smooth mid-range game and steadiness helped him, at 6'3" and 200 pounds, Stais Boseman was abetted by his versatility and physicality. As an indication of his uncommon ruggedness and athleticism, in the spring of 2000, after Boseman's senior year at USC, the owner of the Oakland Raiders, Al Davis, called to see if Stais wanted to try out for the Raiders' secondary, even though Stais hadn't played football since high school. Boseman initially took Davis up on the offer, leading to a $175,000 contract offer. But, having turned in a strong senior season on the hardwood, Boseman reconsidered. Thinking he would get picked in that June's NBA draft, he ultimately turned the Raiders down. "My head started swelling up, agents were approaching me," Boseman recalled years later, in a documentary about his legendary high school hoops team.

It was in 1997 as a freshman at Oregon State that I first played against Boseman. He stood out then not just because of his physical, quirky game and because he played in low-top retro Nikes, but because he could find crafty ways to score. He struggled with his long-range shot and wasn't the greatest leaper, but he managed to use strong forays to the bucket and a solid midrange game to produce. And he defended.

People all across California had heard about Boseman well before I did because, as a scholastic athlete out of Los Angeles, much like Dupay, he was a phenom. Stais, though, may have received more press for his play at quarterback than for his hoops. Still, he starred in both at L.A.'s Morningside High and was considered one of the best athletes in the nation.

Morningside didn't offer an ideal academic environment. Indeed, it faced major academic challenges. In the early 1990s the school's roughly half Latin and half black student body carried an average GPA of 1.9—in other words, a D+ average. Characterizing the school's overall academic achievement at the time, its principal said, "I won't say it sucks, but it has a lot to be desired."[11]

No such characterizations, however, applied to Morningside's sports program. As a junior in 1992, Boseman led Morningside to the California state basketball championship, and the team elicited so much attention along the way that filmmakers decided to shoot a documentary about its next season, focusing on its five starters. Narrated by Wesley Snipes, that documentary became *Hardwood Dreams*, a not-so-subtle derivative of an earlier award-winning documentary starring Arthur Agee and William Gates called *Hoop Dreams*. Only *Hardwood Dreams* didn't stop at one installment. In 2004, a follow-up, *Hardwood Dreams: Ten Years Later*, was released. (It aired on *Spike TV,* not to be confused with Spike Lee.)

The first *Hardwood Dreams* featured a young and optimistic Boseman, with alert brown eyes and a mischievous teenage boy's grin. He was characterized as the "Bo Jackson of Morningside," and came across as someone who was willing to speak his mind. During one scene, an adult tried to offer Boseman some advice on dating, saying, "You shouldn't just go sleep with everybody, every June, May, and Sue." Boseman replied, "First of all, I don't talk to girls named Sue and June, first of all. Second of all . . . if I want to lay pipe, I'm gonna lay pipe."

In another scene, this same person asked Boseman's mom about her son's rumored activity. She responded: "I tell him, you can't be having sex with these girls . . . he looks at me like I'm crazy." At another point in the film, Boseman tells the principal, "We want to drink after school . . . that's our business."

Much of the original *Hardwood Dreams* focused on Boseman's struggles to pass the SAT. Boseman explains that he scored a 550 total on his first attempt and then a 610 on his second. To qualify for the NCAA at that time you needed a 700. In response to Boseman's first two scores, a school administrator exclaims on camera: "You get 400 points for just writing your name on the SAT. You're telling me after twelve years I only learned 200 and some, 300 and some, 610 you say he had? Bad, very bad . . . I'm saying Stais Boseman is lazy."

Boseman agreed: "That's true. I'm lazy 'til it comes to sports."

For his third try at a 700, Boseman gets a tutor, Kevin Drexel. In the film, Drexel, rather confident that in a very short amount of time he can overcome what might seem like years of catch-up work, declares, "I can take any kid short of brain dead and get them over 700." Next time around Boseman earned a 680. On his fourth try, though, he scored over 700.

Digger Phelps, the former head coach of Notre Dame and current ESPN analyst, of all people, shows up in the film. He meets with the Morningside team during the season and, darn-near shouting, asks: "Five thousand seniors per year, guess how many get drafted? Less than sixty. So how many gonna sign? Maybe thirty. That's out of 5,000. Get focused. Get ready with a back up. Be better than that. Be both. It will make a difference, with or without you."

For most of the original film, Boseman's father is out of the picture, which had also been the norm for the bulk of Stais's childhood. "I always wanted to see my daddy, one time at least," Boseman says at one point. He gets that opportunity late in the original film when his dad comes to one of his games unannounced. "It was pretty dramatic, man. I mean, the first time you see your father is at a basketball game, it's real bullshit," Boseman said later.

Even though his dad came to one of his high school games, he drifted out of Stais's life again soon after. Looking for answers, at one point in the second *Hardwood Dreams*, Stais visits his father in jail. It's the first time he's seen him in about ten years—his father had spent the previous seven behind bars. During this visit his dad tries to explain that an addiction to drugs had led to his decision to remove himself from the family. On the downside of that approach, his father said, "I wasn't there to cheer you on." In the scene you get a hint of Stais's anger, but you get a stronger sense of his decency and his ability to persevere.

As it happened, *Ten Years Later* aired during the 2004-05 Rockford Lightning season. The DVD jacket says the film reveals if any of the Morningside five had made their NBA dreams come true. They hadn't.

Boseman, though, did come tantalizingly close—and not just the season after he finished his USC career second among the school's all-time steals leaders and on its list of top ten all-time scorers. In fact, several years after this, in 2003, he got closest to the League.

When his name went uncalled at the 1997 NBA draft, Stais thought he was left with just a couple of options: "I could have gone back to school, which I probably should've did. But I chose to, you know, make some money," he said on film.

He played in the U.S. minor leagues and internationally in places like Seoul, South Korea, and Qatar. "North Korea and South Korea really wanted to kill each other. I didn't understand that," he said on film. "I was in Qatar . . . I was having lunch with Bin Laden. Everyone walkin' around with sheiks and shit, lookin' like Osama in that motherfucker." In Qatar he made $1,000 a week. "How many cats make a thousand a week on a regular job?" he asked. "Basketball gave me a lot of provisions and a lot of things I probably wouldn't've seen just being a local kid from the neighborhood."[12]

Playing internationally and in summer leagues, he impressed enough to land an invite to the Houston Rockets' 2003 training camp and fared well. Waking up on the day of the Rockets' last practice before its first game of the NBA's regular season, he couldn't help but get excited. He found out that day, though, that he was the Rockets' last cut.

Jim Boylen, a Rockets assistant coach from 1993-2003, said later, "Stais was as good an athlete as I've ever seen at this level because he could do everything that you needed to do to play basketball. . . . There's no question he's an NBA player. . . . There are a lot of guys that are NBA players that might be better than players in the League. But because of guaranteed money, because of contract obligations, those spots are taken up."

"I was oh so close, man. But you know, so close so far, though," Stais said, in the second *Hardwood Dreams*, of the day he got cut.[13] "I think no one really finds a permanent place in life . . . I'm lookin'."[14]

9

Fortunately, growing up in Indiana, my family gave me a sense of permanence. In fact, in a lot of ways I had a different upbringing than many of the guys vying for a Lightning roster spot. My family, my whole family, was there for me, and as a kid this made me feel free and easy, bold and capable.

Take my brother Kirk. He was three years older than me, which was quite nice since I could learn stuff from him, like funky dribble moves, how to fish, and how to tuck a *Sports Illustrated* into my textbook to make it look like I was studying. Plus, he kept a look out for me, like when I was in first grade, and a muscular-looking fifth-grader got to picking on me on the bus. When we came to the stop at which this kid got off, all of a sudden my brother—even though he was a year younger than this bully—walked off the bus right behind him. As the bus pulled away, I ran to the back of it to see what he was up to. With my face stuck to the back window, eyes bulging wide open, I watched my brother give this kid some of the business and thought to myself, *That's my brother. Don't mess with me.*

And when my brother had a big birthday party in eighth grade and for it he organized a three-on-three basketball tournament, he let me play in it, even though I was three years younger than everybody else. He didn't as much as mention it, but I bet you he knew that it made me feel eight-feet tall to play with them. And when I was in eighth grade, losing a big CYO game to an arch-rival, down ten with just over a minute to go, it was nice to look over at my brother and his friends, who, even though they were seniors, had taken the time to come to my game. This spurred me to lead my team to an improbable comeback. And it was cool when, having capped that comeback with a clutch feed for a lay-up, I glanced over to the stands and saw my brother and his buddies—my heroes—standing up and cheering like mad, coats off because they were waiving them over their heads in celebration.

It was also nice when, after college, after all the hype of big-time NCAA hoops, when I wasn't feeling myself and needed someone to talk to you, my brother was there. When I started talking and a rush of emotion poured forth and I started crying, trying to explain how I was feeling, unsure and untethered, it was nice to hear that it'd be alright.

Sure, to toughen me up when I was seven or eight he might've, for a few weeks at a time here and there, given me a daily brotherly beat-down, which often included acting like he was going to spit on me while he pinned me down, only to slurp the saliva back up. But what older brother doesn't do something like that on occasion.

My older sister, Caroline, was two grades above me in school and made my buddies go googly-eyed. And her friends were some of the hottest women on the planet, as far as I was concerned, which is why it was tight when she'd show up to an Andrean high school basketball game as a senior, dressed in a custom-made t-shirt that let everyone in the place know that I was her little brother. And it was nice when, virtually every time I saw her in school, she would flash a huge smile and give me a hug, even if we'd fought like cats and dogs that morning over something stupid.

Rounding us kids out was a younger sister by ten years, Suzanne, who was sweet as could be. None of us were perfect, but we loved each other, and we knew this always to be true, no matter what.

This is not to say that we didn't have to face tough times or harsh realities. Whether it was hormones, a lack of Vitamin D, or some other thing, as a teenager I'd confront gloomy stretches, would wake up sometimes feeling heavy and have a hard time shaking it. Stressing about it, telling myself there was no reason for it, wouldn't magically change things. But I knew that, for a few hours each day at least, basketball would.

During one of these inexplicable stretches of gloom, in the summer between my freshman and sophomore years, another harsh reality materialized when Paul Rossetti, my brother's close friend, high school teammate, and fellow co-captain, answered the door to his apartment in Fort Wayne.

He was in Fort Wayne because of basketball, readying for the start of his sophomore year and a season that he hoped would help him get his college hoops career on track. He hoped for this because Paul Rossetti loved basketball, was absolutely enamored by the game. He loved to smile too, and he had a gentle heart, which you could sense when you were around him, especially if he was one of your heroes.

And he was the type of guy who, if he came over to your house to hangout with your older brother when you were twelve and you challenged him to a game of one-one-one, he'd say sure, even though he was a full foot taller than you and sixty pounds heavier and could dunk like no white kid you'd ever seen. And he wouldn't just play one game of one-on-one with you. He'd play you in a best-of-seven series and make sure it came down to the last few possessions of game seven. He wouldn't let you win, mind you, because that'd be too much. You wouldn't want that. But he'd let you hang around, make you feel like you belonged. And because of that, all through the games, if you were anything like me, you'd be smiling so big inside that, if someone could've looked right into you, they'd have seen a grin stretching across the whole state of Indiana.

He was the type of guy who would, in the middle of a hotly contested Indiana state high school basketball game, as the referee was handing him the ball for a throw-in and you happened to be walking by on your way to your seat, reveling at the thought of what it must feel like to play in a game like that, wink at you and smile. My heart stopped, my jaw dropped, and my brain sent waves of delight through me when he did that.

Paul Rossetti was also the type of guy who, if you knocked on his door and asked him for help, like a stranger did on that fateful day in Fort Wayne, he'd say of course and let you in. He'd dash over to the phone and hand it to you, hoping to help in anyway he could, trying to suppress the shock at hearing what this stranger was telling him: that he needed to use Paul's phone because his girlfriend had just been raped and Paul's door was the first door he could find to knock on. Only this stranger was lying. It was all a ruse to get into Paul's condo. It's devastating to think how Paul's face must've contorted when he realized that this person would trick someone like that. Of all people, that type of thing would've been unimaginable to Paul.

And it's even harder to think about the thoughts and emotions that ran through Paul while this intruder held a gun to his head and taunted him, tortured him, for well over an hour. Paul probably thought about his parents and his sister and his college roommate, Russ Marcinek, whom he'd grown up playing ball with. And I'm sure he thought about the upcoming season and the fact that he wanted to teach one day and coach basketball. But the animal holding a gun to his head wouldn't care about that. He was on a gang initiation mission. He had to kill someone at random. That person just happened to be Paul.

You might think that torturing Paul and shooting him in the back of the head would be enough. But no, not for this guy. He had to take Paul's gold chain, too, the one with a cross on it from his Confirmation.

Paul's body was left there to be found by his roommate and former high school teammate Russ, a point guard who my friends and I also idolized. A few days later, crying, I'd watch Russ and my brother and other former teammates of Paul's carry his casket into church for the funeral. Paul's jersey, number forty-three, was hanging by the altar. It's the type of scene that gets seared to your brain. It's the type of tragedy that makes you wonder if God plays dice with the world.

But you couldn't let that fear keep you down, you had to keep going, faithful that it wasn't so. That's what Paul would've done. He also would've kept on hooping. But since he couldn't hoop anymore, maybe you could hoop a little extra for him. Maybe you could fight like mad to learn how to dunk, even if it was just half as well as he used to. When you're doing thirty sit-ups, make it forty-three. And when you're picking jersey numbers for the varsity squad, make sure you get number forty-three. Who cares if it's way too big? Play big. Play big for Paul and all the other guys who still want to be ballin'. And when you get to college, wear number forty-three. That way, not only will it inspire you, but when you get on a roll at Assembly Hall against the Indiana Hoosiers on ESPN, and Dickie V. gets all hyped up because of it, maybe someone back in northwest Indiana will think of Paul just like he used to think of you. And that way maybe you can connect the ever-evolving present with the ever-living past.

10

It helps, of course, in the aftermath of a tragedy like the one that took Paul's life, to feel the love of family and friends, to feel like you aren't facing things alone. And in the case of me and my brother and sisters, when it came to the confidence we had in knowing that we loved each other no matter what, we owed this to our parents. Both of them.

It was my dad who, noticing that he had a son with a gift and a passion for hoops, did everything he could to help me get where I wanted to go. Like find a way to get me, as a fifth-grader, onto an otherwise all black team in Gary, Indiana. If that team practiced in one of the roughest sections of Gary, a town that annually ranks among the nation's most dangerous, he wouldn't flinch. He would simply come to every practice. When I needed to get my right elbow fixed and answers were hard to come by, he sought out one the Chicago Bears' team doctors, costs be damned.

And my mom, well she did nothing more than pour every inch of her soul into raising her children so that they would, she hoped, reflect the values that she and her parents and her parents' parents held dear: an appreciation for God and hard work and straight-shooting, for personal responsibility and independence. Growing up she was the family compass, a rock, but a rock that was somehow warm and sun-kissed.

Beautiful, with big blue eyes, a big warm smile, and blond hair, she's the type of woman who takes nothing from anybody. When I was in high school, I went to an Indiana Hoosiers basketball game as a guest-recruit, and my parents and I met with coach Bobby Knight afterward. Only she didn't appreciate it when Knight, still visibly upset about having just lost to Purdue, took me by the back of the neck and walked me over a few paces to demonstrate how he had wanted one of his guards to get a better angle before making a post feed during the game. It wasn't a rough neck grab or anything, mind you, but my mom didn't like anyone taking any of her kids by the neck, and you could see it on her face. When we left the Hoosier locker room, she turned to me and said, "Never play for that man." She had no reason to worry about that, especially since Indiana never offered me a scholarship, but I know she was proud as a peacock when, several years later, we walked out of Assembly Hall with a victory.

I don't think my parents ever expected to have kid who would play major college basketball, but they reveled in the journey when they saw that this had become my dream.

Related to that, my parents paid good money to send me to Andrean High School, which, unlike Stais Boseman's Morningside High School in L.A., excelled in academics. Ninety-nine percent of its students went to college. And though I didn't know it until I got to Oregon State, the teachers at Andrean prepared me for college better than I could've hoped, despite the fact that I was a subpar worker in the classroom. Sure, I read a ton. On a near daily basis I'd bring to school a newspaper or magazine—the *Chicago Tribune, Wall Street Journal, Newsweek,* or *Sports Illustrated*—and devour it, but I rarely read my textbooks. I'm not proud of it. It's just that I was a hard-headed kid in a lot of ways, and it took some maturing before I started applying myself in school.

Still, Andrean was a great place to attend high school. The teachers were kind and caring and hard-working, and you sensed this, even if they stayed on you to tuck in your shirt and wear the right shoes, to stop reading the newspaper and open your book. And my classmates were, for the most part, much the same—kind, caring, and hard-working.

And, oh my, did all of us love basketball. The local newspaper would put our *fans* on its front page. One of those fans was one of my best buddies. He'd gotten cut from the team, but rather than ignore our squad because he hadn't made it, he would dress up like Superman to cheer us on at our games, and fans would hold him over their heads and fly him around the gym, his red cape—with a gold number forty-three emblazoned on the back—fluttering in the air. Our fans were the Cameron Crazies of Indiana high school hoops, the greatest state for high school hoops ever.

On game day, classmates would rush to the gym right when the final bell rang, at 2:45 p.m., to make sure they staked a choice seat in the student section for a 7:30 p.m. tip-off. They'd send each other out for sandwiches or other errands, but made sure that enough like-minded supporters remained near their seats to reserve them were someone to make a move for them. An hour-and-a-half before game time, or even earlier, policemen would park their cars out in front our school, on Broadway Avenue, to prevent any more cars from turning into Andrean's already full parking lot. They'd have to arrive earlier next time, if they wanted to see the Fighting Fifty-Niners.

People loved our team because they could see in our play what they'd felt in their youth and carried with them no matter how old they were: an appreciation for basketball. Not only that, but *our* Fifty-Niners teams played with an element of creativity that only comes along every now and again. To this day, old men who've watched decades of high school hoops, will stop me and say, "I used to watch your team play." Then they'll stop talking, tilt their head down to the side a little, shake their head, and smile.

During a game, once the flow was on, it didn't matter to the fans or my teammates or me if our well-meaning high school coach screamed a lot and we couldn't figure out exactly why. In fact, the fans loved that my game and our team's style didn't exactly align with the style of tradition-bound, Indiana coaches reared on the methods of Bobby "the General" Knight. Our style, my style, was too flashy, those coaches would say, too improvisational, too risky, too daring. But for my teammates and I, and for the Andrean fans, that's where the beauty of the game existed, in those very moments of creativity.

At Oregon State and Purdue, the fans had embraced me in much the same way. They did so, I knew—I could feel it—because my game spoke to them, just like Sherman Douglas had spoken to me years earlier. They knew that the lefty scoop shots, the risky pass that snuck through, the ambitious drive, and the alley-oop dish were things that I must've done thousands of times. And they could sense that I loved the creative possibilities that the game presented, that I reveled in the game's flow, its feel, its beat. In turn, in feeling an appreciation for this from them, I was connected with fundamental elements that are at the core of our existence. I was given a sense of being centered and yet free, disciplined and yet creative, singular and yet united, of being in tune.

My first college coach, Eddie Payne, appreciated my style, as did the Oregon State fans, which is partly why it was so hard to leave Corvallis and why I ultimately let Eddie Payne know I was willing to walk back on.

At Purdue, Gene Keady was a master at being competitive and stamping his rugged personality on his teams, especially on the defensive end, but he wasn't a basketball junkie, in the sense of seeing the game as a free-flowing art form. And in this regard, a lot like my high school coach, we would occasionally lock horns—after an ambitious pass attempt during practice Coach Keady was liable to tell me to "move to Sacramento and move in with Jason 'fucking' Williams" (the flashy Sacramento Kings' point guard), or after a tough loss to Indiana he might very well write "point guard" on the white-board, making it abundantly clear he wasn't happy with my play. I got fired up about that one, told him I didn't like getting blamed for the loss. But a few weeks later, when we made it to the Sweet Sixteen by upsetting Oklahoma, he declared in our huddle that we had "one of the best point guards in the nation." It was his way of saying, "I'm with you."

All told, regardless of occasionally buttin' heads, we respected each other, and we made it work, which is how I came to find myself among the Big Ten's leaders in assists, while shooting over forty percent from the three-point line and averaging double-digits. At Purdue, then, I learned what it took to lead a national championship contender from the point guard position.

And my, was it buckets to play for the Boilermarkers, to feel the roar of Mackey Arena's thousands, to silence a crowd on the road, and to send an alley-oop pass thirty feet through the air, down one against Oklahoma with under two minutes to go in the NCAA tournament, to my road roommate Greg "Gator" McQuay, confident, though not certain, that he would catch it. I was confident because I knew how high he could jump—so high that it looked like he could take a bite out of the rim, hence the nickname "Gator." Plus, I'd been playing with or against Greg since we were fifteen. We'd played on the same AAU team and were on rival high school teams, and I knew he was the kind of guy who could go get something when the opportunity presented itself. Greg had to be. Along with his virtually inseparable brother Gary, he grew up brushing his teeth at the kitchen sink because their house, in one of the toughest parts of Gary, didn't have a sink in its lone bathroom. And, sure enough, he caught my alley-oop pass and flushed the ball through the net.

Greg McQuay majored in art at Purdue, painted his high school team's gym floor, and would get asked at AAU tournaments to paint family portraits for people who had heard of his ability. And like a lot of artists, he is quiet but sensitive. That's why I wasn't surprised when I woke up in the middle of the night in our Tucson, Arizona hotel room, the night before our game against Oklahoma to get to the Sweet Sixteen, to see him awake, painting. I sensed that this was how he dealt with the uncertainty and anxiousness of the time, with the upcoming game and, more seriously, with his brother Gary's battle with leukemia.

Greg's brother Gary—who played with us at Purdue before he got sick—would die two years later. I'd not only played with both McQuay brothers, I'd lived with both of them, and it was an honor when Greg asked me to speak at his brother's funeral on his behalf. We mourned that day, and yet we also celebrated Gary's life. When the pastor spoke, he started passing a basketball around, asking folks to keep it moving, just like Gary would want us to do. And that ball flowed through the pews. This is the type of thing that can happen at funerals in Indiana.

In addition to playing with the McQuays, at Purdue it was awesome to see, in the heart of winter, teammate Brian Cardinal, a rugged, six-foot-eight forward with a buttery shot, diving for loose balls—at a morning practice after a big win, no less—as if it was the seventh game of the NBA Finals. That can fire your whole roster up.

And, oh my, to feel as if time had stopped for a few moments when I was dribbling the ball up the court amid a thunderous sea of red in Indiana University's Assembly Hall, confident that my guys, the Boilers, could get it done. And we did.

There were some rather tight perks at Purdue, too, especially when compared to the CBA. Practicing in Mackey Arena and playing games there, with over 14,000 well-informed basketball lovers behind you, was tight. And on the road, Coach Keady made sure we stayed in the finest hotels and ate at the nicest steak joints. Instead of taking hours-long bus rides time and again, we often traveled to away games in a private plane, which took off from Purdue's airport. Once, after we lost that heartbreaker to Wisconsin and missed out on our Final Four dream, we landed back in West Lafayette late at night to find fans there waiting for us on the tarmac. They wanted to pick us up now that we were down, like we'd been able to pick them up over the course of the season. It made you feel appreciated.

So too did Purdue's private academic center for athletes and its athletic dining hall, at which, after downing steak or chicken cordon bleu or whatever other entrees were offered on a given night, you could always hit up the sundae bar. Don't worry about the dishes.

And the ladies, my goodness. I'm not talking about groupies, mind you, although if that was your thing, there were plenty of those. Shoot, as a college hoops player one—or two—might show up at your door. I'm talking about full-on, emerging women. It was nothing short of ridiculous to see, at least in my case, how college hoops could get you in the same room as—and perhaps a conversation with—young ladies who otherwise you'd have struggled to find a chance to give an elevator pitch to, let alone land a date with. I sensed that my time at Purdue would likely constitute my peak, as far as attracting a mate goes, and fortunately there I met Christy, a salt-of-the-earth gem with a sharp wit and legs that stretched from Miami to L.A. Rarely does a couple constitute two evenly matched people. And the truth is, I married up.

Not that she agreed to date me because I played basketball. In fact, the first time I struck up a conversation with her, as we were leaving study hall, she asked me—trying to be polite and keep the conversation going—what I'd done the previous night. Seeing as the Boilers hoops squad had beaten Xavier, a team ranked in the top twenty-five on ESPN 2, I realized that she either didn't know I was on the team, or at a minimum, didn't follow our squad. But at least, seeing as Purdue athletes would often run into each other, I'd get another crack at it.

I remember, though, several weeks later, leaving her a phone message, my third in as many weeks, telling her that I'd talked with my brother, and we'd both agreed that three messages was the max. Any more would be unacceptable. So this was it. This was my last chance. And then I said, stealing a line from *Good Will Hunting*, that perhaps we could go out for caramels some time, seeing as caramels are as arbitrary as coffee. I thought that would do it. I'd laid it on the line, and with a touch of humor. Only she didn't call. But this is what I mean about being at your peak. Several months later another chance would arise for me to have an in-person conversation with the woman of my dreams. And this time we clicked. Seven years of marriage and three kids later, I realize that it was my life's big break.

College hoops could get surreal in other ways, too, like when Bill Raftery interviewed me after we beat Florida at the Maui Invitational. Here's a guy that my dad and brother and I had watched call games for years, eager to hear him declare that a given team had come out "in the man-to-man," or a player had made a bucket by making use of "the kiss" or had somehow demonstrated that he did, indeed, have "onions." And it was surreal when John Wooden, a former Boilermaker, handed my teammates and I the Wooden Tradition trophy after we knocked off the nation's top-ranked Arizona Wildcats, featuring Gilbert Arenas and Luke Walton. It was John freakin' Wooden!

It wasn't always easy, but at Purdue time and experience helped me to better understand how to lead in a way that I did not do at Oregon State. Together, the fiery Coach Keady and I found a balance between basketball's tactical and rugged nature and its artfulness and fluidity.

But had finding that balance at Purdue, as I'd thought might be the case when I'd decided to transfer there, come at a high monetary cost, in addition to the rotten feeling of having let Oregon State down? Sure, my muscles were bigger at Purdue, but this meant eight pounds or so of more weight when one of my greatest physical assets was my quickness, and it had meant heavier lifting exercises, which, by my third year as a Boilermaker, had taken quite a toll on my already worn knees. Surgery on my patellar tendons came immediately on the heels of our Elite Eight run in 2000, followed by 10 months of intense rehab. Knee work, less gaudy stats, and a tamed style didn't exactly enhance my draft status. In fact it took me off the draft radar.

Maybe no matter what I'd done, I wouldn't have made it to the NBA. But there are arguments to suggest that I very well did miss my shot at the League by leaving Oregon State. Take fellow six-foot point guard Dan Dickau. In 1997, odds-makers would've put my chances of making it to the NBA much higher than his. A year after I'd finished as runner-up to Mike Bibby for PAC-10 freshman of the year honors, Dickau averaged a few points per game at the University of Washington. The next season, watching on television, I got the impression that his coach didn't really believe in him or his style. Dickau then transferred to Gonzaga, to a free-flowing system with a guard-friendly coach who gave Dickau the reins. Two years later he was drafted in the first round of the NBA draft—just a few months after I'd spent basically an entire season languishing at the end of a CBA bench.

But was that all that mattered, the NBA and the money? No, I told myself. Three years in the CBA, though, can help laser your focus upon how important it is, in a winner-take-all professional market, to capitalize on your opportunities. This season would likely be my last chance to do just that.

Andrean High School, 1995-6 season. You had to get to Fifty-Niner games early. We dug our hoops.

Post-game after a Maui Invitational victory over Teddy Dupay and the University of Florida. Playing in Maui for a school like Purdue and having your game called by the legendary Bill Raftery: tight.

11

While McCollum, Boseman, and Dupay made up my competition at the point guard position, the star of the Lightning show was Ronnie Fields, who ranks among the best-known American basketball players to never to play in college or in the NBA.

Although he didn't play in either of those, Ronnie did carve out a long career with the Lightning, earning him the nickname "Ronnie Rockford," but no pension, medical insurance, or certifiable educational advancement.

Still, much of Fields's story makes for a great American tale. Having been raised poor in a single-parent home on Chicago's West Side, it was in middle school that Ronnie discovered that he had a special gift—when he jumped, he seemed to fly. Perhaps it was his unusually bowed legs, which he thinks might've come about after he got hit by a car as a young child and broke both of them. Whatever it was, he could soar, and this enabled him to emerge as a scholastic superstar.

As a freshman at Chicago's Farragut Career Academy, a public high school tucked between African American and Hispanic enclaves, his legend first took off. By the time he finished at Farragut, Fields had scored 2,600 points, nabbed a school record 412 steals, and hammered home an astounding 372 dunks, including the only high school dunk to make *Slam* magazine's "Top Ten Greatest Dunks of All Time." Even more so than had happened with Dupay, the main question being asked near the end of Fields's 1995-96 senior season was whether he would jump straight to the pros or spend a year or two in college first.

And who could blame people for assuming the NBA awaited him? Fields attracted so much national attention for his gravity-defying jams, forty-eight inch vertical, fade-away jumper, and scoring prowess that when he injured his neck in a car accident late in his senior season, people like Jesse Jackson and Bob Costas visited him in the hospital. Describing the pre-injury hysteria about Fields, Farragut coach "'Wolf' Nelson," who had coached Ronnie as a seventh grader, said, "At schools, in malls, everywhere, he was mobbed."[15] Recalling Farragut's 1994 drive for Chicago's scholastic hoops crown, Nelson said, "At the city final four, there were people outside scalping tickets for hundreds of dollars. Ronnie was Jordan-esque."[16]

Fields's "Jordan-esque" potential was not lost on shoe companies. In the mid-1990s the "sneaker wars" between the likes of Nike, Reebok, and Adidas raged, and Fields counted as one of the choicest young jewels. After Fields's freshman year, Nike invited him to Beaverton, Oregon, the home of its headquarters, to play in an elite all-star game designed to feature the nation's top forty high school players. Fields was fourteen.

Soon, Ronnie's prowess led Kevin Garnett to transfer to Farragut from a small school in South Carolina. Together the two, with the help of freshman Michael Wright—who went on to star at the University of Arizona—turned their Farragut team into one of Chicago's most storied high school squads ever. And Garnett certainly did not outshine Fields. If you visit Farragut's high school gym you will find murals of both on the wall—only Fields's mural is about twice as large as Garnett's.

The six-foot-three Fields, who, with his dark skin, bald head, and ability to move with graceful fluidity before exploding upward, seemed puma-like, did not just overshadow Garnett in high school. He overshadowed entire collegiate teams. When DePaul University invited Fields to a home basketball game, fans surrounded him for autographs and pleaded with him to give college a try before heading to the NBA. Former DePaul athletic director Bill Bradshaw said, "He got mobbed . . . No one was asking our players for autographs – just Ronnie."[17] Never had the state of Illinois confronted such a popular high school basketball player.

However, while its hoops thrived, Farragut Career Academy was not a model public high school. As an indication of this, in October 2005, dozens of students gathered outside the school's walls to protest its decrepit condition. Students said that their principal, Ed Guerra, "gets a failing grade" for overseeing a school where rodents roam the hallways along with the students, graffiti covers the walls, the bathrooms are unclean, and the classrooms overcrowded. Walter Ortega, a student protestor, said, "My French class had more people than seats."[18] A shortage of books forced Farragut students to leave their course books at their desks each hour so the next students coming in could use them.

The Ed Guerra in Martinez's story is the same man who was principal at Farragut for Ronnie Fields's last three seasons at the school, from 1993 to 1996. Guerra carried a reputation among administrators as a hard-nosed leader who didn't put up with nonsense, and Fields, in fact, credits him with decreasing the violence at Farragut while he was there. But a 1997 article about Fields in *U.S. News & World Report* portrayed Guerra negatively for saying things such as, "These kids [Fields and Garnett] were not the types of kids who were going to grow up to be doctors or lawyers. They are basketball players."[19]

The author of the *U.S. News & World Report* piece, John Simmons, who had probably read Hobermann's *Darwin's Athletes,* which argues that our sports culture has damaged black America, chided Guerra and others for celebrating Fields as a destined basketball player. And Simmons found ammunition for this argument in those murals in Farragut's gymnasium. He made sure to note that despite the school's financial issues, Guerra had found enough funds to construct the larger-than-life-size renditions of the school's most famous alums. When asked to defend his decision to commission the murals, Guerra said, "Ronnie gave the school a good name."

To be sure, Fields did enhance Farragut's name recognition. Before he and Garnett attended, the school was known to most for little except that less than ten percent of its students read at grade level (perhaps some knew that Pat Sajak and Kim Novak had gone there, but probably not many). In his *U.S. News* piece, Simmons spliced in these types of academic statistics and made sure to note that at one point during his interview, Guerra stared up at the Fields mural and said, "You know he [Fields] jumped over a kid once." Next, Guerra apparently looked out on the court and pointed to a spot underneath the basket, adding, "The kid was standing right there. He was a small kid, and Ronnie jumped right over him to slam. We're paying tribute to Ronnie where he deserves it—in the gym." He then reportedly stopped for a moment, pondered the setting, and told Simmons, "Maybe I should put his grades and his ACT scores up there too."[20] I don't think Simmons could've paid the guy for better stuff.

Garnett's mural doesn't seem to have hurt him, and yet maybe Ronnie's does symbolize the things that led to his downfall: larger-than-life treatment, little or no guidance from a number of adults, and an inept public school system. Combine these with a young fellow who made a number of poor choices and who had a basketball game that seemed stuck somewhere between an NBA small forward, for which GMs considered him too small, and an NBA guard, for which GMs considered him too unpolished, and you have Ronnie Fields playing in the CBA for the better part of a decade.

With his father out of the picture, among those adults in mentoring positions that received criticism in the aftermath of the troubles that Ronnie faced at the end of his high school career, were Fields's high school coach William "Wolf" Nelson and especially Farragut assistant coach Ron Eskridge. Perhaps Nelson, a long-time Fields family friend whom Ronnie defends, just got swept up by the Ronnie hysteria. Minnesota's *Star Tribune* reporter Jim Souhan, who penned an article a short time after Fields's woes began, suggested Nelson had when he reported that in an interview "Wolf" wanted mostly to talk about the two times Fields "leaped straight over a dude and dunked!" rather than what went wrong. Nelson told Souhan, "Everybody liked being around Ronnie, and he let everybody hang around him. He always had the girls, he always had everything."[21]

In 1994 in the *Chicago Sun-Times,* assistant coach Eskridge, billed as a Fields friend and "adviser," gave a sample of the sort of basketball advice he was offering Fields. Before a Nike camp in Deerfield, Illinois, he said, "Ronnie will show he is one of the few people coaches would pay money to come to see. . . . I think he will show he is the best player in the country, better than the seniors, that he could go to the NBA after his junior year in high school because he is doing a lot of things that NBA players are doing now." Eskridge did claim, however, that Fields needed to become mentally tougher, asserting that Ronnie needed to learn not to give "any quarter" on the court by taking on the mindset of Michael Jordan and Magic Johnson.[22]

As it happened, it was Eskridge who would play a key role in two events that turned Ronnie's supposedly surefire NBA success story into a tale about a guy whose nickname would be forever associated with a CBA city.

The first of these occurred at the end of Fields's senior season when he got in that brutal car accident, the one that brought Jesse Jackson and Bob Costas to his bedside. It also gave Fields a broken vertebrate in his neck. The accident took place just days before a state tournament playoff game. Fields recalled: "People who saw the wreck were shocked that I lived—don't even mention that I could play basketball again. . . . I was gonna declare for the draft *the next day*; we had just played our last regular season game against Manley and I had thirty-eight. That day I had done some autograph signings with a teammate at about four or five Foot Lockers. They were giving me shoes and all types of merchandise."[23]

The crash occurred at 1:30 a.m. on a school night. Fields was driving a car that had been rented by Eskridge. Eskridge said he loaned it to Fields as a birthday present. Questions mounted in the press, and the papers even asked Michael Jordan to weigh in. Jordan called Fields "a monster talent" but added, "At 1:30 in the morning, kids are supposed to be home getting ready for school. . . . But this kid's got to learn how to take responsibility. And somebody's got to guide him to make sure he takes better care of himself."[24]

After the *Sun-Times* asked Eskridge to give his side of the story, the paper reported that an "utterly bizarre" and "startling 45-minute Eskridge infomercial" followed. During it, Eskridge said, "Most people I've encountered in my life don't like me. And you know why? You know why they like making me the heavy? Because they're envious and jealous of me. People don't like success, and they really don't like success when you're smarter than they are. Very few people know more than I do. People should pay me to grant them some of my wisdom. I've been around the world twice, and most of these people never get out of town. They cannot think on my level." He also told the *Sun-Times,* "I affect people in a strange way, especially females. They always think I'm too arrogant, like many of the males. . . . It's like these TV guys who've been talking about me. I'm going to take some of their jobs. I look better than they do, present myself better than they do and hold a conversation better than they do. I'm popular. I'm going to run for politics. I'm a star."[25]

Later that summer, just as Fields was beginning to recover from the injuries he suffered in the car accident, more bad news arrived. On July 20, 1996, Fields learned that he'd failed to earn an NCAA qualifying score on the ACT. A disappointed Joey Meyer, head coach of DePaul, who had signed Fields not too long after the crash, called Ronnie to inform him of the test result. According to Coach Meyer, news of Fields's failed test "shocked" the player's mother.[26] Compounding matters, *USA Today*, in the course of reporting Fields's ineligibility, noted that Fields had also missed the filing date for the NBA draft and therefore faced limited options. Basically, he could go to junior college, overseas, or to the CBA.

In retrospect, the mismanagement of Fields seems ridiculous. Former DePaul athletic director Bill Bradshaw, probably as disappointed as Coach Meyer that Fields would not be able to help resurrect DePaul's basketball program, wondered how Fields had made it through high school without attaining the grades or skills needed to attend a university. "I think you have a long line of suspects there who should take responsibility for that. Assessing blame in this case is like trying to figure out where cancer started," he said.[27]

For his part, Fields doesn't blame anybody for his academic struggles, especially not his former principal Guerra. In fact, he credits Guerra with keeping him at Farragut. Fields recalled that during first two years of high school, nearly every day gang fights plagued the school. He said: "Guerra helped end the violence that was separating the school. With Guerra, Farragut became known for more than violence, because he supported us and the soccer team. So the Hispanics and blacks stopped fighting as much."[28]

Shortly after Joey Meyer had informed him of his failing test grade and just a day after the *USA Today* reported that he had failed to register for the draft, Fields spiraled further downward. On the night of July 22, 1996, Fields and two other men gathered at assistant coach Eskridge's apartment. Apparently Eskridge was out of town again. A twenty-year-old woman whom Fields had previously dated was at the apartment too, on a date with one of the other men. According to police reports, this man began having intercourse with the woman in a darkened room. Unbeknownst to her, in the same room Fields and the third man, a twenty-eight-year-old, hid in a closet. Fields then emerged quietly from the closet and tapped the man having intercourse on the leg, signaling him to switch places with Fields. The woman said she didn't notice. But when the third man then attempted to replace Fields, the woman jumped up and screamed. Fields locked himself in the bathroom while the woman tried to bash open the bathroom door with a basketball trophy.[29]

The woman pressed charges, and DuPage County prosecutor Thomas E. Epach Jr. took the case. He wanted to go to court, but the woman preferred to resolve the misdemeanor charges through a plea bargain. Fields pleaded guilty to a misdemeanor offense, leading to a sentence of fifteen days of work detail, an order to undergo counseling, and a fee of $750 to be paid to a woman's shelter. Later, Prosecutor Epach told a reporter, "I took the written statement from him. . . . He was very nonchalant about it. I remember him sitting in the police station eating McDonald's. He had a Nike Camp hoop shirt on."[30] In a few short months Ronnie Fields had gone from the nation's most talked about high school phenom to wearing an orange jumpsuit and cleaning highways. The CBA looked increasingly likely as his next destination.

Sure enough, rather than go the junior college route or to Europe, Ronnie signed on with the Rockford Lightning. ESPN covered his first game but he didn't play all that much, and as the seasons wore on, Fields's sporadic playing time and suspect jump-shot, as well as lingering questions about his character, even though he'd stayed out of further trouble, kept him from getting an NBA offer. Thus began Ronnie's long career in the United States' minor leagues, with occasional stints in South America and the Philippines.

In 2001, Fields's career reached a low point as he found himself trying out for the Lightning yet again. At that time, I was vying for a spot on the Gary Steelheads, and we played the Lightning in an exhibition game. The Lightning were coached by Stacey King, the former Chicago Bull and an NCAA championship runner-up at the University of Oklahoma, and King did not seem enamored with Fields's game. It was kind of sad seeing Ronnie out of shape, playing few minutes, and sort of looking beaten down. Just five years earlier we'd both attended the Nike All-American Basketball Camp, at which I'd watched him win the dunk contest with a nasty 360 degree windmill. But not long after this 2001 exhibition game, Stacey King sent Ronnie home, where he stayed the rest of the season with virtually no offers from anywhere.

Then a peculiar thing happened. The next year a former-cop-turned-basketball-coach with a desire to run and a penchant for the underdog, a man who was also apparently aware that the Lightning owner, Wayne Timpe, liked Ronnie Fields, replaced King at the helm of the Rockford Lightning. Chris Daleo, as he would later do with me, gave Fields a shot when basically no one else would. And suddenly Fields, who had just spent his first winter without basketball in over twenty years, became a centerpiece of the organization.

He would spend at least part of the next four seasons with Daleo (and two more later on in Minot, South Dakota) in a love-hate relationship that solidified his legacy as "Ronnie Rockford."

Fields—with his ability to shoot Jordan-like turnarounds out of the low block, his ability to hang and double-clutch on jumpers in the lane, and his veteran-like ability to play the game at his pace—flourished under Daleo's style. After years of toiling fairly unremarkably as a professional, in his first season with Daleo he became arguably the best minor league basketball player in the United States. By the end of the 2003-04 season he had led the CBA in scoring and steals for two years in a row. He remains the only player to have done this. Heading into the 2004-05 season only one piece of the Ronnie Fields basketball saga remained: would he finally get a shot in the NBA? But as player after player got called up, it increasingly looked like it just wouldn't happen.

12

By nighttime on the third day of the 2004-05 Lightning training camp, my bones hurt and my muscles seemed to be in a near permanent state of cramping. We'd played about five and a half hours a day for two days straight, scrimmaging most of that time. Compounding matters, I'd jacked up my ankle in that third night's session by stepping on Jermaine Williams's foot.

I curled up in my Fairfield Inn bed just off of Interstate 90, while my wife Christy slept in our apartment back in Chicago.

What am I doing here, what am I chasing? I miss Christy. Ah, just see it through, give it a go. Survive. This place is crazy. Life's crazy. I'm not playing that badly. I could make this team. It doesn't look good. I've got a shot. How could I possibly be this sore? I mean this is ridiculous. The hoopin's good though, you gotta admit that. Yeah, it's buckets. My body just has to hold up.

By the end of day three a few guys had managed to establish themselves. Brian "Lubes" Lubeck, a six feet six shooting guard and former part-time model, with blue eyes, a strong jaw, and Ashton Kutcher-like hair, played solidly, while "Ronnie Rockford" had, not surprisingly, showed flashes of brilliance. But as a virtual lock and a veteran, you got the impression that he mainly saw camp as a chance to get in shape and retune his game, rather than as an all-out battle for employment.

Less expected, at least to me, was the play of Brant Bailey, a chiseled, 6'6" guard/forward from Wisconsin Dells who had played for the University of Wisconsin Stevens-Point and finished there in 2000 among its all-time leading scorers, just seventy-nine points away from long-time NBA stalwart Terry Porter's total. Daleo loved the way Bailey played and that he showed up early to training sessions to work on his game.

Bailey worked out all the time and took what seemed like an array of manly powders, which you can buy at most any health food store. His muscles, accompanied by thick veins, bulged out of his skin. They weren't bulky, mind you, more like lean and long and bulging all at the same time—he had sinewy bulk. Even his jaw muscles protruded. His eye sockets, in contrast, were deep-set, and he sported a goatee. He seemed to literally drip of testosterone, didn't tire easily, and, for a white guy, could flush with authority.

However, Brant struggled with basketball sense. On the defensive end, his rotations were odd. You never knew who he might decide to pick up in a scramble situation. On offense, his movements confounded as well. For instance, he rarely passed when he had the ball on the move, not because he was selfish, but because he went so fast and spun so much that he didn't seem able to see anything on the floor except what was right in front of him. And if he didn't have the ball, he would often cut at weird times. He might cut right when someone else was cutting or somehow make you think that he was going to cut and then not cut. Next time around, he might make you think he wasn't going to cut only to suddenly cut. It was perplexing, but to the opposition as well, as if the theory was: to truly be bewildering you must thoroughly bewilder. It became common to see Daleo, looking all confused, yell at Brant, "What're you doing?" Yet Brant played hard and fast and that's what Dales loved most. So he kept him.

Still, in time, Brant caused so much on-court perplexity that among the players he earned the nickname "The Baffler."

Quite sore, I arrived early for day four's morning session so I could loosen up my sprained ankle, only to discover that there wouldn't be much loosening going on.

Our trainer, Brad, came over to inquire about my condition. I told him it was a high sprain and stiff.

"Have you taken any ibuprofen?" he asked.

"I took some Aleve, but shoot, man, I probably shouldn't play. Then again, you sit out a couple of days and boom, you get sent home, so I can't really afford not to."

Trainer Brad was entering his third stint with the Lightning. He'd kept coming back for about $8,000 to $9,000 on average per season, even though he and his wife lived nearly an hour away in Wisconsin.

Though only in his early twenties, he sported a nice-sized gut and a mop of curly sandy-blond hair, and he dressed predominantly in sweat pants and old t-shirts. He basically looked like he'd just rolled out of a fraternity bunkhouse. And I tell you, Trainer Brad was a teddy bear; you couldn't help but like him. You just sensed that he was a good, honest man, even if he sometimes pilfered things at Dales's command.

Being the only other guy, besides Ronnie, who had been in Rockford for all of Daleo's first three years, Brad shared a weird kind of bond with Dales. Brad claimed a measure of distaste for him, but they commonly shared a room on the road, and you could often spot them dining together. Dales, reveling in the tough-guy persona, liked to dispense nuggets of wisdom to Brad. If you happened to listen in on one of their dinner conversations, you might catch Dales warning Brad about various things, like not to have kids.

"Why?" Dales would ask, feigning a shocked-like smirk. "They're too expensive. Don't have kids."

Given the time they'd spent together over the years, by year three Daleo had grown to consider Brad his right-hand man, even though Dales still made fun of him in front of the team for being fat and for the way he ran. In Trainer Brad's mind, despite interacting with Daleo so much over the years, he was able to remain unaffected by Dales, and to a large degree he had, but time and proximity can have a way of working away at things.

It was during this unlikely pair's first season together that Brad started stealing for Dales. On a road trip to play the CBA's Grand Rapids Hoops, Dales noticed that one of the basketballs on the Hoops' ball rack was not marked. He told Brad to take it, to write "Rockford Lightning" on it, and to stuff it in his bag.

By this time, just like the rest of us, Brad had already seen people getting cut with regularity, and I'm sure he realized that defying such an order could bring the ax down on him as well. So Brad obliged—and as time went on, it got easier for him to comply with Dales's demands. Soon, everywhere they went, Brad was expected to check if any basketballs looked ripe for the taking. Brad told me that Dales probably had twelve Wilson CBA basketballs in his office with "Rockford Lightning" written on them. And it wasn't just basketballs. Dales also had Trainer Brad swiping hotel soap and training room material, and he had him messing up visiting teams' travel itineraries.

Once, on a road trip in 2004, beaten down from the CBA grind and Dale's ways, Trainer Brad told me, "I feel bad about waiting for the maid to go in and clean the room so I can grab soap from her cart and run. Earlier this year I had to ride around the Fairfield a couple of times and wait for the maid to go into a room to steal soap from her cart. [For CBA games, the home team is supposed to provide soap for both locker rooms, but apparently Dales didn't like paying for that]. A few times I've just gone to Target and bought soap, just to appease Dales and let him think I'd stolen it from the hotel. I just took one for the team." But financing Dales's appetite for soap could get costly, especially on eight to nine grand per year. As a result, at a Baymont Inn and Suites that season, Brad took close to a hundred bars of soap just to make his life easier.[31]

Apparently, the pinching at the arenas usually went down during our hour-long pre-game shoot-arounds, which commonly took place at about 11:00 a.m.—when there weren't a lot of folks about. Dales would walk around checking doors and wandering into rooms. If he saw something he wanted that looked like easy-pickings, like a towel or something, he'd turn to Brad and say, "We can use a couple of these, right?"

Once, in Michigan, during the 2004-5 season, Dales discovered that the Great Lakes Storm had left their training room open. Brad recalled: "I had to start ransacking their training bag for tape. . . . Coach Daleo was just picking stuff up and giving it to me, telling me what to take. Afterwards I got to thinking, *I don't want people doing this to me, why would I do it to other people?* But I gotta steal stuff. If I didn't he'd bring it up every day on the bus. He'd say, you know, I'm not loyal and all this crap."

It sounded pretty harmless, but you could tell that it nagged Brad a bit. And, as I say, it wasn't just the pilfering. Dales expected Brad to fill up the opposing teams' water coolers with lukewarm shower water before games at Rockford's MetroCentre. Before setting the coolers down behind the visitor's bench, Brad would lug them into the showers in our locker room and go to work. I think this made him feel sort of rotten too.

But again, like most of us, Brad walked around in a perpetual state of fear that Dales would fire him. During the 2004-05 campaign Daleo threatened Brad with the ax almost daily, even though he'd also try, and sometimes succeed, to make it seem like Brad was his guy.

It was during the previous season that Brad might've come closest to actually getting canned. As the story goes, Dales had been telling Brad and another guy who worked for the Lightning, a fellow named Alexis, to screw up the practice times for the visiting Dakota Wizards and then show up to their game-day shoot-around without any basketballs, claiming some sort of miscommunication. The Wizards were in first place in the CBA's other conference and were coached by Dales's nemesis, Dave Joerger, who in addition to youthfulness already had a couple of CBA titles. Nothing got Dales's daubers up quite like ol' Joerger, which is why he wanted Brad and Alexis to mess things up for the Wizards.

Over the years, Joerger sensed that something was peculiar about his Rockford trips. Things like getting the shoot-around times completely crossed or having no basketballs on-hand didn't happen at other CBA arenas. He had an inkling that Dales was messin' with him, but he couldn't be sure.

Anyway, on this night before a Wizards' shoot-around, Trainer Brad, weary of the shenanigans and eager to get home to his wife instead of playing dumb all night, dropped off a couple of basketballs at Joerger's hotel. He had figured it would go unnoticed by Dales, but he didn't reckon that Alexis would see this as an opportunity to shine. Armed with the knowledge of Brad's insurrection, he apparently went to Dales to tell him that his trainer was a traitor.

After the game that night, Dales brought Brad back into the locker room and called him a backstabber and accused him of lacking loyalty. And over the next few weeks or so, Dales went around the Lightning office bragging that he'd come down so hard on Brad that he wouldn't come back next season. But Dales didn't fire him, and Brad did come back. Brad told me he did so to prove that he was the larger man; that he could hang. This sounded like one of my rationalizations.

But Trainer Brad did say, while taping my bum ankle at this 2004 training camp, that the upcoming campaign really would mark his last in the CBA.

"Do you plan on getting a gig at a high school or trying to look for a job at a college?"

"No, I'm getting out of the business."

"Really?"

"Yeah, I can't take it. I can't work for him anymore."

"What are you thinking about doing?"

"Maybe something in construction."

Trainer Brad sounded more serious than he had during my list stint in Rockford when he'd talked about leaving. But then again, it was hard to say if he really would go. The CBA had a peculiar ability to make you want to get out of the basketball business entirely—to go work construction, for example—while somehow also making you want to stay. Even the trainers.

"I mean, we can't keep living on these types of wages," Brad said. "Sarah wants to have a baby. I hardly make any money. What do you think I made my first year, Carson?"

"I don't know, what'd you make?"

"Six thousand dollars."

"For twenty weeks. Yeah, that's not a lot of money. That's actually less than I made my first year in Rockford [broken down per week]."

"I made eight thousand my second season, and got a 'big-time' raise for 2005," Brad said.

"Oh yeah?"

"Yeah, well, for Chris [Daleo] it was big. I'm making eleven thousand five hundred dollars this season."

"That's more than I'm making."

Great. If I somehow make this team, I'll make less than the trainer.

13

O nce my ankle got taped and we all got squared away, we met at half-court for another one of Daleo's pre-practice speeches:

"Fellas, for many of you this is your last scrimmage against each other. We have a short practice tomorrow and then a practice game against Muskegon the next day. And then I'll send some of you home. Troy will come to your room and let you know your flight information and everything, and then he'll take you to the Milwaukee or Chicago airport. Don't ask Troy a bunch of questions like 'Why'd Coach cut me?' and 'What else could I have done?' You're wastin' your time, 'cuz Troy doesn't know.

"The assistants and I talk about players and I listen to their advice, but ultimately, it's my decision because it's my contract. After all, these two guys [he pointed to his assistants, Renaldo Thomas and Troy Farrow] are after my job. I have Troy cut people because it's easier. I've done it myself before, but that doesn't work. A few years ago I got in an hour-long conversation with a guy about why I was cutting him. It's silliness. You're cut anyway. The decision's already been rendered. I got no beefs, you're just cut. Nothing big, you just didn't fit in my system. That's it. No beefs."

Assistant Troy, who was fresh out of college, had played under Daleo for a year at Barat, a small liberal arts college in the Chicagoland area's swanky North Shore. (Before Daleo's Barat stint, he'd coached high school hoops for a few years and been a lower-rung Lightning "assistant," during which he'd admittedly schmoozed up to the Lightning owners, Mr. and Mrs. Timpe.) Troy had helped Daleo enjoy a measure of success at Barat until administrators apparently grew annoyed by the renegade outfit Dales had put together and shut the program down—literally shut it down.

At Barat, Daleo said he would do stuff like pick a player up "off the streets of Waukegan" and get him enrolled. Dales claimed that a key to his operation was to buy flowers for a lady who assisted the woman in charge of Barat's admissions. When the head lady was out of town or away from work for some other thing, Dales would ask the assistant to pull a bunch of strings.

As for Troy's assistant gig with the Lightning, Daleo didn't allow him to do much of anything except receive verbal lashings in times of crisis, sweep the floors, and practice every now and then if someone needed a rest or was injured.

Our other assistant, Renaldo Thomas, from Gary, Indiana, was a middle-aged, generally good-natured guy, who could become a ball of fire when competing. He'd played his college ball at Houston as a member of the Phi Slamma Jamma. With the Lightning, he'd wear flashy seventies-looking suits to games that conjured images of *Sanford and Son*'s Demond. And when Renaldo talked about his college days, he liked to mention the time he dropped a bunch of points on DePaul in front of all his hometown folks during a game that aired on WGN. Any time a guy brings up WGN when reminiscing about his hooping days, you know he's old school.

Daleo didn't work well with others, though, so he didn't give Coach Thomas many duties either. He did, however, put him in charge of the out-of-bounds plays. Those were just about the only plays we had, and they were just about Coach Thomas's only time to shine, so he put his back into them. He had one play in particular that he just loved. It involved a whole bunch of screens and coordinated movement, exactly the type of stuff Daleo hated.

When Renaldo went over this play with us, he would get really excited on account of not having an opportunity to do much else and given that he loved the play so much. As we'd run through it, he'd be on the sideline calling out all these different options: "Curl, if he trails, curl. You see if he goes under, flair. It's unstoppable. Everything you do is right, everything the defense does is wrong. Run it again . . . Yeah, see, you can cut in here if they do that, you see, it doesn't matter—everything you do is right, everything they do is wrong."

We'd run it again and Coach Thomas would pull aside a player and say: "You see what I'm sayin'? If they go there, you can go under. If he goes there, you can curl. It doesn't matter. Whatever you do is right, whatever the defense does is wrong."

14

B y the end of the night-session on day four of camp, I was spent. My bones were aching, my feet were peeling, and my muscles were sore—muscles in my stomach I didn't even know I had felt sore if touched slightly. I don't mean to be all dramatic-like, but I'm telling you it hurt to turn over in bed. No matter which position I tried to sleep in, my legs would start cramping up.

We'd gone hard for nearly six hours a day but, as I say, feeling that sore didn't make sense. It was about then that I finally started to wonder if that darn creatine regimen I'd started after three years of not taking the stuff had been the best idea.

The next morning, a Sunday, it hurt to walk to the bathroom. You should've seen me get there. It was like someone was tasering me along the way.

As I got my stuff together for practice, I turned on the boob tube. I thought about watching ESPN, but I was hesitant, knowing that all I'd probably see would be two guys sitting at a table and screaming at each other—and then I'd have to hear about how it was brought to me by Coors Light. Worse yet, then I might have to listen to some story about T.O. So instead I listened to Chris Matthews, admittedly a yeller, and his panel of insiders, including the indomitable wordsmith Maureen Dowd, talk about the "moral" issue. Supposedly the "moral" issue had just given Bush the presidency. They seemed entirely perplexed. It was as if Bush was their "Baffler."

As I watched, I wondered if it was solely the creatine or a combination of creatine and age that was making me so sore. I figured one thing alone probably couldn't make someone this sore, so it was probably both.

You're only four days in. Think of the NBA guys. They have a longer camp, followed by eighty-two games, and then, if they're lucky, the playoffs.

At practice, with our first exhibition game a day away, Daleo filled us in on the upcoming itinerary. After practice, we'd take an eight-hour bus ride to Michigan to play the (Muskegon) Mayhem—yet another squad with a team name that isn't animate or plural.

In the meantime, aided by Aleve, I loosened up my body enough to put in at least a solid performance at practice. But Boseman, Dupay, and McCollum played well too.

Dales put a lot of weight on preseason games, so as I boarded our chartered bus I thought about how I needed to turn in a strong performance.

We made our way across Indiana and deep up into Michigan, before staying the night a little ways outside of Muskegon at a Hampton Inn, which was a remarkable upgrade compared to the Fairfield. The Hampton was a legitimate hotel with actual hallways. It had comfortable beds and decent towels, an indoor pool with a hot tub, free broadband internet in the rooms and a legit continental breakfast.

Upon arriving, we congregated in the Hampton lobby and waited to be issued our room keys as Daleo excitedly handed out little booklets. Apparently, he'd talked the owner of the Muskegon squad, who happened to own a bunch of McDonald's restaurants, into leaving two booklets with $5 worth of McDonald's coupons for each player.

The next day Daleo walked around checking to see if guys had used their McDonald's coupons. Even if you hadn't used them, you told him, "Yeah, Coach." Showing some thoughtfulness, he liked to hear that you did. He'd even start doing the math in his head for you: "It's nice, huh? If you can save $10 of your $20 per diem, then tomorrow when I give you $20 you'll have $30." CBA economics.

I got paired up to room with Dupay that night, and we spent a good deal of the evening acting like we were drawing up Thomas-like out-of-bounds plays in which whatever you did on offense was right and no matter what you did on defense was wrong. We imagined the greatest players in the world going up against a ragtag group of ballers and yet becoming victimized by these plays because everything the pros did on defense was wrong. Jordan, victimized. Shaq, helpless. Russell, baffled. Then Teddy raised the stakes.

"What would Ditka do against a Renaldo Thomas play?" he asked.

"Oh, that's good. What a battle. Is Ditka on a bus?"

"Ditka on a bus versus the Thomas play. It would be legendary."

"I just can't decide it."

"Me neither."

"It's undecidable, unfathomable, really."

We went on and on conjuring ridiculous scenarios involving Thomas's unbeatable play. And we talked hoops and otherwise shot the breeze nice and easy.

Eventually, late into the night, we got to talking about Dupay's gambling troubles at Florida. At one point in our conversation he said that if Coach Donovan had just once, throughout the seven-month saga, said, "'We fully support Teddy and we're going to stand by him through this process all the way,' it would not have ended as it did." Dupay said that then, he might have fought the charges. He also said that he'd gotten told on for gambling by his teammate Brett Nelson.

Both Nelson and Dupay had come to Florida ranked among the nation's greatest young shooters and while there, they competed with each other for minutes. Initially, they also forged a close friendship. Dupay figured that the pressure to live up to expectations partly motivated Nelson to tell Coach Donovan that Dupay had been betting on Florida basketball games.

Later, Dupay did say he occasionally bet $30 or $50 on football games with students who lived in fraternities, but he claimed that bookies weren't involved. He also pointed out that during his junior year, Florida covered the spread in a ridiculous percentage of their games, something like over 90 percent of them, which should show that no point-shaving took place.

As the NCAA dragged out its investigation over many months, leaving him in the dark through the summer leading up to his senior year, Teddy said he just worked out and waited. Then, when the NCAA finally declared him ineligible and charged him with "associating with known gamblers," he figured he had few options other than to leave school and try to find work playing somewhere. He wished that the NCAA would have at least told him sooner so that he could have gone to pre-draft workouts and played on an NBA summer league team.

When the NCAA's penalty came down, Dupay admitted publicly to making a mistake, but he denied placing bets on Gator games. A year later the Florida State's Attorney released a report based on a four-month investigation that led to the *USA Today* headline: "Documents: Ex-Gator Dupay Bet on College Sports."[32] During the investigation, the State Attorney's office made Dupay turn over his computer and investigators apparently found links to several gambling sites on it. The report pointed to Brett Nelson as the initial whistle-blower and noted that two other players—Udonis Haslem, who went on to Miami Heat fame, and Brent Wright—said Dupay talked about gambling in the locker room. Wright said Dupay told him of a wager that reaped $1,500.[33]

Gator soccer player Joseph Sustaita, an admitted gambler who got immunity from the State Attorney's office for his testimony, said Dupay tried to bet on Florida basketball as well. The soccer player's girlfriend confirmed her man's claims. It didn't help that Dupay apparently made 209 calls to Sustaita's apartment. Nor did it help that Tom Ostrom, the Florida basketball team's administrative assistant at the time, and the guy Brett Nelson supposedly initially told about Dupay's gambling, heard that "Dupay had a message board in his apartment with point spreads on it."[34] Dupay told *USA Today* he thought that University of Florida police pressured Sustaita into squawking:

They were bothering him every day when he came to class. One time, they came and handcuffed him in front of classmates....He was in tricky situation. He had a friendship, a relationship and his life in front of him. If it was me, and being totally realistic and the options were getting kicked out of school, ruining relationships and pretty much ruining your life or tell the investigators stuff about a guy you're not good friends with, you'll tell them what they want to hear. If you read the report, the first four or five times, he said nothing, nothing, nothing. They were really harassing Joe.[35]

By the time the *USA Today* report came out, Dupay was questioning his decision not to fight the matter a year earlier. "Sometimes I wish this went to court," he told the press. "This has turned my life upside down. I was backed into a corner. I couldn't talk about what happened when they showed me the police report, about the people who lied and stabbed me in the back to help themselves."[36]

One guy who did not offer up information to investigators was Kresten Lagerman, who had moved in with Dupay at Florida. Lagerman came out of the whole affair charged with witness tampering, a felony, and unlawful betting, a misdemeanor.

As we hashed it out, Teddy told me that during the course of the gambling imbroglio, he'd remembered an event that took place a couple of years earlier. On a flight to the Gators' first-round NCAA tournament game, he happened to sit by a high-ranking member of Florida's athletic department. After exchanging some friendly banter, the administrator told Teddy he was heading to an annual meeting for athletic departments and mentioned that each year there was an NCAA tournament pool at the event. Then he bent down and pulled out some papers. He needed Teddy to help him with his brackets.

15

The next day we rolled into Baldwin, Michigan—about an hour or so north of Muskegon—bound for the town's high school gym, where our first exhibition game would take place. As the bus approached the gym, Daleo was talking on his cell phone. He jokingly characterized his opinion of Baldwin to the person on the other end by saying, "Hold on a minute. We just saw two moose run across the road, a couple of inbreds overtook our bus, and the cops arrested us for various reasons."

Truth be told, Baldwin is small. It looks like an old, rural Midwestern farm town, akin to the type you might envision during America's early days, the kind of place where maybe a young Abraham Lincoln-type might have chopped some wood. So when we walked into the gym for warm-ups, it was a little surprising to see a notably African American crowd.

Baldwin High School's gym is also small, nothing like the northern Indiana high school gyms that I grew up playing in. It felt cozy, though, as I threw up shots to get loose. We were quite early, so this wasn't yet the official warm-up. After a bit, I sat down and looked up at the banners hanging on the gym's modest walls. By this time Eminen was freestyling over the school's audio system, and Baldwin High's dance team was warming up around half-court. Hanging on a wall was a banner for each of Baldwin's conference foes. One of them was nicknamed the Free Soilers, which was a short-lived political party in the mid-nineteenth century, a kind of precursor to Lincoln's Republican Party.

Now that's a heckuva of a team name. What a place to make my comeback and to play the first exhibition game of the season: Free Soil country, not far from the very birthplace of Lincoln's Party.

I looked back up at the Free Soilers banner.

What would Lincoln think of this scene here tonight? He'd probably be floored to learn that the scantily clad, gyrating dancers are high school-aged, and he'd probably wonder what this Eminem fellow is talking about. He'd probably be happy to see the integrated crowd, though. As for basketball, I bet he'd have taken a liking to it. A tall, lanky kid from Indiana—who knows, maybe he'd have been trying out for the Lightning too. Let's hope not.

I had time to ponder this type of stuff because the Michigan Mayhem were late. And not by merely a few minutes: the Mayhem arrived over a half-hour late to a game they'd specifically located in Baldwin as a way for fans outside of the Muskegon area to get acquainted with the team.

As things went, when the Mayhem players and coaches finally did arrive, they played as they had come—unorganized-like and tardily. I suppose this wasn't all that surprising, though, seeing as we knew virtually none of the players on the Mayhem roster, which was rare in the relatively small world of minor league U.S. hoops. Later on in the season the Mayhem did sign former NBA guys like Darrick Martin and Sam Mack, who apparently didn't need to mess around with training camp.

Since we still had four point guards on our roster, Daleo decided before the game to play only two of us per quarter. In the first, he went with Boseman and Dupay and then in the second, with Andre McCollum and me. The rotation seemed to suggest that Dales had me fourth on the depth chart, but I didn't want to put too much weight on it. This game marked my first live action in a year and a half, so my primary focus was on just showing that I still had it.

Finally, a few minutes into the second quarter, Daleo called my number. Going up to the makeshift scorer's table, if you want to call it that, I went over the plan of action in my mind. *Stay calm, get people involved, don't rush things, take good ones, stay down, good arch, follow through, stay focused.*

Within seconds of alerting the scorer's table of my intentions, a loose ball went out of bounds and I entered the game. And within seconds of stepping onto the floor, a Mayhem put the ball in play. As we often did in Dales's defensive system, another Lightning player and I immediately pounced, looking to trap. We closed in on the offensive player with the ball and soon had him in a tough spot. The ball squirted loose and I turned quickly to run after it. Only, as I did so, I felt a slight pull. Unfazed, I continued to dash after the ball. But midstride I felt another pull. That's when I knew I had to shut her down. It was the rare double pull.

What are the odds? Within the first few seconds of my first live action in over a year-and-a-half, I pull a hamstring and a groin? Was it the freakin' creatine?

As I wallowed in disbelief, the referee whistled a foul on a Mayhem. As we readied for a free throw, I knew what I had to do. I walked over to Dales.

"I've got to come out," I said.

He looked at me confusedly. "What?"

"It's crazy, I know, but I think I pulled a muscle. Two of 'em actually."

"Really?"

"Yeah."

He subbed for me, and I went down to the end of the bench to confer with Trainer Brad.

When I called my wife later that night, I wasn't entirely sure how to explain it.

"How'd it go?" she asked, excited for me.

"Well, honey, it didn't go too well."

"Really? Oh, that's all right. What happened?"

"Look, you're not going to believe it, but I think I tweaked two muscles. I think we're talking about a double pull here."

She felt for me but she had to try not to laugh. "Are you serious?"

"Yeah."

"Oh, honey, I'm sorry. I've never heard of such a thing"

"I know. Me neither."

Really, it was my fault, a silly rookie mistake. Instead of warming up intensely while we'd waited for the Mayhem to arrive, I'd resorted to casually shooting around or sitting down and pondering the Free Soil Party and Eminem and what Lincoln might've been doing had he been a young adult in the early twenty-first century. Combined all together: my year off, a casual warm-up, sitting down for about a quarter and a half, a quick turn and dash, and perhaps even my recent creatine use, a double-pull resulted.

Deciding to shut things down right away was about the only positive thing I did. By doing that, I didn't let the muscles stretch too far, so a chance remained that the injuries could mend within a week. It still embarrassed me, though, having to go over to tell Daleo I was done after just a handful of seconds had ticked away.

Earlier that morning, at the Hampton's continental breakfast, Dales had turned to me out of the blue and asked, "You have a job lined up to teach next spring?"

It seemed like an odd question, considering I was hoping that he'd employ me and that the season ran through the winter into spring. I couldn't tell whether he was testing me to see if I was going to be "distracted" by an outside job during the season or if he was suggesting that I consider other forms of employment.

"Nah, nothing lined up. I would have had to commit to an adjunct teaching gig a few weeks ago, and I decided instead to see this through," I said.

"So you rolled the dice."

"Yeah, I guess I did."

Newly married, I'd rolled the dice, and now I had a double pull.

16

A few days after our trip to Muskegon we played a second exhibition game against the Mayhem, this one in Rockford. Still convalescing from my double pull, I'd spent the days leading up to the game alternating between a hot tub and ice packs. On game day, though, my leg still wasn't ready, so all I could do was watch, which meant that my chances of making the squad plummeted.

It was our first game of the season on our home floor in Rockford's 8,000-seat MetroCentre, a multipurpose arena built in 1981 along the Rock River in downtown. It was an impressive place when first built, but by 2004, what with Rockford's downtown decaying, thanks in part to all the manufacturing jobs that have high-tailed it out of the Midwest, and in part to the tendency that interstate highways have of hijacking river traffic, the place seemed like a lonely salvo to Middle America's halcyon days.

As I sat, inactive, in the MetroCentre an hour or so before tip-off, I let myself get bored and frustrated. At least the Lightning ladies were there to provide some distraction. Sporting skin-tight outfits, they prepared for the game by gyrating to hip-hop tracks in a way that some might not consider exactly in-line with family entertainment. I recognized a couple of the leading ladies from my earlier stint in Rockford, and though I wasn't privy to the nuances of the dance-team world, I figured they were flirting with the same ignominious fate as borderline CBA-lifers like me.

Two of the leading ladies that I recognized from my last Rockford stint had maintained firm, supple bodies, and still showed enough trunk to appease modern tastes. And they danced with uncommon energy, even during their warm-up. I mean, somehow, they seemed really into it.

If only I'd warmed up that way.

It didn't seem like an act, either. They were tireless. During my last stint in Rockford, I'd gone with the some teammates to one of those dance clubs where songs by edgy lyricists like Method Man are followed by the tunes of pop princesses like Britney Spears, and these two ladies had been there, and I'm telling you, on that night they danced with the same frenetic energy that they were warming up with right now before our second exhibition game. This prompted me to start chewin' on things:

Do they take something? I mean, are they doing uppers? Don't be ridiculous. Alright, but look at 'em! It's remarkable that they can just constantly dance like that over and over again, day after day. Where does the energy for that come from? It's exhausting just watching. I wonder if they ever nap? They don't seem like they'd ever get tired enough to take a nap and yet for many years I've felt as if I could nap every single day. What's the difference? You should warm up like that.

Finally, the pre-game introductions started. The lights went down, bizarre European techno music blared, and the Lightning ladies lined up across from each other, creating a kind of tunnel for the Lightning players to run through as the announcer bellowed names.

We proceeded to beat the Mayhem again, though this time the score was a bit closer. Dupay fared particularly well. In twenty minutes, he scored nineteen points, many of which came off of deep bombs. The guy could launch. His performance, however, didn't help my cause.

17

B efore our final exhibition game Dales had already sent a few guys home, like B.B. Walden, a former standout at the University of South Florida. Most notably, though, he'd sent home Jamario Moon, a high-flyer from Alabama who had played on the Globetrotters the previous year and would eventually carve out a long career in the NBA.

When Moon exploded onto the NBA basketball scene early in the 2007-8 season, people wondered where he'd been and how he'd been so overlooked. It seemed wacky to people that someone who was twenty-seven years old and seven years removed from having declared for the NBA draft would suddenly perform so well on the big stage. But the truth is, some guys just get passed over. In the case of the ultra-talented Moon, he stuck with it even though he'd gotten cut time and again. Hours before he made the Raptors' roster, he told the *National Post,* "I've been cut before . . . I've been cut plenty of times. I am looking forward to being here. But if something happens and I am not here, then I understand. It's a business."[37]

At Lightning camp Dales knew that Moon had loads of talent, but he cut him nonetheless because he felt that Moon played passively and settled for the jumper too much, and that assessment, at least given Moon's play during our camp, had legitimacy. Still, there were numerous times during camp that Moon would make a ridiculous, absolutely spectacular play—the likes of which he has since made many times in the NBA and that people around the globe have viewed on YouTube.

Gravity is an impressive force, but Moon defied it longer than most anyone I'd ever played with. When he leapt and glided through the air it looked, for a few moments, like a spacewalk. And yet I didn't think all that much of it when he got cut. I chalked it up to a case of "that's just the way it goes sometimes." I certainly didn't predict he'd be starting for the Raptors in a couple of years or later catching 'oops from LeBron.

One evening during training camp, as we were driving over to practice in a passenger van, I happened to strike up a conversation with Moon. He told me about his small hometown, Goodwater, his lady back in Alabama—who, like my wife, would stick with him through all the professional uncertainty and eventually become his wife—and about how the Globetrotters would fine players for missing lay-ups in warm-ups. He seemed like a solid guy with an interesting story. But we were all busy trying to survive, so we didn't learn as much about each other as we could have.

Of course, once he started showcasing his hops in the NBA, all types of people became interested in learning more about Moon. They learned that his hometown consisted of one stoplight and that he'd been a celebrated high school star at Coosa Central High School with plans to go to Mississippi State, only to see those plans fall through when he didn't qualify academically. Instead, he set about cleaning up his academic record by attending a prep school, Mt. Zion Christian Academy, a basketball powerhouse. But he soon tired of the structure there and went home. He spent a short stint out West at Compton College in California only to return home again, and then he enrolled at Meridian Community College, not exactly a hoops hotbed. There, Moon played in just seven games, averaging over twenty points and eight rebounds, and then he declared for the NBA draft.

Declaring did not end up looking too smart. As Moon explained it, once he'd finally made it to the Toronto Raptors: "I was one of the kids who just got caught up with the wrong people, trying to listen to a whole lot of different stuff. There was NBA talk in my ear . . . it just got crazy. I didn't know what to do. If I had to tell the kids coming up to do one thing, it'd be listen to your parents first. You're going to make your decision but get your advice from your parents—don't go outside your family like I did."[38]

The core of that family was Moon's parents, Ruby Thomas and John Moon, who, though not wealthy, worked hard to provide for Jamario. "I've got a lot of stuff planned for my Momma," Moon said after making it in the League. "When I was coming up, I used to want to go to all these AAU camps and different camps and we didn't have the money to do that. But some kind of way, they'd find a way to do it. They'd have fish fries and sell all kinds of sandwiches and different stuff to raise the money for me to go."[39]

As people watched Moon perform well enough to max-out his NBA deal with the Raptors and then sign another, he humbly said, "There's not much difference between the play in the NBA and in the CBA. There are guys there that can play and a lot of guys who could start if they were put in my position."[40]

18

O ur third and final exhibition game pitted us versus the Great Lakes Storm in Birch Run, Michigan. For some guys, like me, it was a final opportunity to make a case for a roster spot. For others, like Muntrelle Dobbins, a veteran power forward who, milking his CBA rep for all it was worth, had shown up to camp several days late, the game was another chance to get in better shape.

Now if you'd happened to watch our workouts in these final days of camp, without any prior knowledge, you would've been surprised to learn that Dobbins was a roster lock. That's because he specialized in doing the bare minimum at camp. One time Dales tried to make us actually run sprints for conditioning, which was quite rare. I guess Dobbins reckoned his days of running sprints were in the past because he proceeded to dog it in epic fashion. I kid you not when I tell you that, as guys would head from one baseline to the other, he'd come up ten or twenty feet short of his mark and simply turn around and start "running" down to the other end. Only he wouldn't quite make it to the baseline coming back the other way either. About twenty feet or so short, he'd simply turn back around again and head the other way.

It was absolutely absurd and awesome at the same time. Dales just took it. The bottom line was that, for whatever reason, Dales thought Dobbins could win him games, and Dobbins knew it. So Dobbins did about what he wanted during camp. You had to appreciate it in a way, watching a guy expose the façade of a guy like Dales.

While Dobbins could get away with his shenanigans, at our last exhibition game I needed to focus on doing everything I could to land a job. I'd felt pretty good at practice the previous day, helping my confidence level as we'd boarded a charter bus for another long drive.

Upon arriving at our motel, we didn't have much time to catch up on sleep because our game was slated to tip at eleven o'clock the next morning. Pretty quickly after shutting it down, we would be hopping back on the bus to get up some shots up before the tip.

That next morning at the gym, it felt like a practice session more than a game. But it didn't matter. I needed to get something done regardless of the hour or the feel. Playing well probably wouldn't get it done. I needed to play great.

As it happened, I played almost half of what turned out to be a nip-and-tuck affair, which we lost by a few points in overtime. And in my first extended live action of camp, I played solidly, dropping in ten points and dishing out four assists. My legs held up fine. In fact, I felt somewhat quick and springy, and my mid-range jumper felt good. But I wasn't convinced it'd be enough.

Boseman, judging by Daleo's treatment of him, appeared to have made it, while Dupay had played well throughout most of the camp and had stayed healthy. Dales liked Teddy's jumper and that Boseman could muscle guys with his physical defense and hard drive to the basket, both of which helped Dales overlook Boseman's erratic shot. And, to Stais's credit, he hadn't exacerbated his shortcomings from the three-point line by launching a bunch of threes in camp. Instead, he'd driven and demonstrated passable midrange accuracy.

As for our opponent in this exhibition tilt, the Great Lakes Storm, they had all the markings of a solid CBA team, unlike the Mayhem. Three players in particular impressed. For one of the three, Mark Jones, a 6'5" thirty-year-old veteran wing with a solid European resume but no NBA experience, the 2004-05 season was basically his last shot at the League (in March he would sign with the Orlando Magic). Meanwhile, Kasib Powell, a 6'7" rookie swingman who had spent his college days with Bob Knight at Texas Tech, wanted to prove that NBA squads had made a mistake in not signing him (Ultimately, he, too, would make it to the League, a few years later). The other Storm standout, Jackie Butler, was perhaps the most interesting of all.

A thick and strong 6'10" nineteen-year-old, Butler landed in Birch Run, Michigan, right out of high school. Rather than starring on a big-time collegiate team, he'd turned himself into another example of why most top-flight scholastic players should not declare for the draft right out of high school. The CBA has seen plenty of guys who jumped too soon, whether high school phenoms like Korleone Young or collegiate ones such as Marcus Taylor, but the difference with Butler was that he could dominate. During the game I found myself wondering how he'd gotten bypassed by the NBA. I figured that maybe at this exhibition game he'd just happened to enjoy a really good run. Some nights a

CBA guy can look like a world-beater, the next a rec-league junkie. Time would tell.

Even if Butler did end up making the League, though, his decision to bypass college had already proven costly. Instead of getting a free education, tons of individual attention, and a chance to star on the national stage, he was playing against people like "The Baffler" and me in Birch Run, Michigan, in front of approximately thirty-eight fans. No joke.

He played well enough to make you think that had he gone to school, he could have turned himself into a first-round pick, which would've meant guaranteed years with an NBA team. Getting to the NBA through the Storm, if he could pull it off, would mean that any future contract he'd obtain would almost assuredly result in less money and fewer, if any, guaranteed years.

19

Following this final exhibition game, we drove back to Rockford, arriving at about 3:00 a.m. Given that Trainer Brad had as much access to Dales's ear as anyone else in our operation, during the ride I'd asked him for some guidance about my fate. The forecast he returned, though somewhat murky, was largely unfavorable.

When we pulled into the Fairfield, Daleo stood up at the front of the bus and announced that practice, for those who made the cut, was slated for 11:00 a.m. He also said, "If you get cut, Troy will knock on your door with your plane ticket in hand and give you the word."

I walked up to my motel room and tried to sleep, hoping that nobody would knock on the door. To my surprise, I awoke without having heard a thing except for the cars roaring down Interstate 90. So I went to practice.

Straight away I noticed that point guard Andre McCollum was not there, but oddly, eleven people still remained, including three point guards: Boseman, Dupay, and me. CBA rules stipulated that the opening day roster consisted of ten players. One of us still needed to go. Technically, Dales had until 4:00 p.m. to send in his official list of players, and it looked like he intended to wait until the last minute.

We stretched in a circle at half-court as Daleo spoke. He congratulated those who had made it and said: "As long as you work hard you'll get every chance to keep your job. If not, I've got Lawrence Nelson [a 6'11" center from Tulane] waiting in the wings, Marshall Phillips waiting in the wings, and I still have one point guard to cut today, and whoever that is will be ready to go if I have to send one of you home…"

Great. You shouldn't have gotten your hopes up. You're an idiot. Trainer Brad knows the deal. You're done.

The subsequent "practice" was more like a shoot-around. I went through the motions distracted, reckoning that my goose was cooked.

But since a sliver of hope remained, I vacillated between accepting reality and telling myself I still had a chance. After about an hour, the workout mercifully ended and I went back to the motel to await the word. Finally, at about 3:00 p.m., with final CBA rosters due in an hour, Troy knocked on my door. When I answered, he looked at me knowingly, and then let me know I'd been cut by the Dales.

After receiving the news and getting my stuff together, I went down to the Fairfield lobby and shot the breeze with Teddy, who had made the squad. After a bit, we wished each other well, and I gathered my stuff and hit the road. Driving east along I-90, across the dwindling farmland to Chicago, I thought sentimentally about the end of a nice ride—the Elite Eight, the Garden, Mackey Arena, ballers like Paul Rossetti, and all the rest. Getting axed by the Dales wasn't the best way to go out, but I had to face up to it.

20

To the people on the outside, it's not that big a deal if you make a CBA squad because they don't really know anything about the league. They just know you're trying to play in some league that nobody knows anything about. So they assume you should make it. But if you get cut, that's news. That's when people start looking at you a little sideways, wondering what you're doing back at home.

In the first few days after I was cut, my wife and I went to my parents' home to enjoy the Thanksgiving weekend. Extended family, close friends, and even casual acquaintances would see me and pause a moment, as if to say, "You're not supposed to be here, are you?" Some just came out and asked, "Aren't you supposed to be playing for some semi-pro basketball team?"

I could only nod.

"Oh, don't worry, you'll find something."

Getting the CBA ax also forces you to adjust from the cutthroat world of professional sports to regular life. Initially, this can seem easy. I spent that first weekend resting up my sore hammy and eating great meals as I hung out with my wife and family, and on Monday I played noon ball at a local YMCA. But I knew what was coming. It came that Monday night when I settled into our couch back in Chicago and the fear of the monotony of regular gigs, of a long, slow fade in a cubicle seized me. I'm not saying it was sensible, I'm just saying it was there. Maybe it was that internship I'd done for Schering-Plough during a college summer. I'd gotten stuck in a windowless office shadowing some guy who seemed unhappy and mainly liked to track the wages of the firm's upper-level managers, which were posted on financial websites. It was the type of gig that made you think monkeys had it good—out in nature, swinging from trees, eating bananas, and lying in the sun.

I worried that before I knew it, I'd wake up one day to find myself as a forty-five-year-old vacuum salesman, completely and utterly out of shape, uninspired by work, and wondering where my youth had gone and who had chopped my balls off.

For whatever reason, running around with grown males throwing a round ball in a metal rim helped keep my fears about this sort of decline at bay. I'd tell myself I lacked maturity and ingenuity and that it was ridiculous to think hoops was necessary, but it didn't matter much.

Late Monday night, actually in the early hours of the next morning, as I continued to wallow in my malaise, Dupay called me. I didn't pick it up. He left a message: "Hey, you're probably sleeping, but I just wanted to tell you that me and the boys were talking and I've got a new one for you: Ditka versus a hurricane. Ditka, Ditka. I met some ladies tonight and I asked them to tell me who would win: Coach Thomas's out-of-bounds play in the middle of a hurricane or Ditka? It was Ditka."

The next night the Lightning played the Sioux Falls Skyforce in South Dakota and they got pounded by thirty-one points. I'd been online checking the score every twenty minutes or so. The loss put the Lightning record at 1-2. I hit the pillow, thinking, *Maybe at some point they'll need me.*

That morning at 4:00 a.m., my phone rang. Hopping out of bed, I darted for it but just missed the call. The number left on caller-ID wasn't familiar. I checked my voicemail. Though hard to make out, the voice on the other end sounded like Daleo mumbling something akin to, "Get ready, I want you back."

I played it over a few times but couldn't make it out with certainty. Whoever it was, he sounded tortured and distant.

Baffled, I sat there and chewed on it.

Sure, Daleo might call at some point, but five and a half days into the season? That would be awfully quick, maybe unprecedented. It had to be him, who else could it be? Play it again…What is he saying? I have no idea. Whoever it is, he sounds rattled. Shoot, it's got to be him.

Finally, at 6:00 a.m., I decided to put in a call to the unknown number.

"Hello."

"Hello, who's this?" I asked.

"Troy. Who's this?"

It sounded like I woke him up. They were still on the bus, completing the nine-hour drive from Sioux Falls to Rockford.

"This is Carson; did you call me?"

"Oh, hey, what's up Carson, what's up? Umm, uh, no, I didn't call."

"Really?"

"Naw."

"Oh, because somebody left a message on my phone from this number."

He was silent for a few moments. "Oh, maybe that was Coach Daleo. I don't know; I let him borrow my phone earlier. I'll go get him."

I waited on the other end wondering what the heck was going on and what was taking him so long. Finally, Troy got back on.

"Coach told me to tell you to stay in shape."

Is this guy serious?! You call me at 4:00 a.m. after cutting me to tell me stay in shape? You have got to be...

"Okay," I said.

About twenty minutes later, Troy called again.

"Coach wants to know if you are still interested in playing, if you want to come back."

Here it is. I can walk away. Any reasonable person would recognize how goofy this is. If Daleo's found a scapegoat five days into the season, who's to say I wouldn't be next? The time has come to move on to the next phase of life. I have an opportunity for closure, a chance to say thanks, but no thanks. Ahh, but what about the fade? This is an opportunity to escape the malaise. And what about that championship? Nobody cares. I get to hoop.

"Yes, yes, I'm interested."

"All right then, we have practice tonight at 6:00 p.m. at Christian Life, and Coach wants you to come."

"Is he offering me a contract?"

"Yes, same conditions as your training camp contract."

Ten minutes later, my phone rang again. It was Daleo.

"Can you play pressure defense?"

Are you insane? What a stupid question. You're off...

"Yes."

What else am I gonna say, "No? No Coach, I don't think so. I can't play pressure defense."

"I need pressure. We're getting no pressure," Dales added.

"I can do that, Coach."

"We just got beat by Sioux Falls by thirty-one."

"Really?" I feigned. I've got some pride.

"You didn't know that?"

"Well, I saw you were down by fifteen or so at halftime, but did…"

"Yeah, well, then all hell broke loose. The ball was going everywhere, everything was chaotic…"

He sounded deranged. I didn't know if he was talking about the game or his mind.

"I can't talk anymore, I'm getting sick," he continued. Then he hung up.

Within a few moments, the phone rang again.

"Carson?"

It was Ronnie Fields.

"Yeah, is this Ronnie?"

"Yeah, yeah, what's up, man?"

"Nothing much…"

"Yeah, well, Coach wanted me to holler, you know, and talk to you, you know, about pressure defense. 'Cuz, you know, right now, we aren't gettin' any ball pressure."

Great, I'm talking pressure defense with Ronnie freakin' Fields. It's 6:00 a.m., and I'm standing in the kitchen in my briefs talking to Ronnie Fields about pressure defense. He doesn't pressure the ball much, and he rotates like a square tire, and he wants to talk pressure defense?

"All right, Ronnie, sounds good. Yeah, I can do that."

21

That day the Lightning released Dupay after just three games and that evening I headed to my new job. Of course, you certainly couldn't blame the losses on Dupay. As I'd find out soon enough we had bigger problems, especially with the chemistry between our "stars:" Ronnie Rockford, who seemed to have an insatiable appetite for isolation plays, Boseman, who was trying to learn to play with Fields, and Dobbins, who needed to get in shape and spend a good month or two refining his game but didn't have the time seeing as the season was underway. But it was Dupay that got axed.

I showed up to practice a bit early to put up some extra shots. Trainer Brad was already there, and he welcomed me back. Then I got to my shooting workout. It felt good to feel the leather in my hand after a bounce, knowing I had a team again, to keep my wrists in close to my body as I shot, to hold my follow-through, and to listen to the ball flow through the net. I got a nice groove going. It was melodic and soothing, a reminder of why I wanted to hoop.

Daleo arrived by and by, and then Troy strolled in. When my workout ended, Troy came over and handed me a big envelope with my contract inside. Only a few other players had arrived by then. Sitting down on the bleachers next to Brad, I opened the envelope and started to sign the different copies of my contract. Before giving it back to Troy, though, I checked the salary box just to make sure everything remained the same. I found the wage box and saw that it had been changed. Daleo had decreased my pay by $25 per week. Troy must've seen me checking it out, because just then, he came over and said, "Oh yeah, Coach Daleo told me to tell you he cut $25 from your pay." Then he walked away.

"Can you believe that shit, Brad?" I said.

"What a dick," Brad said.

Let it go, who cares about $25, for crying out loud? But it's the principle. He's seein' if he can treat you like a booch. He can't. I'm nobody's booch. If you let this fly without raisin' a peep, the same garbage that occurred last time will start all over: all the yellin' and hootin' and hollerin' the minute anything went wrong. Fuck this, stand up, be a man.

Jacked up, I called Dales over. He was across the court, keeping his distance, when I motioned for him. He pretended to suddenly notice me as I did so, and then he scurried over in short choppy steps as if he was eager to solve any problems. He looked at me condescendingly, like he wanted to help.

"What? What now?"

He's playing dumb. This guy is your boss. This is ridiculous.

"Well, Coach Daleo, I'm checking the numbers here...and, uh...well, it looks like...did you dock me $25 a week?"

He kind of tightened up and took a seat on the bleacher. "Yeah, I figured since I cut your ass after training camp and everything, not to mention you cussed me out that one time, I'd cut your pay $25." Then he paused. "Why? Was your phone ringing off the hook? Was the Michigan Mayhem calling you?"

"That's not the point. I just think you could've mentioned it when you called."

"Well, fine, don't worry about it. We'll just call it, then. Thanks for driving by. Don't bother signing it at all. Nice working with you."

He took me by surprise, playing his cards like that. I didn't expect to be cut again before even signing the contract. A lot of folks probably would've told him off right then, but I just kind of looked at him incredulously. Daleo glanced over at Sydney Holmes, who was nearby getting taped by Brad, and said, "Right Syd? 'Nice working with you, don't worry about it. You can just head on back home.' Isn't that how it works?"

Syd was just a rookie making half of my weekly wage. He just hoped to stay on the roster. You could tell he didn't want to get involved, but he couldn't afford to test Dales.

"Yeah, I guess so," he said.

Finally, I caught my balance.

"Well, I don't think it has to be that serious, but...I mean, if you want me to..."

Right in the middle of my big stand, though, Dales changed gears.

"No, you know what? You can have it. Even though you cussed me out back in Grand Rapids and I cut your ass for a second time a few days ago, you can have it. Write it in; you can have it," he said.

"It's $25, it doesn't have to be that serious. I was just saying, you could've told me…"

"Don't worry about it. Write it in. Do as I say."

"I mean, it's not that big a deal."

"Write it in. Do as I say."

"Fine."

22

A few days later, I stepped into our nondescript locker room in the MetroCentre's bowels for our game against the Gary Steelheads, which would mark my return, finally, to live regular season action. My new blue and gold Lightning uniform hung in a locker room stall. Sewn on the back was "Cunningham" and the number twenty-four, which I settled on since the Lightning didn't have a jersey with Paul Rossetti's forty-three.

In college, getting your uniform was powerful. Seeing Purdue on the front carried weight. There had been so many great Boilermaker teams with so many great players—John Wooden, Glenn Robinson, and Rick Mount. In the CBA, though, especially if you'd been there for a stretch, uniforms didn't resonate the same way. Partly because, with the turnover, it wasn't all that uncommon to see jerseys without last names (not enough time between the transaction and the next game to change out the lettering). Still, it was cool to see my uniform hanging there, a sure sign that I was back. And it seemed fitting that the first game in my championship mission would come against the CBA team that was not only adjacent to the town in which I grew up, but had darn near run me out of the league a few years earlier by not playing me.

Midway through the first quarter Daleo called my number. My hammy and ankle had healed up nicely by then, and I'd gotten in some good work the previous couple of days. Plus, by the time I entered the contest Lubes, The Baffler, Williams, Boseman, and Fields had helped build a nice cushion. All of this helped me feel more comfortable out there. Running up and down a few times, my legs felt good, live action even better.

We won the first quarter point. (To discourage loafing, each quarter in the CBA was worth a point. In total, you could win seven points per game: four for winning each quarter and three points for winning the game. The scheme worked pretty well.) And we took the second quarter point, too, thanks in part to a late tip-in by our recently acquired seven-foot center Guy Rucker, who, following his collegiate career at the University of Iowa, had played a stint for the NBA's Golden State Warriors and overseas.

Having lost the third quarter, the overall lead ricocheted back and forth in the fourth. Even though it was just my first game back, I started to get nervous on the sidelines thinking about Daleo's quick trigger.

We need to win this thing. It's your first game, relax. Dupay lasted three. You didn't shoot well. It'd be nice to win this thing.

With about ten seconds remaining and the score knotted up, Lubeck drilled a fadeaway jumper to put us up by two. Gary tied it up, though, with just less than three seconds remaining. Daleo then signaled for his seventy-fifth timeout of the game.

Though not prone to calling plays, in this huddle, Dales decided to draw one up. It was kind of a goofy drawing that he put together, with a mass of lines indicating people running here and there. But in my experience, this wasn't all that surprising. It's hard to draw when you're nervous. Even at Purdue it wasn't unusual for Coach Keady to get all nervous at the end of a tight game. His black marker was liable to scoot around unpredictably. In fact, the managers nicknamed his board the "Ouija board" and his marker the "magic marker." Usually, you could figure out what Keady meant, but you had to focus as that marker meandered about. Same thing with Dales's play this time. Basically, it boiled down to getting the ball to Ronnie.

As it happened, before we went back on the court, Dales put me in the game, essentially to stand on the three-point line away from the action, with the outside chance that the inbounder or Fields encountered such duress that they would need to toss it to me.

Near the right-hash on our half of the court, Boseman readied to put the ball in play. When the ref handed it to him, Fields came running from underneath the basket to the right-side. Boseman threw him the ball, and Fields, deep on the right sideline and facing away from the basket, caught it, spun, and threw up a three all seemingly in one motion. It was a ridiculous shot, and yet somehow it swished through the bucket. In a way, it was vintage Ronnie. Although he could hoard the ball and disrupt team chemistry at times, he could also make spectacular plays like this one.

After Gary launched one last desperation heave that fell short, victory was ours, and I went nuts, jumping up and down like I was thirteen again, watching The Rocket Ismail return one for the Irish.

And the Rockford crowd, which could get livelier than you might guess, went nuts too.

It was hard to say on a given night how many people would make up a CBA crowd and who those people might be. Sure, on some nights you might attract just a few hundred people or less, but on the right night in Rockford you could draw close to two or three thousand fans. And out west, say in a Bismarck, N.D. or Boise, Idaho, you were liable to draw even more. And those crowds, especially out west, could get to sounding and feeling a lot like a college crowd.

Among those fans, whether in Rockford or Bismarck, were families with young kids, some of whom knew all about hoops, others of whom had just come out on a lark. Maybe they couldn't afford a Bulls game or maybe their kids were young enough not to care about the difference. These families just wanted to be together, carefree and entertained for a couple of hours, and had paid hard-earned money to do so. In a CBA crowd, you might find, sitting alone, an older woman who had some way or another gotten into her local team. Sitting alongside her, perhaps a twenty-something couple out on a first date, hoping a basketball game would give them a good shot at getting things started off right. Some spectators were simply hardcore hoops fans, who knew good ball when they saw it and sought it out. No matter whom they were or where they came from, though, on nights like this in the MetroCentre they were all up and cheering right along with us.

Sure, Fields was still playing selfishly and Dobbins was still not in form, but when you win like that you can forget about stuff like that, at least for a bit. Plus, as alarmist as it might sound, winning a game like that was huge for everybody, especially if you shot two for twelve like I did. Looking for some solace, I tried to focus on my four steals, but really, before Ronnie's three, I'd reckoned Daleo might pull the plug on me again. Those worries went right down the bucket with that game-winner, though.

Following our on-court celebration, we piled into the locker room, smiles all around. Coach Thomas kept saying, "Ronnie Rockford, Ronnie Rockford, oooh-oooh Ronnie Rockford..."

Daleo was all fired up and excited too. He had this weird, almost evil-looking grin on his face as he talked, hyper-fast, about the various plays down the stretch. Sports can do wild things to a fellow. What a transformation. Only a few days earlier, he had mumbled inarticulately into the phone that he was sick and couldn't talk.

Don't get swept up in it. Don't get too high or low. Things can change overnight. Stay even.

2004-05 Rockford Lighting during a break in the action. Dobbins to far right, Fields far left. Forward Jermanine Williams, uniform number 1, Stais Boseman, number 32, and rookie Sydney Holmes, number 12. To the right of Holmes is Brant "the Baffler" Bailey, and to the Baffler's right is Greg Claussen. I'm in between Brian Lubeck and center Guy Rucker (who is on my left). You can see Coach Daleo offering insight, and the back of Coach Renaldo Thomas, in the dark suit.

23

We trained in Rockford for a couple of days before embarking on the seven-hour drive to play the Great Lakes Storm again in Birch Run, Michigan. The itinerary for this road trip had us hopping back on the bus immediately after the Storm game for a drive to Muskegon, where we'd arrive at about 5:00 a.m. for a night game fourteen hours later. Then, we'd get on the bus again for a six-hour ride back to Rockford.

Rather than driving up with the team on Tuesday afternoon, I talked Daleo into letting me attend a previously-planned history seminar, with the understanding that, after it, I'd drive myself to Birch Run. I was nervous asking him if I could do it, but he seemed fine with it. So at about 9:00 p.m., in a driving rain-snow-sleet storm, I settled into my little Toyota for the long ride. The storm stayed with me virtually the entire way and the visibility was awful, so I had to go incredibly slow. I considered calling it quits on numerous occasions, just pulling over at a Motel 8, shutting it down, and checking things out in the morning, but I powered on and landed at the Birch Run Knights Inn at about 3:30 a.m.

It was too late to spend any time on my diary, which I'd been keeping off and on pretty much ever since I'd started playing in the CBA—something about the league just made me need to start writing; maybe it helped me cope.

I opened the door to my room and saw Trainer Brad tangled up with his covers, trying to sleep in one of the moon beds with nothing on but his tighty-whities. He woke up enough to mumble "Hello." Then he chuckled and asked, "Can you believe this place?"

Later in the season guard-forward Marshall Phillips would sum up the Knights Inn best when, stepping into the "lobby," he turned to me and said, "Carson, watch out for Mr. Bates tonight." And Phillips hadn't even seen the rooms yet.

For this season, the Knights Inn won the always competitive race for "worst hotel/motel in the CBA." The entire structure was musty and broken down, and even the outdoor walkway from the parking lot to the rooms was slipshod. It rolled as if whoever had poured the concrete did so while daydreaming of Scotland's majestic hills or had put it down lit. The rooms themselves contained no clocks. That's rare. No way to set an alarm, no way to check the time. No clock. And the beds had lumps all over. I don't mean a slight bump here and there, more like craters everywhere. I'm not a terribly particular fellow, but I'm telling you, it was like sleeping on the moon or something. And the television broadcast about six channels, and that's putting it generously.

Still groggy and rolling around with his head smashed in his pillow, but waking up a little more, Brad said, "Worst hotel in the CBA, hands down." He reflected a moment before adding, "And that's keeping in mind that I stayed at a place in Sioux Falls just last week that had holes in the dry wall and a television set with an actual dial rather than a remote." He raised his head up above the pillow, taking in the whole scene, and reaffirmed it: "Yep, worst motel in the CBA."

That night in the locker room, as we suited up for the game, no one seemed aware that a CBA record was about to come perilously close to falling. My first inkling that this might happen came during warm-ups, when I noticed the exceptional lack of people in attendance.

After warm-ups, I took a seat on the bench. The game—once the lights came back on, the overly sexualized lyrics that had been blasting away ceased, the disco ball was raised back up to the ceiling, the dancing ladies, with tantalizing evidence of their G-strings showing just above their low-cut, skin-tight pants, left the floor, and a ridiculously loud PA announcer finished screaming the starters' names as they ran out onto the court—was about to start.

At least the blaring music wasn't techno. In Rockford, they made you sit through a long routine featuring the Lightning's dancing ladies that was often choreographed to a thumping European techno track.

All that civilization and Europeans want to stand in a dark room and listen to the same beat pound their heads over and over and over again? It's amazing.

Perhaps the most memorable CBA pre-game routine of all-time took place in Rockford during the holidays, when the director of the Lightning gals decided to have them gyrate to a bunch of jazzed-up Christmas tunes. In tight black stretch pants with thongs peeking out, and a tight-fitting Lightning shirt and a Santa hat on, they danced to a re-mix of the "Little Drummer Boy," for crying out loud. I heard that a fan wrote a letter to Lightning brass wondering how in the world the organization could hire people to dance to the "Little Drummer Boy" like that. Apparently, there is a line.

Back in Birch Run, on this near-record-setting night, once the PA guy stopped screaming, my fan count could finally get under way. I'd started the count a few years earlier, during my first stint in the league. It could make for a nice diversion, and an exciting one, because it's nearly impossible to predict when an inordinate number of people will decide not to come to a CBA game. On this night they did. The total number of fans in the stands prior to the tip-off came to seventy-eight. As low as this was, though, in 2002, at a road game in Rockford when I was a member of the Gary Steelheads, I tallied a pre-tip count of seventy-six.

Still, sprinkled in a CBA crowd, no matter how small, could very well be some powerful figures in the basketball scene, like executives and scouts from the NBA or Europe, former coaches out looking in an unofficial capacity for somebody, or raters of minor league talent who wrote up reports on players that basketball executives the world over subscribed to—in other words, guys who could make or break your basketball dreams.

On opening night, when I'd started for the Lightning a couple of years prior, for instance, I remember catching a glimpse of B.J. Armstrong, a former All-Star guard for the Bulls who was working in Chicago's front office, and future Bulls G.M. John Paxson. That type of thing can't help but get you to thinking, *What if I play big tonight?*...

The seventy-eight people in Birch Run on this night, however, didn't see the Lightning play big. We got down early and pretty much stayed down. A couple of times we came within striking distance, but not much more. I did shoot well, though, which I figured might help me survive for at least a few more days.

This was yet another interesting thing about the CBA realm, particularly for role players: If you, by chance, could manage to play well in the games you lost and save your bad games for the games you won, your chances of survival could increase. But it was a delicate balance. If you were having a bad game, you always ran the risk of playing so badly that it looked like you were the main reason behind the loss. That was terrible for your cause. At the same time, you could play well enough to get a lion's share of the credit for a win.

During their convincing thumping of us, the Stormers' Jones, Powell, and Butler all stood out again, but Butler shone brightest. It was sad in a way, watching him play in front of so few, knowing he belonged in front of thousands of screaming fans in the SEC.

Before ending up in the CBA, Butler had spent some time with the Minnesota Timberwolves, but the squad ended up cutting him. It was in Minnesota, in fact, facing the daunting task of making a crowded roster, that Butler admitted, "I should have gone to college. That's what I tell everybody out here . . . I regret it. I should have gone to school for two years, maybe three, then come out. Everything would have been right then."[41]

It was a few years earlier, in 2002, that Butler surfaced on the national basketball radar as a high school junior in McComb, Mississippi. That year he gained distinction as the state of Mississippi's best prep player, and in 2003 he made the McDonald's All-American team.[42] During his junior year season he committed to Mississippi State, but then his name emerged in an NCAA recruiting scandal involving Auburn. Soon after that, he failed to earn a qualifying SAT score (when paired with his grades). So after his senior year, he decided to attend prep school. He made a brief stop at one school before ending up at Coastal Academy in Virginia Beach, Virginia. There he averaged 29 points and 17 rebounds and committed to Tennessee. But then he decided to sign with some genius agent and declare himself eligible for the NBA draft.

Butler went unpicked on NBA draft day, but he did get that invite to Minnesota, where, without a guaranteed contract, he battled for a spot on a crowded roster. Ironically, it came down to him and another high-schooler, Ndudi Ebi, whom the Timberwolves had picked in the first round, meaning Ebi was owed three years of guaranteed money, making Butler's job of supplanting him especially difficult.

During this Wolves' training camp, with Butler's waiver looking imminent, reporters started churning out stories about how bad a decision he'd made by declaring. Minneapolis's *Star Tribune* characterized Butler's story as "the darker side of the NBA's youth movement." Not all the news was bad for the big fellow, though. Flip Saunders weighed in around that time, saying, "He's going to play in our league. I don't know when, but he's going to play in our league. He's got enough talent. He's got great hands, a big body, and he really has a feel for the game."[43]

In Birch Run, a near-record number of people missed the opportunity to see that Flip had been on to something. Rather than looking like the poster child for why declaring for the draft straight out of high school is a bad idea, Butler again did his best to look like another kind of poster, an extremely rare kind: that of the high school phenom who declares himself eligible for the draft, proceeds to get shunned by every NBA team, then mounts a furious comeback in the CBA and eventually makes it to the League.

He had come into the contest averaging an impressive 21.5 points and 12 rebounds. Even really good big guys with NBA experience, such as Sam Clancy, Olden Polynice, and Dickey Simpkins, didn't necessarily put up those types of numbers in the CBA. And against us, Butler built upon his impressive stats. He banged down low with men who had as many as ten years on him, hitting jump hooks, fighting for space, and talking a little trash. It was pretty vicious down there and Butler delivered most of the viciousness.

Reading the statistics in the locker room afterward, Daleo boiled. Every now and then he'd pull his attention away from the stats and say something, like, "How could you let a high school kid 'BEAST' you?!" Then he might holler, "How?!...I don't understand. How could you let a high school kid 'BEAST' you?!"

Starting in on something else, he'd stop and ask again: "How could you let a high school kid 'BEAST' you?!"

He also threatened a number of players' jobs, Brant the Baffler's in particular.

"Fuck, Brant, you're killing me. Didn't they teach you rotations in Division III? You're making it hard—I like you, but fuck; you're making it hard on me. Make it easy on me. Shoot, do your fuckin' job, man. Just do your job and I've got no beefs. Fuck, control your group."

It didn't stop there. At random intervals, whether in the locker room, on the bus, or back at the hotel, Daleo would rehash specific plays from the night over and over again, asking a guy why he'd done this or that.

"Brant, what were you doing when you left your man?" "Carson, why'd you go double?" "Stais, did you feel like you had it?" "Ahhh, Brant, what were you doing?"

You never knew where he'd pop up. You could be stepping off the elevator or getting on the bus and boom!:

"Brant, didn't they teach you rotations in Division III? Man, just do your job." Or it might be, "Carson, Why do you defy me?"

"Didn't intend to Coach."

Fortunately for us, our next game was against the winless Mayhem in Muskegon and it was only a day away.

If we win, perhaps he can turn it off.

24

In the locker room before the Mayhem game, assistant coach Renaldo "Everything you do is right" Thomas called us together for an impromptu team meeting. Given our 2-3 record, he sensed not only that we needed a win but that our chemistry was off. He wanted us to hash things out before it got worse, and he started this process by talking about keeping our heads up and coming together. He encouraged us to "pull for each other" rather than "rip on each other" and to "go out there and have fun." Then, looking disgusted, he railed, "I've never seen anything like it, what's all this infighting? We got to pull together."

Not so cryptically, he was referring to the brewing drama between our stars: Fields, Boseman, and Dobbins. Boiled down, the gist of the conflict was: Who should have the ball? Ronnie Rockford, who could still make spectacular plays, wanted to take most of the shots and repetitively run isolations, which basically entailed him getting the ball, waving everybody off, and then shooting a fadeaway jumper. Boseman didn't like this. He wasn't as combustive to team chemistry, but he tended to dribble for long periods of time at the top of the key and look people off before making a foray into the lane. Still out of shape and having difficulty getting his shot off, Dobbins was simply frustrated. Plus, he didn't like the Fields wave-off isolation or the Boseman dribble option. He wanted the ball more.

As "Everything You Do Is Right" spoke to us about it, though, he didn't address the issue by actually mentioning any players by name. He talked mainly in generalities.

Suddenly, Ronnie stepped forward to take the floor and proceeded to ramble about "pulling together" and "sticking with the system." He went on for several minutes but never really said anything, didn't offer specifics or talk about players by name, or acknowledge that, based on his on-court tactics, "the system" appeared to be: toss the ball to Ronnie for an isolation. Instead he talked in such a rounded fashion that it made Renaldo's speech seem kind of specific. By the time Ronnie was done, my head was spinning from trying to discern some cohesive strain to the past several minutes.

During the meeting, Daleo paced back and forth in the corner of the locker room. Every now and then, he would look at his watch. You could tell he could barely take it. He prided himself on not engaging in much of any pre-game talk, let alone "meetings." He preferred to keep his pre-game remarks to about a minute or two.

When the meeting finally concluded, though, he stepped to the middle of the locker room to address us. He looked pretty serious.

"Remember the freaking out-of-bounds plays and know what defense we are in. Ask yourself, 'What defense are we in?' You have time to ask yourself, 'How much is an ounce going for nowadays? When was the last time I got a piece of ass? Why is Coach such an asshole?' You should be able to find time to ask yourself which defense we are in."

Dales then announced that he intended to start the game with three big guys, a departure from his usual strategy of running the snot out of people. Still mad that we had let a high school guy "beast" us, he wanted us to assert ourselves in the paint. He told the guards to dump the ball down to the big guys. And he told the big fellows, "Beast somebody! . . . Fuckin' beast somebody, man, do your job!"

When he finished, everyone except Daleo—he never joined the pre-game team prayer—gathered for an "Our Father."

For some reason during warm-ups, my legs felt great. Maybe it was the speeches. My legs felt so good, in fact, that in our layup line, I started thinking about taking advantage of the situation by throwing down a few dunks. Some guys, like me, don't know when a good dunking day might arise. At this point in my career, I may only have had five over the course of a year. Plus, the young ball boys wanted to see something. So I caught the ball on the wing, got squared away, and swooped in for a simple one-handed jam. It went down with relative ease. The ball boys smiled.

Ooohhh, this is a good day.

After a couple more basic jams and with the ball boys getting eager for more—they'd started requesting different types of dunks—I got to considering more sophisticated throw-downs, like the two-handed reverses I used to do in the old days.

I knew I couldn't come anywhere near taking off from the free-throw line, as one of the ball boys had requested, but I figured I could still step it up. I decided to start with a two-handed jam. Lining it up from the left side, I ran in, and took to the air. With room to spare, I threw it down—but by then my enjoyment had already been curtailed, because as I'd left the floor, I'd felt my groin stretch. Sure enough, upon testing the groin with several high-leg jaunts and a few defensive slides, I knew that I had another pull.

You've got to be kidding me. Pulling a muscle in warm-ups? Who does that? Actually, you did it once with the Steelheads. That's true. Still, you've got to be kidding me.

I spent the rest of the pre-game cautiously gauging how far I could stretch the groin without causing any further damage. I also tried to calm down by focusing on simply surviving the game and then getting ice and heat for the next few days. I didn't want to tell anybody, but I had to get some help. With the tip-off only minutes away, I found Trainer Brad near our bench.

"Brad."

"What?"

Pulling him to the side, I quietly said, "Dude, I pulled my freaking groin."

"What!?" he tried to whisper.

"I know, it's crazy."

"How bad is it?"

"It's not that bad, but it feels like it could tear further if I stretch it. Should we tape it or something?"

Brad thought about it.

"I think I've got a sleeve."

He rummaged through his stuff and found it. How he originally got the sleeve, I probably don't want to know. I put it on and he reinforced the sleeve with tape. I tested the groin again, and it seemed like I could get through the game.

Dales's decision to start three big guys, Williams, Rucker, and Dobbins, along with a backcourt of Boseman and Fields, did not end up looking like one of his finest coaching moves. Despite all the speeches and the new strategy, the Mayhem began the game with an 8-0 run. Our squad seemed deflated.

We lost the first quarter by four points, which wasn't so bad, but then at the end of the second quarter, Robert Griffin, formerly of the University of Iowa, hit a three to give the Mayhem that quarter point as well. This just set Dales on fire. In the locker room at intermission, he put on a grand performance.

He stormed in, immediately picked up this humongous garbage can, and threw it against the wall of one of the bathroom stalls. As it happened, I was in that stall taking a leak. From underneath, some garbage spilled into the stall by my feet.

He's a little upset.

Not satisfied, Daleo banged the chalkboard with his fists. Then he turned and looked for whatever he could get his hands on to throw at the wall. By this time I was back out in the main locker room area and able to see the antics. He found a chair and chucked it. He picked up a dry-erase board and threw it against the wall. Only it refused to break, so he picked it up again and chucked it at the wall a second time. But this was a CBA dry-erase board, tough and weathered, and sure enough it still wouldn't break. This made him more livid. He bent down and grabbed it, intent on destroying it. He stood up for a moment and then started pounding the board into the ground like a maniac until, finally, it broke.

A momentary lull followed as Dales seemed to gather himself, but then his rage returned. He picked up the garbage can again and slammed it against the wall, littering more banana peels and other garbage across the floor. All the while he shouted things like:

"How many times have I said to keep it out of the middle? How many times have I said to keep it out of the fucking middle? Robert fuckin' Griffin, a former Rockford Lightning Free Agent Camper who I sent home, I took my family out to eat at Francesca's with his $75 entry fee . . . laughing all the way. Robert fucking Griffin nails a three to win the quarter, former Rockford Lightning Free Agent Camp attendee Robert fuckin' Griffin. He paid $75! I sent him home and took my family out to dinner and I sent him home."

After Dales' antics, we opened the second half on the wrong end of a 13-4 run, and wound up losing the game. I played poorly, shooting a paltry three of ten from the field. My leg didn't feel terrible during the contest, but the groin surely didn't help matters. The low point came when I caught a nifty feed underneath the bucket from Ronnie, proceeded to elevate for a layup, but somehow got blocked by the bottom of the backboard.

During the contest Daleo voiced his dissatisfaction with the way I ran the club. He screamed from the sidelines, "Control your group!" and asked "What are you doing? What are you doing? Jesus Christ! What are you doing?" Then, he turned to the bench to tell the rest of the guys that I was wacky.

He wasn't satisfied with my defense, either. Once, as I headed to my seat on the bench, having been yanked from the game yet again, he asked, "What are you doing? What are doing? Why are you letting Darrick Martin get the ball? I thought we went over this. Why do you defy me? Control your group."

The only positive was that I survived the affair without doing further damage to my gimpy groin.

Back in the locker room after the debacle Daleo spared us a repeat performance of his antics at halftime. Instead, he opted for a somber tone, as a way to let us know just how serious the situation had become. Bringing his voice low, almost in a whisper, he said, "I've never seen anything like this. I mean, I've never seen anything like this at the professional level in my three years in the CBA. I mean, just run my shit. Listen to the 2003 CBA Coach of the Year? Naw, fuck him. I'd rather do my own thing. I've never seen anything like this in my three years in the CBA, never seen anything like it."

He paused and threw his hands down as if he'd had enough, and then he stepped aside in dramatic fashion.

As I got to taking my tights off and we all started putting on our traveling gear, Dales paced back and forth in a short path in the corner of the locker room listening to his messages on his cell phone. Suddenly, he stopped, held his hands up, and shouted, "Listen to this. Harold Ellis [a scout for the Atlanta Hawks] is asking me 'What page is Carson Cunningham on?' My friend Harold Ellis calling me, asking me, 'What page is Carson Cunningham on?'"

Harold Ellis? Did I used to watch him knock down jumpers on WGN? That might be Dale Ellis? Who's Harold Ellis?

I couldn't pinpoint him, but I thought I knew the name. Later I learned that Harold Ellis, before becoming a Hawks' scout, had played in the NBA for three years. He had a master's degree in sports administration and was working on a PhD in sports psychology. At one point, *ProBasketballNews.com* had rated him as the second-best coaching talent in the minors.

Great, freaking Harold Ellis is going to get me fired.What are the odds?Harold Ellis called Chris Daleo to ask him what page I was on. What page am I on? Page 235 in The Rise of the Vulcans. *What fucking page are you on? Who gives a shit what Harold Ellis of the Atlanta Hawks thinks? What page are the Atlanta Hawks on? They stink. They are one of the worst franchises in the history of franchises. Stand up, be a man, tell Old Dales that if he and Harold Ellis are long-time friends, then maybe Harold*

Ellis rates basketball players like he picks friends. The fuckin' Hawks, they stink.

I just sat there and kept quiet. Eventually Dales got on to some other topic and guys made their way out of the locker room to the bus.

Of course, since I'd driven myself to Michigan for this road trip, I had to drive the Corolla back, which only angered Dales further. I knew me not being on the bus would bother him the whole way. And every time he got annoyed by it, he'd think about Harold Ellis and my generally poor play and who knows, maybe he'd cut me the moment I got back to the Fairfield.

Trainer Brad joined me for the long ride. Prior to the game, Brad, happy to get away from Dales anyway, had asked me to drop him off at his grandmother's house on the way to Rockford. That way he could get to O'Hare more easily in the morning in order to catch a flight with his wife. She had a business conference in Hilton Head, South Carolina, and he was joining her for it. He'd cleared the trip with Daleo months earlier, before even signing on with Rockford for the season, but with the losses adding up, Dales was now giving him a bit of a hard time about it. Before we left Muskegon, he'd asked Brad, "Why are you abandoning me now?"

On the ride back, Trainer Brad told me that Daleo was mad that I had arrived so late at the Knights Inn the night before. Apparently, all day he kept telling Brad, "That's not what we agreed upon." Brad also said that Dales wanted to make moves but had neither confirmed nor denied that I was on the block. Dales did, however, tell Brad, "He's terrible, out of shape. I mean Harold Ellis called me to specifically ask what page he was on."

It was nice to get some information from Brad. Having at least some indication of the scenario made me feel less vulnerable, even if the news wasn't positive. With Brad heading to South Carolina, though, I knew I'd soon lose access to inside information about my fate, let alone the therapeutic opportunity to simply talk things out with him. During his time away, I could be axed without warning, which, though the result would be the same in the end, seemed worse than knowing about it in advance. Plus, one of Dupay's biggest beefs was his failure to get in any parting shots at Daleo before he got cut. Had he known in advance, he might've been able to deliver some prepared remarks. That sounded like something I'd like to do as well. Taken altogether, then, it felt like Trainer Brad was abandoning me too.

25

We had a few days before our next game, which meant Dales could mull over the road trip even more. This practice took place at the Gateway Center near downtown. Some wealthy Rockfordians had founded the center, and it functioned like a Boys and Girls Club, with an emphasis on helping the underprivileged. The family that owned the Lightning, the Timpes, donated money to the Gateway Center, which is why, I imagine, we were allowed to workout there.

We endured a hard practice, which included going over our plays, as few of them as there were, in live action about a million times. Still, playing competitive five-on-five, even if it was just on one half of the court, was fun. And it made sense to work on our plays because at this point in the season we hadn't been running them too well. Shoot, even our out-of-bounds plays weren't getting run correctly. You felt bad for "Everything You Do Is Right" because he worked so hard on them and really thought there was nothing you could do that wasn't right. A key part of the problem with our plays was that usually when we called one, whether an out-of-bounds play or a regular one, Ronnie Rockford simply ran over to one side of the court to post up for an isolation.

When I first played with Ronnie, during the 2002-03 season, he didn't seem so disruptive to team chemistry. But since then, as I say, he'd developed an acute affinity for the isolation—around the wing, near the three-point line. It was hard not to give it to him there because once he was situated, he would wave his arms up and down and call for the ball and basically sink down in a crouch, all the while messing up the action for everybody else.

Once he'd receive the rock, he would usually back down his defender using his booty, while he surveyed the court and pointed at people to go to various places. Then, most commonly, he shot. But if a double came and he found it disruptive enough, he would pass, at which point he preferred you to shoot and score, which gave him an assist. (CBA players could get quite selfish about assists—myself included. A classic example of this was Sean "Smush" Colson, a former Houston Rocket and CBA hooper, who, after assisting on a play, would often run back down the court near the scorer's table to tell the stat man not to overlook that he'd just gotten an assist.)

Anyway, as we practiced our plays in the Gateway, Dales ripped on just about everybody, especially Brant Bailey and me. At one point, as I started a play at the top of the key, Dales came near me, shaking his head. "Boy, what a disappointment you've been," he said. Later, he told me to "do something, so people don't think I'm crazy for bringing you back." Given my shooting percentage, he probably had a point there. And he repeatedly asked Brant, "Did they teach you rotations at Stevens-Point? I thought they coached guys in Division III." At one point he suggested, "Maybe you should go back to Europe."

Later that week, we practiced hard again, this time at noon. A number of players showed up right at noon and some showed up even later than that. Dales said he expected us to be there at least fifteen minutes early. At around 11:50 he'd started walking around the court in random loops, nervously muttering things to himself. At one point, when he happened to loop by Lubeck and I stretching near mid-court, he broke out in a wide, crazy-looking smile and said, "Looks like we have a player mutiny here." Then he took off again, murmuring incoherently.

A couple of times he stopped pacing to yell at Troy, who as an assistant was supposed to be at practice at 11:00 a.m. but had walked in right about 11:45. At one point Dales suddenly looked up and hollered, "Troy! Sweep the floor!" Then he brought his voice down so Troy couldn't hear and added, "My fuckin' assistant . . . late. Do your job! Fuckin' Troy."

Finally, at about noon the four tardiest players rolled in. Two of our leaders, Dobbins and Boseman, brought up the rear. At first I figured that Daleo, his fuse lit, would lay into the guys hard, but he didn't say much except "Let's go."

Should've known better. It's easier to yell at Troy.

In fact, when Dales saw the four late players through the windows, walking from the parking lot toward the entrance to the Gateway Center, he seemed to let out a sigh. It happened just for a moment, but it indicated the guy's vulnerability.

The scenario hinted at yet another odd tendency within the CBA realm. Though elusive and susceptible to permutations based on a player's performance, his relationship with other stars, and his relationship with the head coach, in a general sense, the rule goes like this: If certain conditions qualified you, then the less respect you paid to rules, the more respect you got. These conditions were fluid, however. For instance, sometimes veteran status increased your freedom to break rules, but in other cases, like mine, being a veteran had little effect.

When practice ended, I put up some extra shots again. I needed the work, seeing as my shooting percentage was so woeful, and Daleo liked it when a guy stayed after anyway. He hung around the gym as I shot and as Troy gathered our practice gear to take to the laundromat.

As I got my stuff together to head out, Daleo indirectly indicated that I was not facing an imminent firing. He mentioned that Marshall Phillips was coming in from Chile and that he planned to bring in a rookie, Branden Bender, a power forward who'd begun his collegiate career at Louisville only to leave and then play one year at Cincinnati State Technical and Community College before ending up at Robert Morris College in Chicago. At first, while Dales explained this, it made me quite nervous about my prospects, but then he said that to make room on the roster he intended to trade Greg Claussen, one of our big men, for a draft pick and "cash considerations," which I later learned amounted to $100.

In addition, it seemed another roster spot would soon open because Guy Rucker, who had continued to perform well for us, was on the verge of being disallowed from playing in the CBA until a problem with his former team in Croatia got resolved. Rucker had signed with a Croatian team for about $6,000 a month during the summer, but I guess it didn't hit him that he'd actually have to live in Croatia until he got to Croatia, because soon after arriving he apparently began to milk a knee injury until his squad finally sent him packing. Shortly after that, he joined the Lightning. But now the Croatians were crying foul. They wanted cash and Rockford didn't want to pay.

Daleo then told me that Keith Closs, a 7'3" center who had played on the Los Angeles Clippers for three years and in college at Central Connecticut State, where he had bested Hall of Famer David Robinson by setting the NCAA Division I records for blocked shots in a season (6.36 bpg) and blocked shots for a career (5.87 bpg), was coming to Rockford.

Hmm, I wonder whose roster spot he'll take?

Dales was on a roll that afternoon. He got my hackles up even more by claiming that Teddy Dupay kept calling to see about coming back. Then, out of the blue, he leaned in, hesitated a moment, and said, "You know, I shouldn't hide things from people. I should tell the guys the truth. Brad is at a fat farm with his wife trying to lose weight."

For a moment my wheels spun: *Maybe the conference Trainer Brad said his wife had to attend is a cover? He is overweight, especially for a young guy.*

"Come on, you can't be serious," I said.

"He is. His wife got nervous after Brad got back from the physicals and all his numbers, his cholesterol and everything, were high. She signed them up for a fat farm."

I figured he was lying then since Brad had told me he'd planned the trip for months.

But then again, who makes something like that up? Maybe...

At the start of our next practice, Dales made a few comments about defensive rotations and reiterated how bad we had played in our last game. He characterized the performance as disgusting and reminded us that we'd just given the previously winless Mayhem its first victory in franchise history. Then he looked at all of us standing around him in a circle and said, "And finally, Brad will be gone until Saturday. He is at a fat farm. All right, five blues, five whites, run whirl, half-court."

26

At the end of practice, Daleo pulled me aside to me ask if I'd join him by taking over what was supposed to have been Dupay's spot as a guest "star" on 104.9 FM's early morning radio show. This rock station's morning show featured a popular deejay, Jim Stone, his sidekick, Double T, and their voice of reason, Kristin. Seeing as I get a kick out of being on the radio, even if it's kind of lame, I agreed. And, truth be told, it didn't seem like it'd have been a smart move to reject Dales.

Our first appearance took place the next morning. To start it off, Stone asked a bunch of questions about our recent losses, prompting Daleo to break down the shortcomings of various players, including myself. As if that weren't enough, Kristin, a young, nice-looking red-head who gave traffic and weather reports and sometimes lingered for extra banter, also started critiquing our play. Apparently, she'd played high school ball.

It had been quite a transition, seeing this Kristin take on the role of basketball analyst. Before our segment, she'd played a pivotal role, as you might assume, in a game named "What's in Kristin's Box?" The game called on Kristin to shake a box that contained something inside. Listeners would then phone in to guess what was in Kristin's box, and host Stone would give clues to help them out. "It's hard" or "You can eat it" approximate the nature of his hints, real classy stuff. And now this red-head with something in her box was questioning our offensive sets and the team's energy level.

Dales took Kristin's comments in stride, though. After she'd started in on her critique he'd started laughing and asked, "How about the alley-oop pass this guy [pointing to me] threw to Stais Boseman…another *point guard*!"

At the time, the pass had seemed like a good idea.

As our appearance neared its end, the deejay asked, "So, what was it like to be sent home cut and then get called back a few days later?"

For a moment, Stone caught me flat-footed, calling me out like that, but my situation was pretty uncommon so I could hardly blame him.

"Well, it was a bit odd, but I'm used to the CBA, so in some respects it was not that odd," I said. "In my first year in the league with the Gary Steelheads, we went through something like forty-seven players in one season. So you just kind of roll with it."

Walking out to the parking lot after the show, I had a few moments to gauge Daleo's mood. He told me that Rucker's reinstatement appeared likely and confirmed Keith Closs's imminent arrival. He also hinted that Dobbins's days were numbered.

That night I found myself on the radio again, this time on 1440 AM as a guest for the "Chris Daleo Coach's Show." Each Monday night all the players were expected to show up at a "restaurant" for the show. Most of us would, except for Ronnie Rockford and occasionally someone else, like Dobbins, thereby increasing their manliness quotients.

You might not guess it, but the "Chris Daleo Coach's Show" enjoyed a following, albeit a modest one. A group of maybe five or six, most of whom, admittedly, appeared as if they'd recently emerged from a 1980s time machine, would show up each week at the various places that the show taped. These diehards occasionally struck up conversations with us, which was always slightly uncomfortable, because while you wanted to be nice, you also couldn't help thinking in the back of your mind, *What is this person doing here?*

On this night Daleo spent most of his time trying to talk players into going onto the show as a guest. The more guests he could recruit, the less time he had to spend on the show himself, so he worked us hard. Everybody acted reluctant, but I kind of wanted to go on.

Before we went live, the guy set to interview me told me he'd worked in the media and covered the Lightning for nearly twenty years. On the air, he mentioned some former Purdue Boilermakers who had played with the Lightning or in the CBA over the years, like Everett Stephens, Troy Lewis, and Jimmie Oliver. Then he asked me what it was like to be sent home only to be called back a few days later.

Another comedian.

The funniest part came when the interviewer, plowing through his list of stock questions, got to the one about a player's hopes of making it to the next level. At first he just rolled on through the question like he probably had hundreds of other times, maybe thousands—remember, it'd been nearly twenty years:

"Now, of course, it's everyone's goal to parlay this opportunity into something better, hopefully a shot at the NBA, and so for you…"

Right at that point, as he moved to the meat of the question, the meaning of the words he was saying started to register with him. Apparently he found it absurd, because he hesitated and sputtered, "Well, you never know," and "You know, the NBA is often looking for role players." Finally, mercifully, he rounded out his question, the gist being, "Do you hope to parlay this into a chance at the NBA?"

Rather than give him a hard time for having such a difficult time getting the question out, I blathered on about how you never know and about role playing and potential opportunities in Europe.

27

'm not kidding when I tell you that we played the Mayhem next. There were only eight teams in the league, and several of the cities cost a lot of dough to travel to. So, if it seems like all we did was play the Steelheads, Storm, and Mayhem over and over again, we kind of did.

No matter who we were playing, though, we needed a victory on this night, and we got the must-needed home win, 98-93. But unfortunately I played terribly again. Other guys picked up the slack, like Boseman, who used his ability to muscle people to the basket effectively, and Ronnie, who delivered clutch baskets to help us pull it out. Still, our chemistry floundered. Even if I somehow managed to survive the season, it didn't seem like we were playing at a championship-caliber level and therefore my championship mission would not be accomplished. Something needed to change.

In the locker room post-game, guys passed around stat sheets. I didn't really want to look. My woeful shooting line read one for six, which brought my shooting statistics for the season to eleven for thirty-six, or just under 31 percent, a ridiculous percentage for a professional basketball player—unacceptable, really. The only thing working in my favor was the "save your bad games for the wins" rule, but even that seemed to be wearing thin. Dales was so excited about the win, though, that he barely even mentioned my name.

Maybe he won't notice.

For the time being, at least, Dales stuck with me.

Management expected us to go to JD's Sports Bar and Grill after the game to mingle with the fans and eat tacos. The Lightning brass had struck some deal with JD's to host these post-game gatherings. During our home contests, the PA announcer would remind the crowd approximately a thousand times to join the Lightning players at JD's after the game.

As it happened, this Tuesday evening was Karaoke Night at JD's. As we walked into the place, a group of its predominantly male patrons was singing along with a guy on stage who was belting out a tune by the eighties rock band Poison. We went straight to the back room and the free taco bar. Players talked about who got dunked on and rated the ladies that were hanging out by the nearby pool tables. A few of the ladies would peer into our room every now and again, and it didn't take long for a few of the Lightning to see about getting together with them.

None of us made it to the front of JD's again to hang out with the people singing heavy metal love ballads, except when it was time to leave and we had to walk through the place. This wasn't what the Lightning brass or JD's had had in mind when they'd conjured up the partnership. They wanted us to mingle more and encouraged us to do so. It seemed like the patrons up near the karaoke didn't mind our lack of mingling, though, because as I walked by them on my way out, I heard an inebriated fellow on stage change the lyrics to the eighties song he was singing. His version went something like this:

I am at JD's Bar and Grill with the Rockford Lightning,
This sucks, it's all fuckin' dudes, where are the Lightning Girls?

28

As we stretched for practice at mid-court the next day, one of our new guys, Brandon Bender, asked rookie Sydney Holmes where our trainer was. Without hesitating, Sydney said in earnest, "Oh, he's at a fat farm. He'll be back next week."

With our record at 3-4 after seven games, we were preparing to play, for the first time, a team in the other division, the Sioux Falls Skyforce, which came into the MetroCentre with a league-leading 8-1 record. The squad looked poised for a championship run and was coached by Daleo's nemesis, the thirty-one-year-old Dave Joerger. Joerger had already won two CBA titles as head coach of the Dakota Wizards and had won CBA Coach of the Year. If his name got brought up, Dales was liable to say, "Fuckin' Dave Joerger, who gives a shit."

It was especially funny to see this rivalry bloom because the two were so different. Having played at and graduated from Minnesota State University-Moorhead in 1997 and gone straight into a minor league professional assistantship gig, Joerger was young in basketball coaching years, while Daleo, in his late forties, was on the older side for the minor leagues. You knew it irked Dales to see a guy who was younger than some of the players he coached having such success. More than that, though, their styles were entirely different. Dales wanted furious action and risk-taking, while Joerger's squads focused more on team defense and offensive sets.

Playing against Joerger's teams, you got the impression that he really enjoyed to draw up these sets and the various options each could spawn, as opposed to Dales, whose concern for sets mostly involved how to blow them up with traps so that his squad could get to running. While Joerger's more traditional style was not all that original, it was more readily embraced by the coaching establishment than Dales's. Plus, Joerger seemed to get along with that fraternity better than Dales, who was more like a lone wolf, which, truth be told, I could appreciate.

Related to all of this was an attitude amongst establishment coaches that since Daleo's style wasn't to be taken seriously, Dales wasn't to be taken seriously. And you could sense that this annoyed Dales, a lot like it annoyed me that a guy like Joerger wouldn't give me the time of day as a player when I knew full well he couldn't hang with me on the court if he had to take that suit off. And not because I had a lot more talent than him, but because I figured I'd played hours and hours and hours of more ball than him. I didn't blame him for going into coaching once he couldn't play anymore, and I even sensed that, economically, this is what I should've been doing, if I was going to stay in the game. But I was a player and that's the way things were, and it's annoying to most any player when a coach won't give you the time of day.

To get to the MetroCentre, Joerger's Sioux Falls squad had driven through the night. In addition, the team had just lost one of its star players, David Jackson, who supposedly jetted off to Turkey for a guaranteed $300,000 per year. (It was always hard to tell what amount a guy had really signed for, and some overseas teams were notorious for not paying anyway. Plus, not all Euro-deals were guaranteed. As it turned out, Jackson was back in the CBA a month later.) Seeing as they'd driven all night and didn't have Jackson, we should've pounced early. Instead, after a bunch of unsuccessful isolations and bickering, we found ourselves down again.

True, we were playing a bit short-handed too, seeing as Dales had counted on Guy Rucker's services but we didn't have him. It wasn't that Rucker still hadn't gotten his clearance from Croatia to come through. He had. In fact, Dales had spent a couple grand to help Rucker get the issue resolved. It's just that, upon getting his clearance, Rucker showed himself to be one of the smartest minor leaguers I've come across. The ink on that clearance barely had time to dry before he pulled a fast one on Dales by signing a deal to play in Korea, supposedly for $17,000 per month.

Now that's a true vet.

Still, even without Rucker, it seemed like we would enjoy some advantages on this night, and yet there was the Skyforce, scoring points at will, while we ran isolations, waved people off, and then came back to the huddle and started pointing fingers. Ronnie would sit down on the bench and say something like, "Shit, ya'll motherfuckers need to come to play," prompting Boseman to roll his eyes and Dobbins to shake his head. Then we'd go back out there and the same thing would happen all over again. We were spiraling.

Near the end of the first half, as a Sioux Falls player streaked toward the basket with the ball, Ronnie Fields reached out to swipe at it. Ronnie then grabbed his thumb and immediately called time-out. He walked over to the bench, nonchalantly held up his left thumb, and said, "I'm done."

It was a disgusting sight. His left thumb had broken in such a fashion that it looked to be jetting off of the bone that connected the thumb to his hand, at an unnatural right angle, and part of the broken bone was sticking out of his skin. He displayed marked calm about the whole thing, though, didn't even seem to be in much pain.

As play resumed I watched Trainer Brad delicately clean up the blood around Ronnie's dangling thumb and heard the PA announcer use the MetroCentre's sound system to put a call out for the team doctor to come to the Lightning bench. A few minutes passed and nobody came. So over the loudspeaker the PA man called for the doctor again. Eventually, he got the message that there was no team doctor, at least not on this night.

We ended the first half down 56-49. My line at that point stood at one for three from the field, which actually improved my shooting percentage for the season.

As I walked into the locker room, I saw, off to the side on a training table, a couple of recently arrived paramedics wrapping Ronnie's hand in thick bandaging. While wrapping it, someone had to hold up Ronnie's thumb so it didn't dangle. The digit looked straighter under the bandage. I wasn't sure if they'd pushed it back into place or not. But again, Ronnie still seemed quite cool about it all. He told us he felt fine and to go out there and win.

And that we did. From the start of the second half, our energy level was high. We created havoc on defense, which led to steals that we turned into buckets on the other end, and guys ran the floor hard and shared the rock. It seemed like a new team out there. We scored sixty-two points in the half and took both quarters en route to the win.

A key catalyst was the affable, thoughtful, and immensely talented Marshall Phillips, who, as Dales had predicted, had recently arrived from a Chilean league. Phillips was from Atlanta and had played his college ball, or at least the last two years of his nomadic college career, at Appalachian State. Standing at 6'3," he was swift and powerful and well-built but not bulky. If you didn't watch it, he might slice in for an offensive rebound, rise gracefully, and then throw down a deafening dunk on your head. He had strong and yet rounded cheek bones that complemented his steady brown eyes and mustache. He looked a bit like a black Tom Selleck, back in his *Magnum P.I.* days, and his game featured a rare combination of rugged athleticism, craftiness around the tin, and just enough range to constitute a threat. And he played smartly. Only his size kept him from the NBA.

Marshall grew up in the projects, and didn't even play organized high school basketball. But that doesn't mean he didn't play a lot of hoops. In fact, in his teens, basketball helped save him from gang-life. And now he'd already given indications that he could very well help us save our season.

And Phillips wasn't the only one to shine. In one stretch of our offensive outburst, Lubeck came up with a steal at mid-court, drove down the middle of the lane, and hit me with a pass on the baseline for a bucket. A few plays later we forced another steal, Sioux Falls hesitated, and Lubeck took off running. I threw him a lead pass that he caught before leaning in for a one-handed slam. The crowd went nuts. I jumped up and down. My endorphins were firing. I'd come alive.

As mentioned, our goal on defense was to speed the opposition up with our traps. The philosophy behind the traps wasn't necessarily that we'd always get the steal. Rather, that we'd get the other team to shoot quickly or at a minimum we'd take them out of their flow so that they'd find themselves shooting from unusual spots. And on this night we were active and rotating well enough to make it work. In turn, we'd create numbers advantages on offense. And since we played fast virtually all the time, we were used to capitalizing on these.

It wasn't just all fast breaks either. On nights like this, our offensive rhythm carried over to our half-court action. We moved the ball quickly, drove and dished smartly, hit the post and cut, and generally played with vim and vigor. The fans dug it. And it was nice to give them stretches of hoops like this.

To boot, and probably not by coincidence, on this night my legs felt good and my mid-range jumper was on. By the end of the night my line read eight of twelve from the field for sixteen points. The win put our home record at 4-0 and moved us to .500 for the season. We'd beaten the league's top-ranked team and taken down Daleo's nemesis, Joerger—yet another CBA coach who wouldn't give me a shot.

29

The next afternoon we loaded up the bus for another eight-hour ride to the clockless Knights Inn. After nightfall, near Flint, Michigan, our bus turned off the highway and meandered through what seemed like a one-horse town. Though it seemed desolate, at least in the dark, this town did have a Greyhound bus station that we pulled up to. Dales got off the bus to walk inside. Moments later, he came out of the lobby with a freckled, 7'3", part-black, part-Cherokee giant, Keith "Boss" Closs.

Before joining our squad, Closs had been playing in the ABA for the Motown Jammers. In fact, on the night that we picked him up at this Greyhound station, he said he'd played in a game with the Jammers, or at least part of a game. According to Closs, the contest never finished because at halftime, the referees learned that their paychecks had bounced. When they refused to go out for the second half, the Jammers folded—as an organization. A few days later a buyer did swoop in to get the team on the cheap, but by then Boss Closs was with us.

What a sight he was. He struggled to walk to the back of the bus because at 7'3" he had to bend down so much. And yet he was as skinny as he was long, which made him seem even taller than he was. His hair was picked-out into a wild-looking 'fro, and his skin, while just dark enough to make you think he was black, at the same time appeared so light and freckly that he seemed white. As the season went on, it'd kill me to watch other people watch Closs. They couldn't help but stare with their mouths agape. As I would also come to learn, Boss Closs had tremendous hand-eye coordination, remarkable timing on blocked shots, and, un-hobbled by his length, the ability to move smoothly.

While Dales had given me a heads up on the possible arrival of Closs, Lubeck could barely believe it. He hadn't seen Closs in two years. Back then, Lubeck played in the United States Basketball League

(USBL) and his team had played against Closs's Pennsylvania Valley Dawgs for the championship. (The USBL season ran in the spring, so a lot of guys would play in it after the CBA season.) Lubeck's family had come into town for the championship game, and Lubes's dad went out behind the stadium before it got underway. Suddenly Closs appeared, pulled out a pack of Kools, and asked Mr. Lubes for a light. They shot the breeze as they smoked, and Lubes's dad got a kick out of it.

Oddly enough, before seeing him again at this Greyhound station, I'd had an even more random run-in with Closs. It occurred during the summer of 1999 at Venice Beach. Closs had spent the 1998-99 season with the Los Angeles Clippers and taken up residence in southern California. My brother, who was trying to make it in Hollywood, also lived there during this time. One morning during a trip out west to visit my brother, I went with him to Venice Beach to see about getting in some hoops on the courts that Woody Harrelson and Wesley Snipes had made famous in *White Men Can't Jump*. When we arrived, we saw Keith Closs playing. It was just a regular Sunday morning and an NBA player was hooping outdoors with regular folks.

We arrived at the Knights Inn and congregated in the lobby as assistant coach Troy tried to check us in. The lady at the front desk was giving him some trouble. She wanted him to provide a credit card because the Knights Inn had encountered problems with CBA players stealing things like towels and pillows and other stuff.

"Like, a lot of stuff," was the way she put it.

Troy stared at her blankly. You could see him trying to process the idea of somebody stealing from the place. Troy also knew that Dales would not offer up a credit card, and he didn't want to put up one of his own.

"You should have warned us to have something ready before we arrived," he said, angling.

"Well, you can check in this time, but be prepared next time," she said plainly.

During this exchange, "Everything You Do Is Right" took a look around the lobby, sizing things up. He shook his head and asked, "Who would steal something from here? The towels hurt the skin and the soap does not even foam up. I brought my own."

"Maybe we don't have clocks in our rooms because they were all stolen," Lubeck deadpanned.

Having spent a good part of the evening and early morning hours familiarizing himself with Flint, the next morning Closs showed up late to the bus for our morning shoot-around. His first Rockford Lightning shoot-around and he was late.

At this shoot-around, Coach Thomas went to work again on Sydney Holmes's shot. Holmes played hard but was undersized and struggled mightily with his shooting. And his form didn't help. He pulled his elbow in so far it caused his right hand to slide out far to the right and his wrist to flail out at an odd angle. But, as I say, Syd worked hard and was a good teammate and this made you pull for him, and "Everything You Do Is Right" had made fixing Syd's shot his mission. Once he took on this mission, though, just about every time Syd shot the ball during a shoot-around, Coach Thomas would offer a comment. If he missed, Coach Thomas would commonly say "Damn." If he missed badly, Troy might chime in too with a "Dang, Sydney." Then, "Everything You Do Is Right" would bark instructions. One of his favorites was, "Don't throw it; you're throwin' it." So, each time Syd missed, you were liable to hear a series of the same comments:

"Damn."

"Dang, Sydney."

"Don't throw it, shoot it."

And you just had to love Sydney because he wouldn't get impatient with this. He'd listen and just keep shooting.

If Sydney made a shot, Coach Thomas would say something like, "There you go, way to shoot it." But oftentimes Syd would miss the next one, prompting Coach Thomas to say, "Damn, there you go again throwin' it. Don't throw it, shoot it."

Sometimes it seemed like, by the time a shooting session ended, "Everything You Do Is Right" and Troy had Holmes so tied up he could barely draw iron.

30

That night "Boss" Closs suited up with us for the first time. He looked long out there in warm-ups with his skinny limbs and his unpicked, unkempt 'fro rising well beyond 7'3". And the 'fro had hop to it, too. As he'd run up to the basket, it'd seem to bounce up and down. Then he'd elevate and lay his hand about two feet above the rim for a fingertip roll.

And was he ever thin. It's hard to gauge how much a 7'3" guy weighs, but you could see how he might not register more than 211 pounds, if that. I say 211 because that's part of the reason he'd gotten suspended and eventually cut from the Los Angeles Clippers. He couldn't keep weight. A clause in his contract had stipulated that he stay above 212 pounds, but he just couldn't manage it. I doubt the drinking helped matters.

Being "underweight" is an odd way to exit the League, to be sure, but I suppose Closs's route into it had been just about as odd. After leading the NCAA in blocks for two straight seasons at Central Connecticut State, Closs entered the 1996 NBA draft. But Commissioner David Stern didn't call his name on draft day. "I was very, very disappointed not being drafted," Closs said later. "I left school on some bad advice. I wish I would've stayed. It would have helped a lot. But, I can't look back. I can only go forward."

In his first season as a professional, 1996-97, Closs played with the Norwich Neptunes of the Atlantic Basketball Association out of Connecticut, a league few have ever heard of. The following summer, though, he landed a spot on the Portland Trail Blazers' summer team, and in two games he outshined the fifteenth pick in that year's NBA draft, Kelvin Cato. But Closs's strong play did not mean Portland would sign him. As a first-round selection, Cato had roughly $3 million coming to him—guaranteed for three years—which, from the point of view of the team, had apparently made Closs expendable.[44]

Other teams took notice, however—the Clippers in particular. And after Closs further demonstrated his shot-blocking abilities that summer, averaging 11.6 points, 7.3 rebounds, and 4.4 blocks for the Lakers' summer league team, he signed a five-year $8.5 million deal with the Clippers. It was striking for an undrafted rookie with one year of minor league experience to land such a contract, an indication of his immense talent. It paid him more money than many first-round picks received, and, with the first three years guaranteed (the last two subject to a Clippers' option), it offered first-round security.

Excited about the signing, Clippers' Vice President of Basketball Operations Elgin Baylor and the legendary Bill Fitch, the Clippers' coach and a former Marine drill instructor who once scheduled twenty-one two-a-day practices in a row, touted Closs's potential.[45] "I'm not saying he's going to be as good as Kareem," Baylor said. "But when Kareem came into the league, he was skinny but very strong. So was Bill Russell. Keith doesn't need to necessarily build his upper body so much as his legs. We're working on that now."[46]

In a mid-October, 1997, exhibition game Closs showed further promise by scoring nine points, grabbing eight rebounds, and registering five blocks. But problems also arose early on. By the first of November, during the preseason, he had already missed a number of workouts. First, his grandmother's death, according to Closs, had led to about a week of missed workouts. The absence left him out of shape, which prompted him to tell reporters after an exhibition game, "I was tired in warm-ups." He didn't attend another workout a couple of days later, this time without informing Coach Fitch, opting instead to go to a cousin's funeral. Trying to explain why Fitch did not know why he'd missed practice, Closs said, "I called the wrong person."

By early November both Fitch and Closs sounded eager to put any issues behind them. When asked whether he was ready for the season, Closs said, smiling, "Oh, yeah…My teammates have helped me with certain things. It's going to be a hell of a season. I'm ready."[47]

Problems with tardiness continued, though, and Closs delivered inconsistent play while Fitch gave him inconsistent minutes. He did show flashes of brilliance, like the time in January—in front of a meager NBA crowd of about 4,000 fans—when he scored twelve points in the second quarter of a win over the Vancouver Grizzlies. But even then, issues unrelated to basketball infringed. Sometimes it was superficial, like when reporters focused on Closs's hairdo. A reporter for the *Daily News* called the "mini 'Afro puff' braids" on Closs's head "outrageous" and wrote that they made "the Allen Iverson and Rasheed

Wallace corn-row style appear conventional." Fitch said he hoped haircuts could affect a guy's caliber of play, while Closs declared, "It's a new look. I can't worry about that, I've got to get more rebounds."[48]

Though he and Fitch had a tenuous relationship, taken altogether, Closs did enjoy a measure of success that first season. He played in fifty-eight games and averaged 4 points and just under 1.5 blocks, which was just enough production to enable him to become, thanks to his eccentric persona, the odd kind of celebrity that only Los Angeles can create.

And this popularity brought with it the kind of perks that only L.A. can, whether it was access to beautiful models or getting placed on a list of celebrity guests, among them Paula Abdul, for a cruise from Marina Del Ray to Catalina Island to celebrate the release of Wayman Tisdale's jazz album *Decisions*.

But for Closs's second season with the Clippers, Fitch was gone. In the ever-revolving Clippers coaching carousel he'd been replaced by Chris Ford (the same guy that would later, according to Dales, offer Dales NBA coaching jobs). Ford didn't gel with the Boss. In turn, Closs's playing time decreased dramatically; he registered just eighty-seven minutes in fifteen games the entire year.

With his career on life support heading into the 1999-2000 season, Closs said, "I've got to treat every day like my last day." He explained, "I didn't prepare myself the last two years." When asked why not, he responded frankly, "A sour attitude and immaturity."[49]

There were plenty of doubters, but in this third season Closs again became somewhat of a cult figure with the Clipper faithful as he turned himself into a legitimate, productive member of the rotation.[50] But on January 19, 2000, five days after a shouting match had erupted in practice between Ford and Closs, the coach suspended the Boss indefinitely, citing a "series of problems."

Tardiness and a lack of communication had continued to count among these "problems." As an example, just before the suspension, Closs had missed a game because of, quite understandably, the birth of Keith Closs III. But the problem was that he hadn't contacted team officials to tell them why he'd missed the game.

This first Ford suspension, though, lasted only one game before Closs made "peace with the team."[51] Yet issues continued to sour the relationship between Closs and Ford. In early February, late in a game against Golden State, Closs waved his arms up and down on the bench in an attempt to "incite the crowd into a 'We want Closs' chant." Ford by all accounts did not join the chant.

Daily News reporter Scott Wolf claimed that earlier in this same game, during halftime, Closs had shown his interest in playing by strolling onto the court and launching a three-pointer before he "chatted with a friend"—as opposed to warming-up in earnest.

Wolf didn't just lambast Closs, though, he also accused Ford, whom he characterized as a "two-time loser and perennial retread," with losing the team. And he put even more of the blame for the Clippers' woes on the team's owner, Donald T. Sterling, as well as on Elgin Baylor. Wolf had reason for complaint. For the previous fourteen years, the front office had presided over one of the worst major professional sports franchises of all time, perhaps worse than Ellis's Altanta Hawks.[52]

Just before the Clippers' woeful 2000 season came to an end—the team finished that season with a 14-68 record—the Closs saga took one of its most bizarre twists. On Los Angeles radio stations and elsewhere, stories of Closs's involvement in a brawl outside a Southland nightclub started to circulate, and rumors that there was video footage of the incident spread. On April 18, Closs confirmed his involvement in the fight, and eventually an unnamed Clippers employee admitted that during the melee anywhere from four to twenty guys had browbeaten Closs.

Dales liked to point out that you could watch the Southland nightclub beat-down on the Internet. He claimed that on paydays in L.A. thugs used to walk Closs to check-cashing places and force him to cough up his earnings.[53]

In a way, the brawl only added to the peculiar aura surrounding Boss Closs. In an interview with ESPN's Dan Patrick, former NBA standout Steve Francis, who would later enter a professional basketball game in China with an ice pack on his ankle, picked Closs as the NBA's "goofiest" player because of the brawl. Francis told Patrick, "It was Keith Closs last year. Definitely Keith Closs. But this year, I don't think anybody will ever take his place..."

This prompted Patrick to reply, "So nobody's going to take Keith's place...Why was he the goofiest?"

"Did you see that videotape when he got in a fight? I mean, that was goofy."[54]

In early October of 2000, during preseason, the Clippers indefinitely suspended Closs for "a lack of physical conditioning." By that time Alvin Gentry had taken over the Clippers' reins.

Closs thought he'd come to camp in shape but that the Clippers' brass had said otherwise in an effort to get out of their contract with him. The Clippers did schedule meetings with a team doctor, Tony Daly, to have Closs assessed, but Closs said that at their first appointment the doctor did nothing to examine him. The second time Closs supposedly took a treadmill test before meeting with Dr. Daly in person.

Worried because he'd heard that the Clippers' executive vice president, Andy Roeser, had been telling Dr. Daly that Closs was out of shape, Closs asked Dr. Daly what he should be expecting next. "He [Dr. Daly] said, 'I don't know why [Roeser] puts me in the middle of this stuff,'" Closs told the *Daily News*. Basically, Closs figured the Clippers were squeezing the Doc to deem Closs unfit to perform.[55]

As it happened, Closs's departure from the NBA led to a series of gigs in various parts of the world. He even endured a one-year hiatus from hoops. And yet he could still play by the time he joined the Lightning, and he made a huge difference for us immediately by blocking shots wantonly and even stroking a jumper or two. At least once a quarter he did something that made you shake your head and think about how he didn't belong in the CBA.

As I say, Closs's first game with us was against Great Lakes, and his potential was made clear right away. My shooting, on the other hand, reverted to inaccurate in this game, while Dobbins performed even worse, taking some of the attention away from me. He finished four of seventeen from the field with eight turnovers, and his play looked worse than these stats suggest. He was getting blocked by guys who just a year or two earlier he'd have dominated. As much as he might've tried to mask it by disrespecting Dales or otherwise looking frustrated, it was apparent that he'd let his frame get unfit and his skill set go dull. Dobbins knew the game and, when fit and polished, could present match-up problems for most anyone. But at this point he looked like an old vet ensnarled in the underbelly.

Even with my shot coming up blank and Dobbins playing poorly, with eight seconds to go we were up two, and I found myself at the free throw line for a pair. In other words, I had a chance to clinch the thing, and in somewhat dramatic fashion. Oh, Dales would dig it.

Crazy things can go through your mind when you shoot big free throws. It could be anything: *What if I miss? Look at that gorgeous lady. Don't mess up.* Over the years I'd adopted a saying that I'd run through my mind on free throws to avoid this: *Let's go baby, yeah, right over the front of the rim.* A shooting guru from Valparaiso, Indiana, named Skip Collins, who had borrowed the tactic from another Indiana shooting legend, Virgil Sweet, had recommended this—along with limited movement to decrease the chance of error—and it had helped me sink big ones in high school and as a Boilermaker. But this time, as I readied to shoot at the line, a series of random thoughts popped into my mind and distracted me. The sequence went something like this: *Let's go baby yeah, right over the…Can this few people make this much noise? I didn't think anybody was here. How's that possible? Should I be furthering this goofball Daleo's cause?…*(By this point I was clearly distracted and should've started my routine over right then. But I continued…) *right over the front of the rim.*

Now, as I say, I'd mostly moved past letting distracting thoughts get my daubers up on the line, but this caught me a bit. Plus, I hadn't shot a pivotal free throw for well over a year.

Coming off of my fingers the shot actually felt good, but it hit the front of the rim and fell short.

Oh shit. You idiot. You could be done. Don't miss the next one. How unacceptable. That's ridiculous. You could be done. You're only two of nine from the field to begin with. Don't compound it. Hit the next one. Remember Sinatra: "down in May, back on top in June." Stay focused. There's nothing you can do now. What an idiot! All right, focus on the routine. Let's go baby yeah, right over the front of the rim.

This second free throw felt horrible coming out, but it went in.

The make put us up three with only a few seconds left. Great Lakes inbounded the ball to guard Mark Jones, who raced up the court. Smothered by defenders, he managed to get off a ridiculous turnaround three-pointer from about twenty-five feet. Sure enough, as the buzzer sounded, it sunk straight through the hoop, sending the game into overtime.

We lost in the extra session. So, though we won the first three quarters of the game, we lost the contest 4-3 in standings points. That one free throw turned a potentially humongous win, into a loss. If I'd hit both free throws we would've won the game 7-0, I'd have greatly enhanced my job security, and we definitely wouldn't have had practice the next day, a Sunday afternoon. Instead, back in the locker room, Daleo promptly scheduled practice.

What a terrible miss.

31

Another long bus ride brought us to the Fairfield at about 4:00 a.m. We thought practice loomed in about six hours, but just before stepping off the bus Daleo told us he'd give us the day off.

Our next game was several days away, though, meaning everyone had plenty of time to mull my miss. I'd broken two major CBA laws with one missed free throw: I played quite poorly in a loss and did so with plenty of time before our next game. My odds of surviving the waiver wire felt low.

As if this wasn't enough, on Monday morning I met up with Daleo for our early morning radio show and everybody, Stone, Double T, Kristin, and Dales, hammered me about the free throw. It was a blast. But when Daleo said, on the air, "At least you still have a job," my spirits lightened a little. It sounds crazy but he said it in a way that was comfortable enough to make me think my job was safe.

When the radio show finally came to an end, Stone gave Dales and me $30 worth of Don Pablo's gift cards, which lightened Daleo's spirits. As we strolled out to the parking lot behind the station, it seemed like the gift cards had suddenly caused him to forget about the missed free throws.

At our workout that afternoon, as guys practiced shooting free throws, Dales walked around to each basket telling everybody about the gift cards. When he got to my bucket he said, "That's like four meals, huh, Carson?"

Four meals with $30 of gift cards?

"Yes, that's right, Coach."

A bit later, we broke again for free throws and Dales came around another time. "Hey, Lubeck, did Carson tell you? We got gift cards from Don Pablo's for like $30. Carson, that's like four meals, right?"

"Yes, Coach."

32

The next day, following practice, Trainer Brad gave Closs and me a ride home to the Fairfield. Along the way we went through the Burger King drive-through. Keith ordered three Whoppers Jr. How he couldn't hold weight I don't know.

On the drive Keith told us about his three years with the Los Angeles Clippers. He said that during his last year with the team he made $1.8 million. I couldn't fathom such a thing. "Man, what did that check look like every two weeks?"

He thought about it for a minute. "About forty-five thousand after taxes."

"Gosh damn! Every two weeks."

"Yep."

"You got any left?"

"Nope."

"How'd you spend that?"

"Paying for a house, partying…"

"You bought a house?"

"No, I leased one. Plus, family came out of from everywhere. People calling me, 'Hey Keith, could you fix this?' 'Keith, this is your cousin.' 'Oh, yeah? How are you related to me again?' 'Oh, from such and such.' 'Sorry, buddy, I've never heard of him.'"

Keith would give five-hundred dollars to homeless people he'd pass on the street, like it was nothing. He figured he had a roof over his head, while the homeless guy was sleeping under freeways.

I couldn't keep from chewing on $45,000 every two weeks.

How could he spend it all?

For years I had grinded on something closer to $700 every two weeks. That first $45,000 monster would blow me away, and then to think another one would come along, and then another two weeks later.

That's insane. No assets? Richard Pryor struggled to spend that much money in Brewster's Millions *and he was trying.*

By and by, Keith got to talking about Bill Fitch, his first coach with the Clippers. Apparently, Fitch was full of piss-n-vinegar. According to Closs, one time in Philadelphia, in a game against the Sixers while Keith sat on the bench, Coach Fitch challenged him to a fight.

"We were getting blown out. My cousin was killing us..." Keith explained.

"Wait, your cousin? Who's your cousin?" I asked.

"Employee number three. Allen Iverson."

"Really?"

"Yeah."

His cousin is Allen Iverson?

Closs continued, "Coach Fitch turned around, looked at James 'Hollywood' Robinson and me, and then said to me, 'It's all your fault.' I wasn't even playing. Then he asked, 'You want to go?' And he held up his thumbs and said, 'I was in the Marines. I may be old, but I'll take your eyes out in a second.'"

(Coach Fitch was known to have a wry sense of humor. In *Cavs: From Fitch to Fratello* Fitch relayed the time, as coach of the woeful 0-14 Cavaliers, that he showed up to the stadium without his NBA identification pass for a game against the Warriors in San Francisco. When the security guard balked at letting him in, Fitch referenced the Cavs' record and asked, "Why would I tell you I am the coach of the Cavaliers if I really am not?" The security guard thought about it and promptly let him in.)

33

B ack in the MetroCentre, following a practice, Daleo turned
melancholy. Most of the guys had cleared out by then, but seeing
as I needed to improve my woeful shooting percentage, I had
stuck around to put up shots. Daleo stayed until I finished. Then we
walked back to the locker room.

I mentioned to him that I'd heard from John Mueller the other
day. Mueller, a big, strong, 6'10" center from Marquette, had played for
Daleo a couple of years earlier during my first stint with Rockford. At
Marquette, he'd spent most of his career as a role player and no one had
really expected him to play professionally, Mueller included. Educated
as an engineer, he figured grad school would come next, but at a
workout the summer after Mueller's senior year, Daleo took a liking to
him. So Mueller played in Rockford for a season before catching on
with a USBL team. The next year he ended up with a nice gig in
Australia's top league.

Apparently Daleo thought he deserved credit for keeping Mueller's
career alive, because when I mentioned Mueller, Dales sighed for a
moment and got a disappointed look on his face. He started to wax
philosophical. "You know what, this business is garbage, it's terrible.
It's a bunch of people stabbing you in the back: agents, coaches, players
. . . nobody gives a fuck about anybody. It's a horrible business, the
CBA. You know, I'm not looking for much, just a little respect. Just a
little thank you or a phone call from a guy just checkin' in."

"You haven't heard from Mueller?"

"Nothing. And I'm not asking for much, just a little thank you.
Coming out, everybody thought he was a bum. But Dales saw
something. I gave him a shot when nobody would give him a shot. And
nothing. This business is garbage. There's no loyalty, people stabbing
each other in the back. It's a horrible business."

Home game at the Rockford Lightning's MetroCentre, during the 2002-3 season. We scored a ton of points that year. Future biomedical engineer John Mueller is in the background. He's buckets.

The next morning I got to practice extra early, still hoping to overcome my propensity to miss shots. When I walked onto the floor, Brant "The Baffler" Bailey was already there tossing up shots. He arrived earlier than any other player, virtually all the time. He was unbeatable, like a bewildering Rambo.

Daleo came out of the locker room a short time later, all wound up. He walked over as we shot. "Where are my assistants, fuck? Coach Thomas, Troy, where are you?"

He didn't talk about Renaldo much. I asked him what he thought of him.

"Are you kidding me? I'd fire him tomorrow if I could."

"Come on."

"What," Dales stated as much as he asked. Then he took a look at me and said, "You think I'm kidding? He should be getting here earlier. And when he is here . . . I didn't hire him to sit around and talk about unemployment benefits. And I didn't hire him to hang out at Shooter's."

I just kept shooting.

"I don't need anybody. Think of your first year here . . . when it was just me and Shaman."

"Where's Shaman now?" I asked.

"Who knows? I told him not to go to the Steelheads, but he didn't listen. Last I heard, he was doing something for Chicago State."

"Shaman. What a character."

"Yeah, he knew nothing, absolutely nothing. But he'd listen. He'd do as I say. And he was on time."

Craig Shaman loved basketball and was a competent task-completer, but he did endure a lot as Dales's assistant. Say, for instance, Daleo was in the middle of one of his speeches, about THC or an out-of-bounds play or some other thing, or maybe he was just telling us about something as simple as the itinerary, and he paused for a moment. Well, during one of these pauses, only every now and again, Shaman would interject with a quick comment, something harmless, like letting us know what time to get on the bus. The problem with this was Dales didn't seem to like it when Shaman spoke to us. Sure, sometimes Dales would let it go, but other times he'd get real irritated, and it seemed like it would get Daleo particularly mad if Shaman mentioned basketball. In these instances, as soon as Shaman started to talk, you could see Dales kind of cringe. He would do this exaggerated pause, tilt his head down a little, tighten his lip in disgust, and shake his head a bit. You could see him boil. Then, right in the middle of Shaman talking, Daleo was liable to say, "Shut up Craig, I'm talking."

One time at practice Shaman had the misfortune of trying to say something at a moment Daleo found particularly annoying. I don't think anybody remembers what Shaman said, just Daleo telling him to "shut up" and to "go sit over there [on the sidelines]."

Shaman marched right over to the sidelines, sat down, and watched the remaining forty-five minutes of practice. Apparently, the next season—I wasn't there—Daleo did the same thing, only this time Shaman had to wait outside in the cold. He could've excelled in a lot of different industries, but he wanted to make it to the NBA, just like the rest of us, so he dealt with it, knowing, as you sensed at times that Dales did, that he helped the Lightning operation run, and hoping, I imagine, that one day he could end up as a director of basketball operations for the Chicago Bulls."

As I shot around, probably with my tights on, Dales finished recalling Shaman's stint and then went back to talking about how he wanted to fire Coach Thomas. I think he even mentioned Mueller not keeping in touch with him again.

As he talked, I mainly just nodded, trying to gauge whether or not he intended to cut me. Our next four games were at the MetroCentre and we needed wins, bottom line. All in all, we'd posted a paltry record since my return.

34

Fortunately, we played the four-game home stand with the same kind of energy that had propelled us in our recent comeback against Sioux Falls. In our first two games of this home stretch, we ran the floor like madmen, shared the rock, dropped plenty of buckets, and helped out on defense, even the Baffler. Keith Closs swatted shots prolifically and Boseman was strong and under control, while Lubes and Phillips knocked down threes. When we played like that, the game rolled along nice and smooth, in a way that reminded you of why you loved it. Rather than feeling all "cramped and smothery," like an office job can do to you, this made you "feel mighty free and easy and comfortable."[56]

Marshall Phillips, perhaps more than anyone, continued to show how valuable a pro he could be. He could rebound and score effectively down-low, while also operating on the wing well, and he could defend just about anyone. His game was an uncommon mixture, then, of just about everything. But his game made sense if you knew his back story.

Moving with his mom from project to project during his high school years in Atlanta, Phillips consistently had one major focus: make sure you've got enough money to eat dinner. It's not as if the threat of missing dinner arose each day, but Phillips relied on his earnings for a lot of his food, and the threat that he might have to go without arose regularly enough to spook him. That's why Phillips didn't play high school basketball. Practice cut into his ability to make money, to secure his primary needs.

As far as his versatile playing style, Phillips explained, "I played in the park, and when you play in the park you've got to be able to do anything. I played for money." A lot of times he'd play two-on-two, which forced him to recognize the mismatch and exploit it ferociously. Food was on the line.

And it wasn't just hoops that could bring a small amount of financial security. He was a small-time hoodlum, too, who would resort to petty crime every now and again to make money. He sensed that he risked going down the wrong path, in a real bad way, even though his mother told him to make good choices and did what she could to get him to do so. Basketball helped guide him down a better course, and he's grateful for it.

His break came when he was discovered at one of the parks he frequented, by a young basketball-junkie assistant from Campbellsville University, an NAIA school in Kentucky. The assistant had heard about a six-foot-three workhorse from Atlanta who didn't play organized ball, but could play with anyone. He'd asked around and was directed to a park. It didn't take long for him to figure out that Marshall Phillips was the player he needed.

An older neighborhood guy, who probably regretted that he'd passed up opportunities in his life, told Phillips that this was his chance, and that he had to take advantage of it. In fact, he told Phillips that he'd give him cash, fifty dollars here, one-hundred dollars there, if he just stayed in school and graduated. So Phillips applied himself in his last year of high school, not just during the regular school day, but in night school and summer school. Something in him realized that this really was his chance to get out of the Interstate-285 ring that project kids from Atlanta didn't always venture beyond.

Within months, Phillips found himself on a predominantly white, Baptist campus in southern Kentucky. It was the first time he'd ever dealt with white people on a daily basis, and the school opened his eyes to the world. It let him know that not only was there a big world out there with a lot of possibility, but he was smart enough and talented enough to excel in it.[57]

At his first college basketball practice, when the coach told him to get down into triple-threat position, Phillips froze, puzzled. He had no clue what this common basketball term, used to describe holding the ball near your waist and bending your knees so that you are ready to shoot, pass, or dribble, meant. He was raw, plain and simple. But a great thing about sports is that it doesn't matter how raw you are if you can play. And in his third game at Campbellsville, Phillips showed that it didn't matter if you didn't know what a "triple-threat" position was either. He pulled down thirty-three rebounds in that game, a school record. Within a decade he'd play in junior college at Appalachian State, in the CBA, in Mexico, Puerto Rico, Venezuela, and Italy. By his career's end, you could add France,

Germany, and Lebanon to that list. Of all of these, the best league in terms of the quality of players, he would tell me, was the CBA.

Along with his talent and desire, Phillips had an understated, workman-like approach, both in how he played and how he interacted with folks, which was effective. He learned early, he told me, that if you're the biggest drug dealer in the projects, you're probably going to get caught or killed. He saw this and applied it to his life. The limelight wasn't for him. If he scored forty, he planned on being the first guy back in the locker room. He didn't want a lot of attention; he simply wanted people to say, at game's end, that Marshall Phillips is a good guy and plays hard. And, unlike his father, he wanted to be there for his family. As his teammate, you sensed these types of things about him. And in his own quiet way he'd managed to steer our team onto a smoother course, one that was leading us to victories.

As we readied to win our third game in a row, a problem did arise, however, when Boss Closs missed a shoot-around. During this missed shoot-around, Daleo paced up and down the court ripping Troy (basically to himself) for not knowing Keith's whereabouts. At one point Dales told Renaldo they needed to bring someone in to replace the Boss.

Apparently, Closs had drunk too much the night before. Getting to know the guy a little, I'd come to learn that he was the gentlest fellow you'd ever meet—when he was sober, that is. He had a ready smile and would slap you five or pat you on the back more than anybody I'd ever played with. And he loved the fans. He'd talk with kids and joke with ladies; he seemed to have time for anybody. You got the impression that they gave him something he needed, just like he must've given them something they needed. But the bottle called to him something fierce. And I'd heard that when he answered that call, he could turn into one mean and erratic Gulliver.

That evening, in his pre-game talk, Dales laid into me. It shouldn't have surprised me that right when things got to rolling along all nice and smooth-like, the current would start to turn a bit. I suppose Closs's absence at the shoot-around had caused Dales's sour mood, and he probably figured it easier to start in on me than go after Closs. I knew he'd be irritated with me anyway, because a local newspaper from my hometown had just written a piece about how I played ball and went to graduate school. Daleo had, of course, read it. He found just about every article written on any of us. That way, if he liked it, he could put it on the Rockford Lightning website and email-blast it to whoever it was that signed up for the Rockford Lightning mass-email list. I reckoned Daleo would take the article personally, since I talked about graduate school in it—even though by this time I'd finished my coursework and was just chipping away at my dissertation. And sure enough during his pre-game rant, Dales said I needed to start rotating better on defense and a bunch of other stuff, "or else it would be more book time and less play time. You'll be gone." Then he reminded me with apparent seriousness, "You're in the big-time now."

Fortunately, we played well as a team, and I turned in one of my better performances of the season, dropping in twelve points and dishing out five dimes. I also reached a milestone by raising my shooting percentage just over forty percent. Granted, for most professional basketball players that's no milestone, but you take what you can get.

I matched up against Darrick Martin in the contest, and during a lull in the action a Lightning fan yelled out to him, "Why are you wearing NBA socks? This is the CBA." I guess the fan didn't know that Darrick Martin, who seemed like one of the classiest fellows in the league, had spent more time in the NBA than a lot of the guys in the NBA. (Within a week of this ingenious fan's statement, Martin got called up to the Clippers, and about a week after that, he drained pivotal shots in a Clippers win over the Sonics.)[58]

Although I'd played well, at halftime Daleo gave me a hard time for not throwing the ball up the court quickly enough on the break. "I mean, Brant was ahead and you didn't send it, and he's a white guy, so it can't be a white-black thing."

Players just shook their heads and laughed uncomfortably, kind of a "this guy's jokes are out of left field" chuckle. Smiling bewilderedly, Renaldo said, "Why's it got to be black-white thing, man? Shoot, look at Keith: he's more like orange anyway."

Daleo continued with his halftime spiel. A short ways into it, Boss Closs leaned over and whispered to me, "Carson, you fat racist." Then he flashed his wide grin and busted out laughing.

35

After the win we had a day off. Before practice the next day, Daleo summoned us to center court to announce that Stais Boseman had earned player-of-the-week honors and that Brandon Bender had gotten cut.

Following practice, I got trapped in the locker room with Daleo and Trainer Brad. I'd taken to devising ways to avoid Dales but somehow failed in this instance. Sure enough, Daleo started in on me, just as he'd done all practice, saying "Less time in Chicago and more time in the weight room. The first time you played here you were lighter and I think a bit stronger; now, I see more fat. Less time with the wife and more time at the YMCA."

Dales then stepped out to go get something, prompting Trainer Brad to pull me aside as he and I walked out: "Too bad he knows you're married; he will probably use that against you. You know what he told me last season? That I'd be divorced in eight years. Who says that to somebody?"

Riding the emotional wave of our winning streak, the next day, in between the morning shoot-around and our game that night, I decided I finally had to let a small college near my hometown know that I planned on passing up a new offer to teach a couple of history courses during the spring semester. I reminded myself, before officially declining the offer, of my goal to see the season through, to finish my basketball playing days on my own terms—and with a championship. It was a gamble because if I got axed by the Dales I'd have no income, but, given our recent success, it actually seemed possible to see the season through.

That night's game carried particular significance because it was our last home tilt before Christmas. If we won, Daleo would likely approach the holiday with liberal inclinations. If we lost, he was liable to schedule workouts straight through. Marshall Phillips, for instance, who since coming back from Chile had barely seen his wife and daughter, was already angling for the opportunity to rent a truck and drive straight to Atlanta on the night of December 23rd. If he made the trip, he planned to arrive back for our shoot-around on the morning of December 26th. But Dales acted like he wasn't much into holidays, not even Christmas. One time someone asked him what he bought his kids for Christmas. He kind of scoffed and said, "Nothing."

"Nothing?" I asked.

"Nothing. I don't buy presents. My wife can do that."

"Well, that's the same thing. They're from you."

"Nah, I don't buy presents."

So no one knew if he'd give us the 24th and 25th off or not. To increase the likelihood, winning our last two games leading up to the holiday seemed crucial.

In this final home game before Christmas, we faced Great Lakes, which had emerged as our main conference rival, with its three starters who would eventually make it to the NBA. But the Storm had just endured losses on a tough western swing, which had helped us capture first place, and we capitalized on their fatigue by taking the first two quarters. I turned in a solid first-half performance knocking down midrange jumpers, speeding up the game's pace, and hitting free throws. You could feel our energy and our rhythm.

In the second half my playing time increased dramatically because Stais Boseman got ejected, early in the third quarter, for having elicited two technical fouls. His problems started when he told the referee, in rather strong language, about his objections to a call. The ref charged him with a technical for his efforts, which prompted Daleo, sensing that Boseman's anger was mushrooming, to sub for him. But the tide had started rising within Boseman and Daleo's attempts to curb it proved futile. The second technical came when Boseman, taking his time as he made his way toward our bench, decided to pick up a telephone at the scorer's table and slam it down.

With Boseman out, I played virtually every second the rest of the way, and not too shabbily, either. As the game wore on my confidence increased. Pretty soon I was busting out some of my moves from the olden days; double-crosses and behind-the-back forays to the rack. I sliced into the lane feeling super swift, like the old days, dropping it off or pulling up. My endorphins were firing.

Oooooooh. Feelin' good today. Would Pat Riley ever actually take notice? I can still do this. Focus, you cheeseball.

With a few minutes to go and the game basically even, I felt pretty good about our chances. But then I ran out of gas down the stretch. In the waning minutes I missed two bunnies and committed a costly turnover. We had plenty of opportunities to win but ended up losing by two. Our winning streak was now suddenly over, and I'd gone from looking good to dreadful in a couple of minutes.

In his post-game speech Daleo laid into just about everybody. He called out guys for giving up offensive rebounds: "Fuckin' beast somebody!" He got on people for messing up rotations: "Brant, what the fuck are you doing?" And he laid into me for the late turnover: "Carson, you're making it hard on me."

Then he started in on a tirade about how he always gets to shoot-arounds early and how he doesn't understand why some guys don't constantly work on their game. "I am here before anybody else at shoot-arounds. I don't understand. I would be doing everything I could to get out of here. Instead, guys are happy with making their $450, $550, or $650 a week. This is a joke league. You should not want to be here. You win a few in a row and you think you're King of the Hill making $500 or whatever a week? I don't understand. You should be figuring out a way to get to Korea to make $10,000 a month, or get $30,000 for ten days with an NBA call-up. But no, 'Can't come in coach, I'm big-time, making my $550.' I watch more tape than my assistants combined. I don't sleep. I'm doing everything to move up. You should be in here every day working on your game, trying to move on. I don't understand why some of you guys keep playing in this league, why you are here."

That night, my wife informed me that she was pregnant.

36

In the Gary Genesis Center's visitor locker room, prior to our last game before Christmas, Daleo went over our strategy, which basically consisted of, as usual, pressing and rotating on defense, and pushing it on offense. If the break proved fruitless, we were to run one of our three or four plays. It was all pretty straightforward. During the briefing, Keith Close leaned over and whispered in my ear, "Carson, you fat racist."

Things went well enough in the first half, thanks in no small part to Close, who proved pivotal yet again. In a revealing instance of Close's ability to affect a game, during the third quarter the Steelheads' Paul McPherson—a former Phoenix Sun from Chicago who in a high school all-star game years earlier had dunked on me in spectacular fashion—went up for a layup on the right side. Sensing pressure in midair, the left-handed and bouncy McPherson glided underneath the bucket hoping for a reverse lay-in. Boss Close, realizing McPherson's intention, moved over, reached out for the ball, and pinned it against the backboard. It took a moment to register with both the crowd, which eventually gasped, and with Close, who, upon fully realizing that he hadn't jumped and therefore didn't need to land, simply held the ball against the backboard, and then crossed his legs and smiled. For a moment he looked as if he could've been chilling on Venice Beach. The crowd fell out.

It wasn't the night's first gasp-inducing maneuver from Close either. Earlier in the game he'd caught a pass at the NBA three-point line and taken two strides before hammering home a dunk. As CBA'ers, we'd all seen guys do crazy dunks, like take-off from very near the free throw line at a shoot-around on a high school court. But, just like the crowd, we were stupefied by this loping jam by the Boss, and not only because he took off from so far away, but because most of the time he preferred fingertip rolls to dunks.

As I say, for those fingertip rolls, Closs would rise up and extend his arm real high like the Statue of Liberty and then let the ball roll right off his hand into the hoop. Daleo hated this. He'd yell at the Boss to dunk it, which would make Closs want to roll it even more. Once, Closs did the fingertip roll and then ran down the court screaming, "I ain't dunkin' Chris [Daleo]! There's the fingertip roll." On the loper, though, Closs flushed it, and his performance on this night in Gary forced you to ponder why he was still in the CBA.

Even though we won, and all anyone wanted to do was go home for Christmas, Daleo babbled on and on about the stat-line in the post-game locker room. When he got to my numbers, he said, "Two for four from the field, two assists, two steals, but one of four from the free throw line? Stinky. You're tired. Too much going to and from Chicago. Too much time with the wifey. Talk to some of your teammates. They'll hook you up with a nice piece of ass in Rockford. Stop going to and from Chicago."

He went through the next guy's line and the next and then over the team stats, with commentary along the way. It was excruciating. It seemed like he wanted to stall because he knew everyone wanted to leave. As he kept on, players would steal glances at each other and roll their eyes, but only when Dales wasn't looking. When he finally did finish with our stats, you could see the energy among the players shift to go-mode. You got the sense that some of the guys were about to darn near sprint out of the locker room, especially Phillips. He still had to drive to Atlanta, for crying out loud, and Dales knew it.

Only we couldn't sprint out of there because when Daleo finished with our stat-line, he moved right on to the Steelheads' line.

Unbelievable. We won. Who cares?

He proceeded to go over each person's stats on the freaking Steelheads. And of course he added commentary as he went along: "He's fat," or "He had nothing," or "He's a good player I have to give him credit," or "Too much Coke." It numbed your mind listening to him. Nobody gave a hoot. We wanted to go home. Fifteen minutes later, mercifully, he finished. And then he gave us both Christmas Eve and Christmas day entirely off.

Hallelujah.

37

S pending forty-eight hours in the real world can really mess with a
CBA'er. Normalcy beckons. Most alluring were the reasonable
conversations you encountered with rational human beings.
Instead of encouraging me to hook up with a groupie, people asked me
how my wife was doing. It was all so different. Part of me wanted to
stay away, to never go back, but by the thirty-second hour, about the
time I had downed my twentieth cookie, I started to get restless and to
think about the fade. So I turned my thoughts to our next game. It
made things easier that my wife remained in full support of me trying
to see things through.

We had a shoot-around at 10:00 a.m. and Christy dropped me off
at the gym before she went to Borders to pass the time. During a lull in
the shoot-around, about midway through, I asked Brad if he could give
me a ride back to Borders when we were done. He looked at me
nervously and sputtered: "Well . . . I can't, you need to, well I need to . .
. I'll talk to you after practice."

"Dude, what are you talking about? Do you have to go somewhere
first or what?"

He said "No" and then looked around a bit nervously, acting like
he couldn't elaborate. I just left it at that and went back to shooting,
wondering why he was acting loopy.

The shoot-around ended at 11:00 a.m. Afterward I worked on my
free throws, while Daleo, a volunteer assistant named Stockton, and
Brad looked on and talked. I took my sweet time trying to fine-tune my
form. After about twenty minutes or so, I decided I'd tossed up enough
shots and headed to the locker room. As I started walking off the court,
Brad came right up alongside me and said, quietly: "Carson, listen, I
hesitated when you asked me for a ride because we received a call that
your wife fainted at Borders. An ambulance came to get her. She's in

the emergency room right now. My brother-in-law Ted will give you a ride."

"What? What happened? What the fuck are you talking about?"

I started running towards the locker room and, as I did, I turned back and yelled at Daleo: "You waited until after a shoot-around? You stupid fuck."

Moving quickly, I got in the car with Trainer Brad's brother-in-law and headed to the emergency room. I probably didn't even have time to take my stupid tights off.

Once there, someone directed me to room three. When I entered I saw Christy lying on a hospital bed, with her lip bloodied on the top and bottom and both of her front teeth badly chipped. It looked like she'd lost about half of each front tooth. Her entire face was ashen white. The nurse had just inserted a catheter for an ultrasound and was trying to draw blood.

"Honey, are you okay?" I asked.

"I'm so glad you're here," Christy said, teary eyed. I felt horrible.

"I'm sorry I didn't make it sooner," I told her. "I didn't know. My idiot coach didn't tell me until after the gosh damn shoot-around."

A short time after the internal ultrasound and blood tests, we learned that everything was fine. The baby, five weeks and a day old, was healthy, as was Christy. She just needed to get her teeth fixed.

With her nerves settled, Christy told me what had happened, and a short time later, Brad came to the hospital with some flowers. He said he'd never felt less human and hoped that I could understand the difficulty of his position. Then the part-time volunteer assistant Stockton showed up. He gave me his number and said if there was anything he or his wife could do, let him know. Before he left he said, "I can't believe the way this was handled."

A bit later the doctor released Christy and the little one from the hospital and we went to the Fairfield Inn to rest. I just laid there, stewing, envisioning myself beating the tar out of Dales, beating the piss right out of him, just hammering away. I got so wound up I called Daleo on the phone.

He must've seen it was me on caller ID, because he tried to sound excited and pleasant-like: "Hello. Is she pregnant?"

"Yes."

"I knew it! Congratulations."

"Yeah, well, thanks. But I have to tell you that I think your decision not to tell me that my wife was taken by ambulance to the emergency room was completely unprofessional and selfish. And if a situation like that ever arises in the future, I expect you to tell me right away."

Dales was silent for a few moments. Finally, kind of weakly, he said, "I had a decision to make and I made it."

"No, it's not your decision to make. You needed to tell me what happened, and it's my decision how to deal with it."

"Okay."

"Goodbye."

Livid, I went back to picturing myself beating him down.

A lot of fellows would've called it off right there, and understandably so—would've told Dales off and high-tailed it out of town. But somehow I convinced myself that one person's mean-spirited thoughtlessness should not the season ruin. Plus, I'd just turned down that teaching job. Feeling a bit cowardly, I stayed on. Christy, again, was for it. She figured I shouldn't quit because my boss was a jerk, and that we'd known going into the season that it wouldn't be all seashells and balloons.

As it happened, her parents and extended family were coming into town to watch our game that night. Pangs of melancholy ran through me during warm-ups. I felt like I was violating the advice a former NBA player had given me over a decade earlier: Control basketball, don't let it control you.

38

That evening we played the Gary Steelheads again. Before the game Closs called me a "fat racist," and complained about how every coach he'd had since Bill Fitch yelled at him to dunk it.

Near the end of the second quarter we came to the sideline for a time-out. Daleo barked a few instructions and then, just before we stood up to take the court, he looked down at me on the bench and said, "Why don't you show some *professionalism* and win this quarter?" I'd figured he would hold my earlier comments to him against me, but I didn't care. I only wished I'd laid into him harder.

In the second half, Daleo got on Closs for "not beastin'" or some other thing and took him out of the game, irritating the usually good-humored Boss. Not too much later, Daleo yanked me for turning the ball over. As I sat on the bench, Keith came over and stood up in front of me, facing the MetroCentre crowd. He made sure he was in plain view of all the people in the crowd just behind our bench. Then, real loudly and slowly, making sure to accentuate each word, he said, "Our coach is a fuckin' prick."

Just in case the fans didn't hear, he said it again, nice and slow.

"Our coach is a fuckin' prick. I am talking like this and facing the crowd so that his wife can read my lips."

A few minutes later Daleo looked down the bench. He did a double-take and seemed confused. Walking briskly, he passed all of us before leaning in to ask the assistant Stockton at the end of the bench, "Where's Keith?"

"He went to the bathroom."

Daleo opened his mouth and jutted his lip up and out to the left. He was baffled. "He did what?"

"He went to the bathroom," said Stockton. "He said he had to go. I told him it wasn't a good idea, but he went anyway."

"Well go find his ass," Dales said.

Stockton came back a bit later without Keith.

"Did you find him?" I asked.

"Yeah. He was in there."

"Is he coming?"

"I don't know. He said he was coming back."

About a minute later the Boss strolled in.

"What were you doing in there, Keith?" I asked.

"I needed to get out of here. I was throwing chairs around, I'm so pissed off."

He didn't seem too fazed, though, back on the bench.

Dales put Closs back in the game, and straight away he started swatting shots. One play in particular stood out. It involved McPherson again, who I guess had a stubborn streak, because he'd raced down the lane and tried to elevate for a shot over Keith once more. This time the Boss effortlessly tipped it and then caught the ball in midair with a big smile on his face. In the meantime, McPherson's momentum had carried him out of bounds. Keith looked at Paul standing out-of-bounds and couldn't resist. Rather than throw an outlet pass up-ahead, he lightly passed it to McPherson, who had no choice but to let the ball hit him as he stood out-of-bounds. Sure, some fan probably griped about showboating and grandstanding and all that other jazz, but I tell you it was pretty funny. Most of the fans got a chuckle, and that's all Keith wanted.

Thanks again largely to Closs's control of the paint we won the game. And yet you could sense that we might not have him much longer, since his relationship with Daleo was rapidly deteriorating and his behavior was becoming increasingly erratic.

As we headed off the court, Closs told Stockton, "I've got the right teammates, right assistants, and right trainer—just the wrong coach."

39

The next night, with the lights down and the Lightning ladies dancing like mad right before we ran out for the pre-game introductions, Closs told me he had a surprise in store. The nickname I'd come up with for Bailey had caught on by then. A few moments later, when Brant ran out on the court with the spotlight on him, the PA announcer boomed, "At 6'6," from the University of Wisconsin-Stevens Point…Brant 'The Baffler' Bailey." In the tunnel, guys rolled.

Dales was concerned about this game because Teddy Dupay had recently signed with the Mayhem. Seeing as he had cut him, Dales figured Dupay would be gunning for us and might catch fire. And in pre-game warm-ups Teddy claimed he planned to do as much. He wanted to knock down some jumpers and then start doing impersonations of Dales to mock him.

But Teddy couldn't find his groove, so he didn't carry out many antics, which in a way was kind of a bummer. Closs took up the slack for him, however.

We started the game slow, which allowed the Mayhem to jump out to a twenty-point lead, to which Dales responded by running up and down the bench yelling, "Look at this, look at this . . . it's pathetic!" At one point he looked down the bench, eyes blazing, and screamed, "You should be ashamed of yourselves!"

That's when Keith decided he'd heard enough and piped back: "I'm not."

"Well, you should be," Dales said.

"I'm not. I'm proud of myself. Maybe *you're* ashamed of yourself."

"Yeah, right, Keith."

"Take some accountability. Stop blaming others all the time," Keith said.

"My game plan was right on."

Keith shook his head. "Take responsibility some time."

"Be quiet Keith," Dales said.

"Maybe you have a self-esteem problem. You got self esteem issues?"

I figured Daleo would lay into Keith big-time for that one, but Dales just took it. He needed a shot blocker so he kept his mouth shut. There was something agreeable about that, Keith being able to get away with it.

Despite Keith and Daleo's exchange, we managed to get in a groove in the second half. It felt like somehow, regardless of any drama, we'd turned the flow of the game completely around and now we were rolling downstream, nice and free. And, as I say, when the hoops gets like that it's almost like you don't have to do anything: the game just moves you along and before you know it, you've overcome a seventeen-point halftime deficit and pulled out a victory.

My first year in the CBA, with the Gary Steelheads, an assistant coach tried to explain the power of "Lady Mo'." We'd just lost a game, and back in the locker room he started in on how important it is to take care of her. He was from the South and had an accent, so it wasn't all that easy for me to make out exactly what he was saying, but the basics seemed to be, "You got to massage Lady Mo', you got to treat her right, because before you know it, she could be gone. She's fickle. She's elusive. You got to treat her right. Take care of her. You gotta recognize how important she is." As he was giving this speech, though, I was lost. *Am I the only one not following this? Who's Lady Mo'?* I asked myself. Finally, a minute or two after he finished, it dawned on me: *Ahh, she's momentum. I get it. It makes sense now. You're a real genius.*

Of course, in addition to treating Lady Mo' well, our comeback was helped by Boss Closs's dominance of the paint again. Plus, Phillips remained a stalwart and Boseman continued to play a more controlled game. Compared to earlier in the year, when Boseman had a stretch during which he shot a bunch of threes, he'd been relying on his midrange jumper more, and his distribution had improved. Meanwhile, "The Baffler" confounded the opposition and Lubes maintained his steadiness. And I played well too. Taking advantage of the big minutes Dales gave me in the second half, I finished 4-for-8 from the field and 4-for-4 from the line for twelve points.

But after the game Dales fumed. Maybe this stemmed from Keith's comments during the game, maybe he was still irked because I'd called him out, or maybe his anger really did result from my decision not to go to the corner on some lousy play. He'd gotten himself into quite a huff when the play happened during the game. He called me over and screamed, "What are you doing? What are you doing? Why?"

Now, I had thought about going to the corner on the play, as I was supposed to, but Stais was dribbling near the spot, and I thought I'd have crowded him by doing so. I tried to explain this during the game, but Dales didn't want to hear it.

Whatever the catalyst, Dales seethed. He went on about all types of things that we needed to do better. Then he went over to the chalkboard to draw up a play, the one I didn't immediately cut to the corner on. As he drew it up he called me unprofessional, and he let it be known that he hadn't appreciated my explanation of what'd I'd been thinking during the game. Putting on a real sarcastic tone, he said: "Carson said, 'I thought I was crowding Stais.'" Then he paused and looked at me, his eyes steely, and said, "That will be your demise."

Dales stopped talking for a few moments after that and went to pacing back and forth in front of us, like he was still seething over something. Then he added, "I don't care to hear your opinion. Some guys like Muntrelle, who have been with me for while, then yeah, maybe. But other than that, I don't care to hear your opinion."

I guess it figured. Just as we won our fifth game out of six and just as I started turning in my best performances of the season, I got put directly back on the chopping block. I knew the league, though, and Dales needed something to fill the vacuum with, so I reckoned surprise was unwarranted. It didn't make sense for Dales to overly worry about Close—he needed him too badly right then. So instead he sat around thinking about being told that he lacked professionalism by a role player.

It seemed like he really was angling to can me now. And yet, though it might sound a little paranoid, I imagined that he possessed enough scruples to know that he couldn't make it look like he was firing me for having called him out for the way he'd handled the situation with my wife. Too many people knew about it, Ronnie Fields in particular. At the same time, I figured feeling boxed in would make Dales even angrier and therefore he'd start re-building a case to send me packing.

Ronnie, although I wouldn't know it till later on, when Trainer Brad told me, was the unexpected wild card. His thumb injury had kept him from playing the previous couple of weeks. But on occasion he'd come to practice and games, and apparently, he'd kept in close contact with the Lighting owner, Judy Timpe, whose husband and long-time Lightning owner, Wayne Timpe, had passed away less than a year earlier. Now, Judy Timpe, word was, liked Ronnie Rockford immensely, just as her husband had, which Dales knew. Indeed, Dales probably figured, since Ronnie had apparently played a role in getting him hired, that Ronnie could very well get him fired. And yet tension between Dales and Ronnie, which could ebb and flow, had picked up during Ronnie's absence, causing a power struggle to brew. Amid this struggle, Ronnie, for whatever reason, had gotten in my corner.

I got a hint of this after my wife had gone to the hospital, when Ronnie called to ask about her. During the call he launched into a spiel about Dales's selfishness and told me that he'd seen Chris do too many people wrong over the years. And he intimated that it would come back to get him.

As for the ownership, it was hard to tell day-to-day how much the Timpe family affected things, especially with Wayne gone. In my first year with Rockford I only saw the Timpes occasionally. One of those times occurred when Wayne and Judy came to a Rockford country club, which on this night was hosting a remote radio broadcast of Daleo's coach's show. This country club had an aura of bygone glamour—it was probably a first-rate joint before American manufacturing went in the tank—but by 2002 the place looked drab. And the country club wasn't the only thing that looked tired: so did Wayne Timpe, as he sat and smoked while chatting with his wife and friends. It looked to me that night as if the Timpes had spent many evenings at country clubs, puffing away with Rockford's well-heeled. But I really didn't know the Timpes, and as it turns out I was wrong. They didn't fancy themselves country-clubbers and weren't showy. Sure, Wayne's company, LKG, generated millions in revenues, but, as I'd come to find out, his wife drove a minivan and he often drove an old Pontiac Fiero. They appreciated their humble roots.

Wayne Timpe did smoke like a lot, though, and the effects seemed apparent. It was lymphoma that would end his life. Before he passed, he'd single-handedly kept the CBA in town by spending millions. He loved both basketball and the Lightning. They gave him something.

For decades, he rarely missed a game, and when a reporter asked why he kept pouring cash into the franchise, the former gas station attendant-turned-millionaire said, "One, I genuinely believe it's a valuable asset to the community. Two, my wife and I are big fans. Three, Grandpa doesn't want to tell the grandkids there's no more basketball. And four, if I quit maybe I would have to look at it as if I failed."[59]

When it came to Ronnie, maybe it was his perseverance that intrigued Wayne Timpe. Whatever it was, he had been a big fan and his wife liked Ronnie, too, and Dales knew it. It couldn't hurt my odds, then, of making it through the year and perhaps to that championship, to have Ronnie backing me.

But could the squad in its present form survive a frustrated Ronnie and an antsy Daleo?

40

Having driven all night, we pulled into the Knights Inn at about 7:00 a.m. for the back end of a back-to-backer. On the ride, Trainer Brad, who had spent a good part of the season rooming with Dales, told me he'd been trying to figure out a way to room with someone else. He just couldn't take it anymore, or so he said: "All he does is talk about CBA players: who's on crack, who's on the block, who stinks, and who back-stabs. Plus he asks me why I got married and tells me not to have kids or he's asking me why I eat so much. I'm tired of it."

"That'd probably get old," I said.

"I've got to be smart about switching rooms, though. He'll hold that type of thing against you."

As it happened, seeing as Trainer Brad did the travel plans, he managed to concoct a reason for why he'd booked Dales his own room, and then he gently encouraged him to take it. Dales did, which meant Trainer Brad ended up rooming with me. But the weird thing was, on this road trip, he and Dales still ended up spending a lot of time together, whether it was grabbing a bite to eat together or walking to and from the bus together.

Case in point, upon pulling into the Knights Inn at about 7:00 a.m., I'd gone straight to bed and awakened at noon, expecting to see Brad in the bed next to mine sprawled out in his whitie tighties, possibly working on some microwavable Campbell's Chunky soup. But he wasn't there. When he returned a bit later, he told me he'd gone to Daleo's room to take care of some business. Apparently, while he was in there Dales told him, "Brad, you know Carson's days are numbered."

"I think he's serious this time," Trainer Brad said. "He's thinking about a trade that would send draft picks to Sioux Falls in return for David Bailey [the 2004 CBA rookie of the year]."

That would leave me on the outside. We'd gone 9-4 since my arrival and had moved into first place—not that I was the catalyst, mind you—but my shooting percentage had climbed above 40 percent and my free throw percentage was now close to eighty and my assist to turnover ratio was steadily improving. I'd just started to feel good out there again. At one point I'd even ran through NBA rosters in my mind: *Maybe I could be role player on the Miami Heat. What if Damon Jones got hurt or something, I could fill a void. Maybe Riley would take a look around the CBA and say 'I just need a guy who can knock down the midrange and get people the rock in the right place and not be an idiot.' And who knows, maybe he'd call my number. Ahh, don't be delusional. But who knows? You never know: Kurt Warner packed groceries, Starks did, too, I think. Maybe that's the key, packin' groceries. You never know. Who knows?*

We lost to the Storm that night 121-111. Basically, the game was a debacle. I'll spare you the details and just tell you that I played quite well until the end when I went for a steal on a post feed to Butler, the powerful young phenom.

Oh, Dales was livid. In his post-game harangue he asked Lubeck, "Why can't you rebound?" And he must've asked a thousand times why I doubled off the post.

"Why do you defy me?" he asked with an edge.

In fairness, the play did come at a crucial time. Despite being down most of the way, we'd clawed our way into striking distance, and Dales had told us not to double the post. I knew this and had stuck with my man on post-feeds up till then. But on this one occasion the man I was guarding had delivered a pretty weak, telegraphed ball to the post that, coming out of his hands, I'd read pretty well. Feeling like I had beat on the ball, by instinct I turned and chased it as it headed toward the low-block in what seemed like slow motion. I reached out towards it and got within what must've been an eighth of an inch, but for some reason I just couldn't get it. Sure enough, Butler was able to corral the ball with his big paws and dart a pass right back out to my man who drained a three.

Worse, I had plenty of time to mull matters in Birch Run's slipshod Knights Inn, because we were slated to play the Storm again two nights later.

Lubeck, the Baffler, Trainer Brad, and I grabbed a bite to eat at a truck stop across from the Knights Inn. Later, Boss Closs stopped by.

Continuing his disciplined attention towards his muscular needs, the Baffler nibbled on low-calorie, high-protein fare. I asked him how his muscles felt, and after clearing his throat just enough to enable a deep, guttural noise to emerge from his cords, he uttered, "Good."

After complaining about being at a truck stop across from the Birch Run Knights Inn, we did some impersonations of "Everything You Do Is Right" and rehashed one of Daleo's classic post-game diatribes.

At one point, I asked Lubeck if he thought about going to Europe.

"I might," he said, "but my agent wants me to finish out the year, to give two good years to the CBA, and who knows maybe get a good summer league invite. Either way if I put up numbers, he says it'll help my stock overseas. Who knows?"

"How 'bout you, Baffler, what's your plan?"

"I'll probably go back to Europe."

"He wants to retire by thirty," Lubeck said, shaking in his head in astonishment. As road roommates, Lubes and the Baffler had gotten to know a good deal about each other.

"What?"

Lubes told us The Baffler's plan.

"I've already saved like a hundred grand," Bailey declared.

"How?" I asked.

"I live at home. I have virtually no expenses. I save just about everything I get."

"Dude, you want to retire with three-hundred grand?"

"That's what I told him," Lubeck said.

"I could buy a house and retire."

"How about kids? Do you want kids?" I asked.

"Sure, later."

"You're gonna retire with three-hundred grand at thirty. You continue to bewilder," I said.

Soon, Lubeck, with smoke lingering in the diner, wondered, "What am I doing here?" Adding, "I'm not going to the NBA. This is ridiculous. I'm in Birch Run with Chris Daleo."

41

The next morning, upon stepping out of The Baffler and Lubeck's room, having shot the breeze with them, Dales happened to be walking by. He stopped and quickly involved me in a conversation about why I'd doubled the post down the stretch. He kept asking, "Why? I mean why? What were you thinking?" Finally, he stated, "It makes it hard on me, you know."

I found this excruciating on a number of levels. As the encounter neared its end, Daleo said, "You need to focus. I don't think you're focused, too many distractions, too many pregnancies, too many dissertations."

"No, that's ridiculous. I'm not distracted."

He kept asking me questions, talking about the same plays over and over again. It wouldn't end. We stood outside in the freezing cold right in front of the door to my room. I just wanted to get inside, but I couldn't find my key. He'd babble, I'd offer a quick response if queried, and then he'd continue on, all while I searched my pocket for the stupid key. I couldn't find it. At one point, he thought I had found my key, and he kind of stepped forward, intimating a desire to come into my room to continue the conversation. Happily, I still hadn't found it. Eventually, he grew impatient and, with the cold burning, said, "I can't wait all night." Then he slinked away.

We had practice later that afternoon. All through it, Baffler Bailey did exercises on the side: tricep dips and crunches and inverted push-ups off the back of a chair and other weird stuff. He wasn't practicing full-on because a few days earlier he'd pulled his hammy something powerful. So he'd turned the sideline into his own little Gold's Gym. As Renaldo barked at Sydney, "Shoot it, don't throw it," we'd point over to Rambo the Baffler in disbelief.

Lubeck could barely get a shot off, he laughed so hard, "Carson, look at that man over there . . . He's a machine."

While we enjoyed watching the Baffler fine-tune his lats and I engaged in a sorry inner dialogue about my prospects with the squad, word circulated that Keith had made the morning papers for his exploits the night before. Near the end of the practice we broke off into small groups, giving me a chance to ask him what happened.

"Carson, the last thing I remember is being on the dance floor," he told me. He said he was at a club hanging out with some of the players on the Great Lakes squad and working on one of his eleven Long Islands when the next thing he knew he woke up under a Christmas tree at a Flint police department.

He figured they had dropped him off at the police station as some kind of prank. He didn't find it all that funny. "They didn't look out for me," he said shaking his head.

What a sight he must've cut when some unsuspecting officer came to work that morning to find the Boss sleeping underneath the Christmas tree.

Later, I read in the paper that Renaldo had come to the police station on our team bus in the morning to pick Keith up. Apparently, the Boss had given the police enough info to prompt a call to Dales so that he could have someone come get him.

When the Lightning's big, chartered bus rolled up to do just that, "Everything You Do Is Right" strolled into the police headquarters. He hoped to get in and out of there quickly. But by then the cops knew Keith played in the CBA, and that he had played in the NBA, and they wanted to talk hoops with him. You can't blame them; Keith was coming around, and when that happens, he's a friendly bloke and he's got quite a tale. Keith, trying to make everybody feel comfortable, was probably happy to regale the cops with stories about his days in the NBA.

At one point, some of the cops requested a photograph, much to the chagrin of Renaldo who wanted to get going. Keith obliged and even tried to bring "Everything You Do Is Right" into the picture. But Renaldo wasn't too keen to get in on a photo like that, with a bunch of cops and Keith Closs after a binger. "Everything You Do Is Right" wanted no part of it. "Hell no, you aren't taking my picture with a bunch of cops," he told Keith on the side. But he didn't want to make a big scene right there in front of the cops, so he decided to act like he would get in on the picture. He joined the fringe of the group only to slip outside the bounds of the lens as the photographer snapped the shot.

42

F ollowing this eventful practice in Birch Run, Daleo noticed that
the Storm had left the door to their training room/storage area
open. He could barely contain his excitement. He asked Lubeck if
he wanted any of the shorts or t-shirts that he'd found laying around.

"I'm good, Coach."

Confused by Lubeck's indifference, Daleo moved on. He told Brad
to pilfer a bunch of items like tape and wrap. Then, as guys got their
stuff together and Brad prepared to load things onto the bus, Dales
asked, "Did you get the some tape? How about the wrap?"

"Yeah, yeah, I got it."

"That's my man, Brad."

It probably didn't cause too much rancor, though—Brad and
Dales cleaning out the Storm training room and all—because the
Storm didn't even have a trainer.

That night in warm-ups, as Keith and I tossed up shots an hour or
two before our second game in a row in Birch Run, Closs stopped for a
moment, looked at me, and said, "I'm the only guy I know who sleeps
in the police station one night and plays the next."

A little later I struck up a conversation with the Storm's Trevor
Huffman, the former Kent State star who tallied 1,820 points in college,
making him the school's all-time leading scorer, and had helped take
the Rockets to the Elite Eight. In 2001 and then again in 2002 his
exploits earned him selection to the All-Mid-American Conference
(MAC) first team, and he won MVP of the MAC tournament twice.
After Kent's 2002 tourney run he made the NCAA's all-South Regional
tournament team. Playing in Germany his first year out of college,
Huffman won his team's MVP award. But, as the *Record-Eagle* put it,
he "really wanted to take a shot at the NBA."

Prior to the 2003 season, Dan Majerle, also from Traverse City,
Michigan, helped Huffman get that shot with the Suns. And

Huffman's performance at the Suns tryout led to an invite to the Suns' training camp and a non-guaranteed contract offer. "I played against a lot of their other free agents. I played well enough to get a contract," Huffman explained.[60] However, he ended up cut by the Suns and back in Europe. A year later he became a point guard for the Storm.

Unshaven, he looked a bit tired and slightly dazed as I went up to talk to him. Apparently, the CBA had shocked him into a weary-looking, confused state. Once we started talking, he told me that having spent the last two seasons in Europe, the prospect of playing in the States had excited him. Then he paused, looked around at the twenty or so people milling around in the stands, and said, "But I can't believe this."

"Yeah, it's crazy. Shoot, our big fella slept at the local jail last night, under a Christmas tree. Worse, word is your guys dropped him off there."

"Yeah, it was in the paper this morning. We haven't made the paper all year long, and sure enough Keith Closs comes to town, sleeps at the police station, and gets the front page. This league man, it's too much," Huffman said. "We don't have a trainer. We don't do any scouting. Our high school player runs shit, tells the coach to fuck off. It's crazy."

The Storm's coach used to scout for the Utah Jazz, but supposedly he quit so he could return to coaching. Apparently he spent a good deal of time in his team's huddles cussing out the referees.

Huffman started reminiscing about a stint he had playing in Venezuela.

Just about everybody in the CBA who'd gotten a gig in Venezuela would end up telling stories about how great it was there. Only the CBA could make someone pine for a country run by Hugo Chavez. It's mostly the women down there, from what I gathered. Even if a guy didn't try to date the women or hook-up with them, you got the impression that the sheer attractiveness of them created an aura of sublimity that generally lifted them up. Hands down, Venezuelan women received the most praise from itinerant CBA ball players.

About thirty minutes before the game we went into the locker room for Daleo's final rousing words. As usual, he started to mow through the game plan, but then out of the blue he said, "And we're gonna open with Bailey in the lineup. We'll test out that hamstring and see what happens. I want you to go hard at Mark Jones, post him up, and try to get him in foul trouble. We might as well get something out of you, even if it's just a few minutes and that thing pops." Bailey looked shocked. He hadn't tried to run on his hammy in three days. He had mainly just worked on the sideline to further chisel his upper body.

When Dales suddenly announced that The Baffler would give it a go, guys shot looks toward Bailey to gauge his reaction. He tried to play off his concern by managing a slight chuckle, but you could tell Dales had gotten his nerves up. As Daleo continued his pre-game talk, Brad shook his head and snuck glances at people as if to say, "What the fuck is going on? I had no idea this was coming."

After we went back out for the last twenty minutes of our warm-up, Brad pulled Daleo aside and told him he estimated the Baffler's hammy at about 2 percent functionality. In warm-ups, the Baffler could barely jog. As he tried to loosen his poor leg, guys ribbed him for letting Dales punk him.

"I'm not playing," he said, trying to sound tough. But boy was he sweating it.

Brad pulled me aside and claimed he would not accept it, that this time Dales had gone too far. He intended to make a stand if Daleo tried to start the Baffler. No one knew what Daleo would do, and you could tell Dales liked that. Not until the lights went out and the disco ball came down, the dancers started gyrating and the PA announcer started screaming, did we learn that Dales had not put The Baffler's name on the list of starters. Brad avoided making a stand and The Baffler's tightly wound hammy lived to see another day.

When the game finally got under way we came out strong, and our fast start helped carry us to a 6-1 quarter-point victory. We only had nine guys, but it didn't matter. We continued to share the rock and run the floor, to get to the rack and drop buckets. The win pushed our record to 11-7 and put us squarely in first place. What a turnaround. We'd gone 8-3 since Ronnie's injury.

Overall, Daleo's roster moves and playing style were proving successful yet again. At the beginning of the year, I'd wondered about our chances. The Baffler seemed like a risky move, Lubes a reach, and I was a stretch too. Looking at our roster eighteen games in, even our standouts Phillips (undersized), Boseman (inconsistent jumper), and Closs (generally unpredictable) had issues on paper. Few coaches would've chosen that group. Fewer still would've run a full-court trapping press and full-throttle offense with it. But Daleo had been choosing motley crews and running since before Mike D'Antoni had made it popular again.

Even Daleo seemed happy. After the win over Great Lakes, he waited to go over the stats until we got on the bus. Of course, he did have plenty of time to work through them on our 450-mile journey back to Rockford. Dales also surprised us by springing for dinner— Little Caesars. And so, we drove through the night and into the next morning with guys chomping on pizza, shooting the breeze, watching DVDs, and listening to music.

First though, early in the ride, Dales faced us from the front of the bus and went over the stats excitedly. He got particularly keyed up when he read Sydney's line: "Sydney Holmes, the big rook from Lewis, who nobody wanted, who nobody thought could play, sixteen points and twelve rebounds, and he played great defense..."

Hours later, with the bus powering toward Rockford, everything seemed nice and smooth, when all of a sudden Dales decided to get up from his seat near the front and lie down across the seats just in front of me. He proceeded to keep poking his head through the two seats he was lying across to ask me odd questions like, "Does your wife think I'm a jerk?"

"No, I don't think so." *It's like 1:00 a.m., what's this guy talking about?.*

"Did you hear from Purdue Calumet?"

"No, not yet. Probably a week or so after the New Year."

In asking about Purdue Calumet, he was referring to a basketball coaching job that had opened there. He'd plugged me for the spot to a newspaper guy, quite gracious of him really. But now it seemed like he asked about it a bunch.

Then Dales started in on the scores of other CBA games and the players on other teams and asking me questions about certain plays that happened during the game. "Why did you do this?"... "Bismarck beat..." His mind raced. I needed to think fast but nothing really came to mind, so I simply got up and walked to the back of the bus, sat down next to Lubeck, and asked him to get some cards out or something.

We arrived back at the Fairfield at about 2:00 a.m. In about fourteen hours we had to report back to the MetroCentre for our third game in four days, this one against the Gary Steelheads. Still, some of the guys mustered the energy to paint the town. It was New Year's Eve.

43

In the first half, the Steelheads capitalized on our weary state—a state that was likely exacerbated by those who had gone out the night before—and therefore at halftime, Daleo got himself riled up again, cussing and carrying on. If nothing else, his ability to conjure such concern was commendable. "The veterans on this team should be ashamed that I have to go to Sydney Holmes, a rookie who makes $300 a week, to get some energy," he declared, before pausing for a bit and then screaming, "$300 a week!"

Closs, unfocused, did not enjoy one of his finer outings. At one point Marshall Phillips won a jump-ball on our end by tipping it right to Closs, who was alone underneath the bucket. Closs needed to just hammer it home, or in Keith's case maybe fingertip it into the hoop, but he momentarily forgot which end our basket was on. So instead of laying it in, he caught the ball and looked down to the other end of the court. A collective gasp emanated from the crowd as fans realized his confusion. Then fans started hollering at him to shoot, trying to reorient him. But by the time Keith realized he was standing underneath his own bucket, the defense had rotated. Challenged, he missed the lay-in.

A couple of days after our loss versus Gary, Dales and I sat down in-studio for our weekly morning radio show. Before going on air, Kristin, of "Kristin's Box" fame, brought up the Christmas tree episode in Flint. She had a newspaper article in front of her, written by Kris Palmer in the *Flint Journal*, which detailed Keith's antics on the trip. Palmer opened the piece by writing, "First-shift police officers arrived for work Thursday to find an unexpected gift . . . er, guest, beneath the Christmas tree in the lobby of the police station. All seven feet three inches of him." And he reported that the bemused officers said that Closs had started out on a chair before somehow moving to the floor underneath the tree. The policemen maintained that Closs answered all their questions, only getting testy a few times, at which point he would declare, "Hey man, I'm from L.A."[61] For background, Palmer also noted that Keith had come to the NBA as a rookie out of Central Connecticut State with high hopes, reflected by his monikers "the Messiah" and "Boss Closs." Then Palmer ran through some of the low lights of Closs's career. He mentioned the 2000 beating outside a nightclub in Los Angeles and the time the Boss drew a suspension from the Clippers for not meeting minimum weight requirements.

What he did not mention, and what he probably did not know, just like I didn't know and no else on the Lightning probably knew, was that when Keith was a baby his father—before he abandoned Keith—would give him beer, to keep him from fussing and to get him to fall asleep. We didn't know that some of Keith's first memories were drinking beer with his dad, or that he didn't have a clue how to get in touch with his father now. And we didn't know that by elementary school, with his brain already conditioned to crave alcohol, Keith would sneak it anytime he could. And if we had known this, we couldn't have related well to it anyway. Who knows what that does to you? When does it hit you that your father not only left you, but before he did he kept you liquored up? He was just a baby, for goodness' sake.

Kristin asked if it was all right to talk about the episode.

"What do I care? I can't stand the guy. He'll be gone in a week or so, as soon as we get a replacement in," Dales said.

And so, immediately after a contestant correctly guessed the contents of "Kristin's box," we started our segment with the Closs story fair game. Before getting to the Lightning, Daleo joked on the air that he didn't receive the gift he had asked Kristin for: "You, under the Christmas tree."

"Instead he got Keith," I said, at which point Kristin segued into the Christmas tree story.

Following a quick briefing of the scenario for listeners, she looked at Daleo and asked, "What happened?"

"I don't know, I guess Keith went out with a bunch of guys from the other team, the Great Lakes Storm, and they dropped him off at the police station . . . Well, we are all in the CBA for a reason."

Then he started in on how some guys need to work on responsibility, some on people skills, and some on other things. "In the case of Keith, he's made a number of decisions that have kept him out of the NBA, which is why we have an NBA-caliber shot-blocker here in Rockford. What I want to know is how Jackie Butler, who I hear is the guy that asked Keith to come out with them and is only nineteen years old, goes out in that town at that age? Who's letting him in places?"

We moved on to other topics and after a while host Stone got around to asking about me. Daleo took the mic, "Well, I'm sticking with him, no matter how bad some of my assistant coaches want me to get rid of him. Carson's been playing better; he's working off a year of rust. And his wife's pregnant."

"Really? Congratulations!" Kristin chimed in.

"Actually, he's mad at me because of how I handled that…"

"Really, what's that story?" I was asked.

"Yes, well thank you, she's pregnant. It's early, you know, but since it just got announced on air, I guess people know."

44

B efore we played Yakima that night, Brad let me know that the trade involving David Bailey, which would leave me the odd man out, was off for now. Brad said he didn't know exactly why it didn't go down, but added, "I know you have one person in your corner, Ronnie."

"Really?"

"Yeah, he told Coach Daleo he wanted to keep you."

Whatever the cause, according to Brad, it seemed as if my job rested upon the unpredictable personnel whims of Ronnie Fields. It wasn't completely new terrain. In Gary, I'd been at the whim of the former Chicago Bull Khalid El-Amin's cardiovascular strength. Back then, as El-Amin's backup, I'd often not play at all. But sometimes, with about twenty-five seconds left in the first half, he'd simply nod at our coach, who would then sub me in. But this Fields situation was different, and it caused a unique conundrum. With Ronnie, it was harder for us to win, but without him, I'd struggle to survive. And, as it happened, that night's game versus Yakima marked Ronnie's return to the lineup.

Making the situation even more peculiar, Ronnie had played a prominent role in my exit from Rockford during the 2002-03 season—which occurred in that post-game locker room in Grand Rapids when I let Dales know I'd tired of his nonsense and his threats. At that time, in addition to Dales's treatment of me, Ronnie's politicking for point guard Kareem Reid had irked me. So after my rant, and after Dales told me I was cut, I had ironically declared "Some guys don't need this shit."

As for Dales and Ronnie, given that they'd worked together the better part of a decade, their personal dynamics confounded: loyalty, power, ego, shared frustrations, and familiarity all swirled, causing occasional eruptions. As I mentioned, during his absence Ronnie had voiced his displeasure with some of Daleo's personality and some of his tactics. Part of the problem between the two also seemed to be frustration on Ronnie's part caused by his diminishing athleticism, a result of some of his injuries and the general grind of playing virtually year-round hoops in the CBA, Latin America, and South America. From Daleo's end, he seemed to want to distance himself from Ronnie, but, as I say, he still realized that Ronnie had played a pivotal role in his hiring and held sway with the owners.

At halftime of that night's 5-2 quarter-point victory over Yakima, evidence of tension between the two mushroomed in the locker room. The rift erupted when Dales got on Ronnie for having taken a bad shot at the end of the first frame. Ronnie started to talk back, and it quickly turned into shouting.

"Fuck that, what you gonna do? Fuck that, you walk around here treating people like garbage, fuck that. It was a bad shot, say bad shot and move on," Ronnie hollered.

"It was a bad shot."

"You always got something to say."

"It was a bad shot."

"What the fuck you gonna do?"

Daleo wasn't ready for a showdown. So he switched gears by reading the halftime stats. He started to comment on some other players, when Ronnie said, kind of under his breath but audibly, "What you gonna do?"

Dales stopped mid-sentence, "Yeah, I heard you."

"You ain't gonna do shit. What you gonna do?"

Dales just started in on the stats again and eventually the storm passed. We knew Ronnie was right; Dales would not do anything.

Seeing Ronnie riled like that, though, made me kind of melancholy. He'd kept his cool the first year I'd played with him in Rockford. With people asking him what could have been and how he'd dealt with his basketball career, as if it was a given that he'd failed, he'd answered calmly. Maybe hope had kept him up, maybe he just accepted things, maybe both. You could argue that even then he'd gotten in Dales's ear too much and thereby combusted team chemistry, but at the same time, he rarely got into heated arguments with anyone, was pretty cool with the referees, and generally kept a level head. Even when I called Dales and Ronnie out for campaigning for Reid to come in and replace me, Fields barely batted an eye, just heard me out, got dressed, and got on the bus. And two years later, when his bone stuck out of his thumb, he merely looked at it and said nonchalantly, "I'm done." But when he and Daleo went after each other after the Yakima game, it seemed like the years in the minors, the years with Dales, had worn on Ronnie.

Over the course of a season, it's common to get tired of your head coach, at least for stretches. But Dales made it especially difficult for guys. I know he did for me. And yet you could tell the game was still ingrained in Ronnie, like it was me.

The moments in basketball when we could, no matter how much traffic we were in, no matter how small the window seemed, or how trapped we appeared to be, find a way to get the ball where we wanted it to go, were the types of moments that had attracted us—and so many others—to the game.

But with Dales targeting my dignity, with myself letting the CBA grind sap my energy, and with the opportunity costs of hanging onto a young boy's dream seeming to escalate by the day, I was finally starting to come to grips with the fact that now the ball was directing traffic. I might've still been able to make it look like I could put a basketball on the end of a string, but really it was me on the end.

Yet I still loved the game. And in a twisted way this is what I respected about Dales, as much as I disliked his antics. And I'll bet Ronnie felt similarly. It gnawed at Dales that he didn't get the type of respect from the coaching community that he thought—and his record suggested—he deserved. Just like it gnawed at me that I knew guys had gone to the League that I could outplay. And yet Dales, like a lot of CBAers, still rose and fell with the game. For some of us, basketball consistently moves us in ways that day-to-day life doesn't. So we hoop on, even if the current has turned against us, borne back—as F. Scott Fitzgerald elegantly put it—ceaselessly into the past.

45

In Gary, shortly before the start of our next game, Daleo ordered Brad to get on his cell phone and call Mrs. Trainer Brad, who was at home in Wisconsin. Dales wanted her to get online so she could continually update him, through Brad, on the score of the Great Lakes game. The outcome of it, along with the result of our game, would determine whether Dales would get to coach in the CBA All-Star game.

Thanks to Mrs. Trainer Brad, before our tip-off we knew that Great Lakes had won the first two quarters. If the Storm ended up winning 7-0, Daleo would need us to win a minimum of two quarter points. And getting to the All-Star game was a big deal for CBA coaches. Next to championships, how many CBA All-Star games a guy had coached was a point of reference to compare with the resumes of CBA coaching greats of bygone years, like Phil Jackson and George Karl.

However, we proceeded to lose the first quarter, and then we dropped the second. Gary scored seventy-two points on us in the first half. Having convalesced from a spider bite that had kept him out for a couple of weeks or so, the Steelheads' speedy point guard Jemeil Rich ran all over the court on us. Dales didn't seem overly perturbed, though, probably because he spent most of the half worrying about the Great Lakes Storm. Every few minutes during the action he'd scurry down to the end of the bench and say "Brad, what's happenin'?"

"Great Lakes up three in the second."

Then, only a bit later, he'd return to ask, "What's the game score?"

"Great Lakes up seven."

"How much time left?"

Momentarily satisfied, Daleo would go back to coaching. Brad didn't dare hang up. He spent nearly the entire half on the phone with his wife.

A few more minutes would pass, and Daleo would come back down to the end of the bench.

"Brad, what's the score?"

At intermission, we went into the locker room rather dejected. With Ronnie back, our chemistry had broken down again. Our motion on offense, in particular, stunk. We resorted to calling a bunch of isolations. To make things even worse, throughout the first half, Ronnie had made a bunch of remarks, whether on the floor or on the bench: "He needs to go here," Ronnie would say, or, "We should rotate like this," or, "We need to do this…"

At the half, Coach Thomas stormed into the locker room, in a huff. At first, he paced around a bit, fuming, his perturbation steadily rising. Eventually, though, the pressure built enough that he let it out, calling out Ronnie without specifically calling him out. "I'm just gonna put it out there. We need to stop talking so fucking much. I can't believe this shit. I've never seen anything like it. We need to pull for each other. What's all this griping about? All this fuckin' talkin'? You guys got a comment for everything. Everyone's suddenly pointing fingers. We need to play together. Fuck all this talking."

After Renaldo's explosion, we went out and played arguably worse in the third quarter, not that Dales seemed to notice all the much, seeing as he couldn't decide whether to focus on our game or the updates from Mrs. Trainer Brad. We'd entered the second half knowing Great Lakes had won the third quarter, and therefore it looked as if they'd win 7-0. With each score update Brad delivered, you could almost see Dales's nerves get to dancing. The worse the reports got, the more frequently he'd scurry down to Trainer Brad for info.

By the time the fourth quarter rolled around, Brad was at least beyond the "anytime minutes" threshold of his cell phone plan. Finally, he informed Dales that Great Lakes had won its game 6-1. This meant that for Dales to be the head coach of the CBA All-Star Game's Midwest team, we needed to win the fourth quarter. As we sat on the bench awaiting the start of the fourth, Daleo implored us, well mainly his go-to guys—Ronnie, the Baffler, Boss Closs, Lubes, Boseman, Phillips, and Muntrelle—to go out there and win the quarter.

We were down twenty-something going into the frame, but you should've seen Ol' Dales coach those final twelve minutes. If you didn't know better, you might've thought it was the NBA Finals. He made defensive substitutions, called strategic time-outs (something he rarely did), and lasered-in on trying to exploit mismatches, mainly by posting Phillips down low. All the while, Dales scurried up and down the sidelines, barking instructions to players and waving his arms as if conducting an orchestra.

I suppose it paid off, because, thanks in no small part to a timely bucket by Fields, we won the quarter point. As the final seconds wound down and it became clear that we would win the quarter, Dales shook Coach Thomas's hand and told him congratulations. Sure, we'd lost the game, but Dales was bound for Gary, Indiana, as the head coach of an all-star team.

Heading to the locker room afterward, I figured that since he'd clinched his All-Star appearance, Dales would ease up on the post-game theatrics. And at first it seemed like he would, but he managed to work himself into a rhythm. Unhappily enough, that rhythm ended up amounting to about a forty-minute speech that covered a whole slew of topics.

At one point he paused for a moment and declared he was going to toot his own horn:

"I have the best winning percentage in Rockford history, had the best first-year record, I won Coach of the Year, won the conference, and last year if 'Snap' Hunter's stupid ass hadn't missed an elbow jumper, I'd have been in the finals. And I take care of you guys. You got problems at home, problems paying a bill, some girl keeps callin' the office sayin' some Lightning player knocked her up, I take care of it. I stay with people. Lawrence Nelson trade, on the table. David Harrison calls me every day. He averaged twenty-nine points for me. I'd bring him in in a New York second, does well in this system. David Bailey trade, on the table. Shit, you do your job, and I stay with people. Stais, you need to go to court, fly back the same day for a game. No problem. You start. Jermaine, Gary didn't play you, didn't want you back, and I know for a fact they didn't vote for you for the All-Star game, and you give me three rebounds and a bunch of weak fouls. Knock someone on their ass! Look, Muntrelle's injured. I ride him. I stay with him. We've only had two hard fouls here all year and both are by Muntrelle. People say he hasn't done this or that. I know something he has done: given me two hard fouls! Brant, nobody wanted him, but I found a spot for him here. Stais, I'm not so sure Great Lakes wanted you back. Carson, no one wanted you, and I stay with you even though you cost me fuckin' games. Keith, you were on your mom's couch for two years. Lubeck, maybe you had an option in Sioux Falls, I don't know. You guys have a place here, and I stay with guys, but you've got to meet me halfway. You need to use this to move on. I give you an opportunity to put up numbers." He paused, turned toward Stais, brought his voice down lower, and said, "I mean, Stais, how old are you, thirty?"

"Almost thirty-one."

"Yeah, see, almost thirty-one. You know the odds of you getting a call-up are slim. You need to use this to get yourself something in Europe or South America for next year, or you could always come back, but realistically, you need to try and use this to get big money overseas. You've got to bring it every night, get up in people's grill. Who cares if Jemeil Rich or Duane Ticknor [Gary's head coach] might not like you? Give 'em some of the business. Get up on them. One thing Carson will do, no matter how odd he is, how many times he makes stupid passes, struggles feedin' the fuckin' post, and does wacky shit with the ball sometimes, he'll get up on people on the press and push the freakin' ball. That's why he's here."

Don't feel happy 'cuz this guy's giving you a compliment, you idiot. He's an asshole. What's your problem?

"I know for a fact Sioux Falls is getting rid of four guys next week. First place, they're getting rid of four guys. Joerger doesn't give a shit. He makes moves, and he wins championships. But you got to meet me halfway. Isn't that right? I go to bat for guys. Brant, I told you if something comes up in Europe for you to go over and get back on track. That's fine. I plug Carson for head coaching jobs. Shit, I tell all these agents and coaches and scouts, this guy can play or that guy can play. But shit, you got to meet me halfway, and you're not. If I smooth over things for a player and back him up for a guy like Chris Ford [the 2003-04 Philadelphia 76ers head coach and former NBA champion player]—who's called and offered me a job the past two years and I turned it down both times, said 'No, I'll stay in RockVegas,'—and then a guy sees this kind of effort? After I've backed you up? They're gonna say, 'That Daleo, he's a fuckin' idiot.' I have to try and smooth over things for Chapman [a guy who rates minor league basketball players], who comes up to me and asks why some guy is sleeping under a Christmas tree. You got to meet me halfway. We need to execute. Just do your job."

46

B ack in Rockford before practice, Lubeck and I went to a local restaurant, Mr. C's, which had given Dales $10 certificates for us. Looking at the menu, Lubes and I got to pondering how we could fully milk our certificates. It registered with us, yet again, that we were pretty poor. We decided you know you're poor when you start thinking about skipping meals. And, as much as I might not have wanted to admit it, ordering cleverly at this place could actually net two lunches.

Sitting there, I opened the *USA Today*. A front-page story immediately caught my attention: "Jayson Williams to Suit Up for the CBA's Idaho Stampede." This was the same Jayson Williams who had become infamous for getting charged with manslaughter in the death of a limousine driver (a case that Court TV highlighted in the summer of 2004), after he'd become famous for leading the NBA in rebounding and for his colorful personality as a commentator on NBC. And, as it happened, that upcoming weekend, we were slated to play his new team, the Idaho Stampede, in Boise.

Lubeck and I arrived at practice nearly an hour early, yet the Baffler still beat us there. The Baffler worked, you couldn't argue that.

We got to tossing up shots and by and by Daleo came out on the court..

"Looks like I'll be battling for rebounds with Jayson Williams this weekend," I said.

"Yeah, you'll play him this weekend. Well, I don't know if *you'll* play him, but Rockford will."

Real freakin' funny, what a riot.

I chuckled nervously.

Dales continued, "Yeah, apparently he met with CBA people at their headquarters and they talked it out. What a joke, what a joke, what a joke...Family entertainment, what a joke. The guy shot an old man, said, 'Oh no, my life is over,' and then left him there to die. What a joke, family entertainment."

"Just don't let Williams show our bus driver around town," I offered.

Dales went back in the locker room. A bit later I went to the locker room, too, to look for a t-shirt—it could get chilly in the MetroCentre.

"Are you mad at me for not stopping practice because you had a cut on your face? Was that unprofessional of me?" Dales asked.

He was referring to a workout the day before, during which I got caught in the face with a 'bow, causing a little cut.

"No, it was a superficial wound. Brad super-glued it up nice for me."

"Good, because I wouldn't want you mad at me."

I got my shirt and got out of there quickly.

After Ronnie arrived, a good ten minutes late, we huddled up to stretch. Dales made some announcements and then said, "And the Idaho Stampede signed Jayson Williams, murderer and felon—good family entertainment here in the CBA. Just don't tell the bus driver to show him around Boise."

He stole my joke.

As we sat on the court stretching in a circle, Keith heard the Williams news from a player (apparently, he'd missed Dales's first announcement), and said, "Really? That's my boy, good for him."

Daleo turned around to look at him. "Good for him?"

"He's a friend of mine."

"Well, that's too bad. He's a murderer."

"No, he's not."

"He killed an old man and committed numerous felonies."

"No, he's not. Was he convicted?"

"Tell that to the old man's family. He's a murderer and a felon."

"I need Gus's phone number," Closs said. (I didn't know who "Gus" was, and I don't think anyone else other than Keith did either.)

"The CBA, what a joke," Dales said.

"He's a good guy."

"He killed an old man with four grandchildren. Shot him, tried to cover it up, moved everybody downstairs, and left him to die. He's a murderer and a felon."

After practice we headed to Don Pablo's for our weekly meet-and-greet Lightning dinner. Usually, you could count on at least four or five fans showing up, along with maybe seven or eight members of the owner's family and friends. But this time, no fans came. Zero. And only about five members in the Timpe group showed up. I felt bad for the Don Pablo's manager or owner who had negotiated the meet-and-greet in the run-up to the season. I figured that person, if he'd bothered to attend, would be annoyed to see us eating tremendous amounts of complementary food while drawing basically no paying customers. The waitresses were annoyed. At this point in the season they carried little hope for a generous tip, and were thereby quite short with us. I felt bad about not tipping more, but then again, most of us just didn't have much.

Later that night I stopped by Lubeck's room. He was a bit dumbfounded because Keith, a former millionaire, had just visited his room asking for $20. Lubeck gave him $10. Word was Keith had run into trouble earlier in the week at a check-cashing establishment when he tried to cash an ABA check from his former team the Detroit Slammers. The check bounced and the folks at the currency exchange contacted the Lightning to complain and ask for their money back. Daleo told Keith about it, but for some unknown reason, the Boss took his next Rockford paycheck to the very same currency exchange. They gladly took the check, and kept the cash for security against the one that had bounced. In turn, Keith found himself tapped out, so he'd hit up Lubes.

Upon hearing Lubeck project the odds of ever seeing his money again, I stopped by the Baffler's room. His agent called while we watched *American Chopper*, and he asked the Baffler if he wanted to head to Poland for four grand a month, with accommodations, mind you. The Baffler wanted five.

He's truly confusing.

Looking around the room, I noticed the slew of jars on his little Fairfield Inn desk. He had what seemed like an array of GNC-type fuels: pre-workout, post-workout, during workout, extra protein, high-calorie, low-calorie.

The next day on the bus, en route to our game against Gary, the Baffler told me he had risen that morning at 7:15 a.m., all jacked up, so he'd gone to the YMCA to lift.

47

Having lost a close game to the Steelheads, during which I at least shot well, we readied for our trip to Boise to meet Jayson Williams and the rest of the Stampeders. Thankfully, we flew to Boise rather than taking a bus. It was our first plane ride of the year and seeing as the Lightning didn't fly much, I didn't take the convenience for granted—as opposed to my first CBA season, with the Gary Steelheads, when I'd gotten a bit spoiled in this regard.

Then again, a Steelhead road trip that included a flight could get quite nutty, so maybe bussing in the CBA made more sense. It's hard to get lost in a bus. Everybody's together in a compartment and can be easily accounted for. But a trip to an airport for a flight, which involves, of course, getting people from terminals to actual planes, is another matter.

The most peculiar Steelhead airport charade occurred the morning after a game in Flint, Michigan. We'd stayed at a hotel in town because we had to get up for an early flight the next morning to Sioux Falls. The plan was for our three coaches, one trainer, and eight players (one couldn't make the trip because of a court date) to catch the hotel shuttle to the airport. But only two coaches, one trainer, and five players made it onto the plane. We reckoned that with five guys, we could at least still play the game.

But then a remarkable thing happened. At a stopover in Minnesota, somehow, two of our remaining five players missed the connecting flight from Minnesota to Sioux Falls. (They said they fell asleep.) So we ended up landing in Sioux Falls with three players, two coaches, and a trainer. The three of us players who did make the flight laughed at the thought of running a true triangle offense and implementing the first ever one-two zone in CBA history. Our assistant coach didn't find that funny. We didn't need to implement the one-two, though, because that night players started to slowly trickle in, and most everybody ended up making it to the game.

This flight to Boise with the Lightning wasn't nearly as eventful, although during it I did read in the *Chicago Tribune* that Darrick Martin—who I'd guarded not weeks ago—had hit three key jumpers down the stretch to win a game for the Clippers. The next night he would score ten points, which made me think he was probably playing himself into a second ten-day contract, meaning another $45,000. If he were to stay on beyond that, it'd mean a guaranteed prorated contract for the rest of the season.

Within a couple of hours of landing at the Boise Airport, word spread at our hotel that Keith had already spent his $105 per diem, that he'd started drinking when the plane landed, had stopped by the grocery store once we'd arrived at the hotel, and then hit up a liquor store. I don't think his list of expenditures included a $10 repayment to Lubes.

The next morning, as we stretched before our shootaround in the Idaho Center, players started talking about various CBA guys we'd played against throughout the season that had gone on to make the NBA. When you're down in the underbelly, this is a common topic of conversation. These talks are both depressing and hopeful. Everyone in the CBA had a couple of guys in mind who they just couldn't believe had made it to the League. It can really gnaw at you if you let it.

By this time in the year, guys from both Idaho and Sioux Fall especially had gotten called up. Indeed, over the course of the season, Corsley Edwards, Britton Johnson, Sam Clancy, Donnell Harvey, and Randy Livingston (whom Sioux Falls had recently signed), would count among these two teams' call-ups, helping them account for roughly half of the CBA's call-ups that year.

The Randy Livingston call-up was one that would get my attention. Not that it was all that surprising. Livingston's rise from the underbelly to the NBA had, by this point in his career, become a kind of rite of spring, a rite that I'd started taking notice of, seeing as Livingston was one of the guys whose ability to make it to the League baffled me. As I say, all minor leaguers have a player or two in mind who they think represent precisely why they should at least get a chance at the NBA, and Livingston was one of those guys for me.

Perhaps more than anyone else, Livingston epitomized the power of the repeat call-up. By the end of his career, nine different NBA teams had brought him up—an all-time record—and yet he'd tallied a total of just 203 regular season games in his more than a decade-long NBA career.

I'd first heard of him back when I was in middle school in Indiana. That's because in 1992, when he was a senior in high school, Livingston was named the nation's co-player of the year, along with Jason Kidd. In other words, he was a super-athlete. But by 2001 he had a bit of a hitch in his gait, on account of having had a couple of major surgeries on his right knee, one during his freshman year at LSU to repair his ACL, the other during his sophomore year to fix a ruptured patellar tendon.[62] By 2001, when he ran it seemed like one of his legs was shorter than the other because he leaned to the right slightly and kind of bobbed up and down. Teddy DuPay could do an impressive impersonation of the gait. He would do the impersonation while sitting in a chair; he'd just tilt a bit to the side, put his hand out like he was dribbling, and bob. It was hard not to laugh.

On the court, then, it made sense to attack toward Livingston's good leg, so as to make him push off the bad one. Taking him off the dribble, when I was a CBA rookie, in fact, helped me tally my first game in the CBA with over twenty points, which might seem a little rotten to admit, but, given that a few months later I was watching him play in the NBA playoffs, I can't feel too bad.

Now, lest you think it, I'm not saying it was only chance and connections that routinely propelled Livingston to the NBA. He played a crafty, cerebral game, had solid ball-handling skills, and, at about 6'3, was a good size for a point guard. Indeed, these attributes helped him play well in the 2002 playoffs with the Sonics, prompting the *Seattle-Post Intelligencer's* Laura Vecsey to headline an article about Livingston with: "A Classy, Classic Guard Makes His Case to Stick with the Sonics."[63] Livingston could play (in 2007 he earned NBDL player-of-the-year honors), so he deserved to be there, but part of it was also that since he'd already been to the show, NBA folks knew him. Plus, his agent enjoyed strong connections, which helped.

Anyhow, we talked about call-ups prior to our shoot-around in Boise, hopeful that somehow one of us could be next. By this point in the season, the CBA had gotten more call-ups than the NBDL and the struggling ABA, and ultimately it would finish the year with fourteen, which kept the CBA's annual average, since the league started keeping track in 1978, at over twenty call-ups per year.

As players chatted, Dales was off to the side, getting nervous because Marshall Phillips's ankle injury suddenly seemed more serious. He'd tweaked it during the previous game but had kept on playing. The ankle had flared up, though, pretty significantly afterward—to the point that now Phillips couldn't participate in this shoot-around and looked doubtful for our game that night. Daleo fumed at Trainer Brad for not telling him earlier.

Dales would pace around the court and pause occasionally to say something like, "Why didn't I know? How bad is it? I could have flown in Brant [The Baffler, still convalescing, had remained in Rockford]. Why didn't you tell me how serious it was? He looked fine yesterday walking around the airport. Now, he's hobblin' around."

Privately, Trainer Brad claimed he had told him.

Regardless, it was bad news for us. Marshall had played so well with us that he probably was our MVP and our main hope of offsetting the effects of an active Fields. If he couldn't go and Fields went into isolation-mania mode, we could go on a losing streak.

With Daleo's head still spinning, we hopped on the bus. Back at the hotel Lubeck told me that Dales must've had a ton of bad karma floating around him, because, "On the bus back from the shoot-around I look up at him and he has a bottle of body wash sticking out of his jacket. He stole it from the locker room."

We had a few hours to kill before the game, so I turned on the television and soon found myself watching two people I didn't know on ESPN talk to each other about Terrell Owens. I could've talked with an actual person on the team or walked around Boise, but instead I sat there and listened to these strangers manufacture disagreements about nothing.

What happened? It used to be Berman and Ley and highlights. Now it's this? The same thing happened to MTV and music videos.

Bored, I left the room early to catch the bus to the game, which didn't turn out to be the best idea either. When the elevator doors opened and I stepped out into the lobby, there sat Dales on a couch. Across from him was Livan Pyfrom, a lean seven-footer from the Caribbean that we'd recently picked up.

Dales liked that Pyfrom could run the floor and anchor our pressure defense by blocking shots, and it was nice to have him on board. We'd played together for a stretch in Gary and again during my first season with Rockford, and we'd shared Thanksgiving dinner together once at my parents' house and I'd stayed at his place in Omaha. We'd meandered through the underbelly on similar paths, and it'd been a bit of a grind for him, too. Once, a couple years earlier, as we were driving near a ramp to Interstate-90 during a day of Lightning training camp, he'd pointed out that he could get on the highway and head straight to Seattle where his wife was. You could tell it was tempting.

On another occasion, he'd run into one of the most peculiar CBA roadblocks I've ever heard of. It happened during the 2001-02 season, shortly after he'd left the Gary Steelheads and joined the Sioux Falls Skyforce, when he and the rest of the Skyforce went on a road trip to Canada to play the Saskatchewan Hawks. Everything seemed fine until it was time to travel back to America. That's when Livan learned his student visa had run out. In turn, he got stuck in Canada while his teammates went home. Eventually, the Skyforce brass decided to just trade him to Saskatchewan. But then Livan could only play home games until his papers got worked out.

While we were sitting there in a hotel lobby in Boise, I asked Livan if he'd settled his plans to travel to Omaha. Earlier, he'd told me he was hoping to go home during the All-Star break to spend a few days with his wife, and I'd told him I could drop him off at the airport in Chicago if he needed. Well, right when I checked with Livan if his plans were set, Dales jumped in and asked, "Is what set?"

We just kind of looked at him.

"Oh, am I being to nosy?" he asked.

"No, I was just telling Livan that I could give him a ride to Midway."

"Where? For what? Nobody cleared it with me."

Livan piped in, "Oh, it's nothing. Just over the All-Star break, I was planning on going home for a few days and it's much cheaper to fly out of Midway than O'Hare. I talked to Brad about it."

Brad, sitting across the way, fidgeted on a love seat, looking uncomfortable that his name had been brought up.

Dales chewed on it a bit and then said, "I didn't know about these plans. Carson's probably the ringleader organizing these plans."

Oh my, here he goes. I should've kept my mouth shut.

"No, I just said I'd give him a ride to the airport, assuming that if he needed one everything had been cleared."

Listen to me, "Cleared?"

"See, I got guys making plans. Carson, you probably are behind this; you probably just want to see my downfall."

"No, I just want to win the next game, and then after that game, win the next one."

It was pathetic. After a few more painful minutes, we finally boarded the bus.

48

In the locker room prior to the tip, Daleo gave us a speech which consisted of him basically threatening people's jobs for various reasons. The pressure of the season, which could be strong, seemed to be spooking him. The Idaho Stampede was rolling, and Dales's nemesis Joerger was leading a Sioux Falls squad that continued to look strong.

Shooting around during pre-game warm-ups out on the Idaho Stampede's home court, Lubeck pulled me aside to point out a lady in the stands who was checking him out. I looked over and saw her smile at him and give a slight wave. You could tell straight away that she was flirtin', that she dug her some Lubes. He tried not to gaze over that way too much, but her brazenness puzzled him a bit.

Carrying on, about three minutes before the tip-off I decided to make a quick run to the locker room. To do so, I had to run the length of the court and cross in front of the Stampede's bench. On my way back from our locker room onto the floor, as I jogged back across Idaho's half of the court, a sweaty fellow reached out to slap my hand. I looked up and saw Jayson Williams. It startled me a bit seeing him in person, but I managed to play it off and say "good luck" or something like that before heading to the other end of the court.

Prior to the singing of the national anthem, we huddled up with Dales to talk a little strategy. We were surprised to see the lady who was smitten with Lubes walk out onto the court to sing "The Star-Spangled Banner." She was kind of buckets. Apparently, by this time, word had gotten to Dales that she dug Lubeck, because while we were still huddled-up, Dales took a long look at her as she walked past. Then he turned to us and said, "She's terrible."

It was a little noisy in the huddle, so he raised his voice a bit and hollered "Lubeck." Lubeck looked up and Dales said, "I got a good look at her close-up. She's terrible." He paused for a moment and added, "All right guys, come on, let's get this one."

Boseman, Ronnie Rockford, Lubes, steady Williams, and Boss Closs ran out for the tip. The game did not go well. Other than Lubeck, nobody played all that solidly. Ronnie missed shots and hobbled up and down the court as if he had an injury to one of his legs—really, I think it was just the mileage. His mouth, though, certainly wasn't injured. He'd come back to the bench griping about various things that "you guys" were doing.

With about forty seconds left in the half, I thought about how quickly the half had gone by and how nice that was. Only a game and a half left and I could go home for the All-Star break. Our team was devolving rapidly, and I missed my wife.

Dales reamed us pretty good at intermission. His rant was complemented by further commentary from my ally Ronnie, who again noted the shortcomings of "you guys." Marshall Phillips just rolled his eyes. Daleo threw some verbal jabs Lubes's way for defensive issues. Then he leveled some choice barbs about my inability to exploit mismatches on the offensive end by getting the ball to the right guy in the right spot.

We opened the second half on the wrong end of a 7-0 run, and it pretty much went downhill from there. Ronnie kept trying to bring up the ball to conceal the fact that he did not want to run the wing hard on the break. And when we tried to "whirl" it up—our three-guard weave that was our staple play—he usually just dribbled over to the sideline and cleared everybody out.

During one sequence I forced a shot that I thought I got fouled on, but apparently, the ref did not. Then on defense we fouled Idaho. As I lined up on the free-throw line, Daleo shouted, "What the hell was that? Nice shot. Put that one in your book."

Did the guy know I was keeping a diary? Did Trainer Brad tell him? Had to be him. Maybe this could help my cause. Maybe Dales will want to be in a book. I don't want Dales changing his behavior toward me in some way because he knows I'm keeping a diary. Well, he hasn't exactly given the impression that he's changing his behavior. I suppose that's true. A book? You're a long way from a book. Maybe some day. Focus on the game, you goofball.

We made a little headway with about nine minutes left in the game, but then I got whistled for a foul on a trap with Sydney Holmes. The call riled Dales. He earned a couple of technical fouls and got tossed, which didn't help matters on the scoreboard, and, seeing as we didn't take any assistant coaches with us on these longer road trips, left us with only one guy to take over the reins: Trainer Brad.

Play stopped for a bit as a fired-up Dales exited the arena, so we huddled around Brad for direction. You could tell by looking at his wide eyes and hesitant manner that he was nervous. He said a few things like, "All right fellas, well, see what you can do," and we took the floor again.

Unfortunately, soon after Trainer Brad's talk, the Stampeders opened things up again. Still, playing for a few minutes without Dales's seemingly incessant commentary proved refreshing. After a bit, we found a rhythm and made a slight run. But then guys on the bench started campaigning to come in the game, namely Ronnie. Brad wasn't prepared for this, and he pretty much folded—any semblance of organization quickly broke down. Maybe this was why Dales thought he had to act like a jerk.

It would've been something, if we could have at least won the quarter without Dales. Instead we lost it and the game, 6-1.

As the clock wound down on Brad's head coaching effort, I sat on the bench wishing that this game was the second of the road trip rather than the first—if indeed this back-to-backer with Idaho was to mark my last professional runs. That way, I could've at least gone out with Trainer Brad as my last head coach. It's sentimental, but like Holden Caulfield and his good-byes, I like going out in a decent way.

By the time we got back to the locker room, Dales had changed into jeans and a t-shirt. I still had my tights on. He was jacked up, and as each guy walked dejectedly into the locker room, he said sarcastic stuff, like, "You didn't win? You didn't comeback and win? Oh, I thought for sure you'd comeback and win since I wasn't there." When Marshall Phillips walked in, Dales said, "Marshall, they didn't comeback? Oh, thought for sure you guys would comeback, since you have all the answers. What happened?"

When he finally got over himself, Dales read the stats. Unfortunately for him, the guys he wanted to lay into actually didn't play all that badly. Lubeck nearly finished the game with a triple-double, tallying twenty-seven points, ten rebounds, and nine assists. Jermaine Williams shot fine, and I finished 4-6 from the field with eight points, four assists, and no turnovers. When Dales read that I had no turnovers he said, "That's probably because you never pass the fucking ball."

While reading the other team's stats, Dales got hot when he came to Jayson Williams. "Jayson Williams, six for ten, with fourteen points, nine rebounds, and two assists... My guy Jayson, the killer. My killer, Jayson."

Now, whatever you think of the guy, Williams could hoop. One spectacular play in particular stood out. It happened when one of the Stampeders missed a shot. As the ball bounced off the rim, Williams swooped in seemingly out of nowhere and elevated ridiculously high to throw in a powerful tip-jam. A foul call on Williams nullified the basket, but, as a writer for New Jersey's *The Record* asserted, "It hardly mattered." The crowd, announced at just over 3,000, went nuts. "That looked just like the Jayson Williams of old, didn't it?" Closs said to the press afterward.[64]

Having put the stat sheet down, Dales repeatedly told us how bad Idaho was and how he couldn't believe that we'd lost. "They're terrible."

Really, though, Idaho was pretty good. With Williams, the team had three players who had spent substantial time in the NBA: Britten Johnson had recently returned from a ten-day with the Indiana Pacers and the previous couple years had been on the Orlando Magic, and forward Sam Clancy had spent a couple of years with the Philadelphia 76ers. But that didn't matter to Dales, he was rolling. "We have one more game here tomorrow and then I can make changes over the All-Star break. Just like last year, right, Ronnie? We got blown out at Idaho, and I said, 'Fuck it, I'm bringing in new guys.' I cut Timmy Winn, who was averaging twenty-one points for me, and brought in Timmy Kisner to dump it in. I changed my style and we nearly made it to the finals. Shoot, I'll bring in new guys and win the championship, and then I'll Xerox a picture of myself to Dave Joerger."

You knew things were bad when Dales brought up Joerger.

49

Boise's arena stood right across a wide parking lot from our hotel, so Phillips, Lubes, and I walked back to our rooms. Along the way, Lubeck wondered why Dales always singled him out. Then he thought about it, looked at me, and said, "Well, you get it pretty bad, too." After a moment or two of further reflection he said, "Well, Carson, if this is your last road trip, I've enjoyed being your teammate."

Back at the hotel Lubeck and I settled into our room. By and by, Trainer Brad paid us a visit. I'd looked at Brad a little sideways since Dales made that comment about my CBA diary. Still, I asked Brad what the word was. He said I was on the chopping block yet again. And this time, he really figured it was the end. "Coach told me he was getting rid of you over the All-Star break."

Right then I started plotting all the things I would say to Daleo before he fired me. "I'm gonna give him a piece of mind, gonna tell that stupid ass he doesn't treat people right."

"You aren't going to tell him how you found out, are you?"

"No, Brad, don't worry."

"Oh man, you've got to tell me when you're going to do it. I want to be there," Brad said.

Trainer Brad was still mad he hadn't gotten to hear Dales and I have it out in Grand Rapids a couple of years beforehand. But Brad was also nervous that somehow Dales would blame him if we had it out again, since Dales already blamed Brad for me knowing that he had waited to tell me that my wife was in the emergency room.

As Brad gave me the dirt, word broke among the players that an impromptu meeting was taking place between Ronnie, Stais, and Daleo down in the lobby. We envisioned them sitting down there talking smack about everybody else. I had a sense that Ronnie might not be backing me anymore. When the meeting adjourned, Boseman came up to our room and filled us in. Other guys had trickled in. According to

Boseman, Daleo had declared that "nobody was off limits," as if anybody would actually believe that. Ronnie wasn't going anywhere. Boseman was dejected as he told us this, because Daleo had told him that he was too quiet.

"He said I was soft, that I didn't speak up enough," Boseman said. "I told him I've never been a rah-rah guy, and I'm not going to start now. At thirty, I'm not just gonna suddenly change. If you have to tell a guy to play hard, it's too late."

Lubeck piped in, asking, "All right, let me hear it, what's he saying about me?"

"Oh, he said you can't play defense. That you let guys go right by you."

Then I mustered the courage. "All right, what'd he say about me?"

"Oh, Carson...," he paused, shook his head, and then said, "I'm just gonna tell it to you straight. He said you were retarded."

Then Boseman looked around all dramatic-like, and everybody started laughing. Even I fell out. "He said that's why nobody else wanted you. And that's why he already sent you home once on a Greyhound bus."

"What? That's bullshit. He didn't send me home on a Greyhound bus. I called one and took it home myself." A fellow has to stand up for something.

"Really?"

"Yeah, it was after a game in Grand Rapids, I told him I was tired of his shit and that he needed to stop threatening me, and plotting moves with Ronnie for freakin' Kareem Reid. That I didn't need this shit like some guys, and I was tired of it. When I was done he told me I was cut."

"Oh, he told me he sent you home on a Greyhound."

"The heck with it anyway, Brad already told me he was looking to cut me. I just want to know when it's coming so I can lay into him beforehand."

Then Lubes asked what Ronnie had said. "He doesn't like me anyway. I know he was talking shit."

Boseman hesitated for a moment, but then said, "Yeah, he was hatin'. When Coach D was saying shit about you, I said 'Hey, Lubeck nearly had a triple-double.' And then Ronnie said, 'Yeah, but so did his man probably.'"

"I knew it. I hate that shit. I hate when people start talking about my defense. That pisses me off, Ronnie down there talking shit."

Dobbins had walked in our room a little earlier. He sat there a while, taking it all in. Eventually, he said, "Same shit as last year. He doesn't like guys scoring more than him. Both you and Stais got more shots than him. That ain't gonna work. That's why Quincy Wadley got cut last year. He was in the top five in scoring."

Trainer Brad gave his take. He told Lubeck that Ronnie didn't like him because Lubes shot more than him.

Stais kept shaking his head. "Shit, he came in and fucked shit up," he said. "We're 9-3 without him and 4-8 with him. You see we got into first place when he was gone."

I didn't let on that somehow Ronnie had been working as my ally. First of all, I didn't know if he still was, and second, I didn't disagree with Boseman's analysis.

We all knew that when Ronnie was fit and cut-in and focused, rather than frustrated and working his way back into form, he could help carry a team to victories. As it stood, though, we could sense that our outfit was reeling.

Stais kept pacing in and out of the room, chewing on what had been said at his meeting with Dales and Fields. "That shit pisses me off; don't attack my manhood again," he said.

"I just want to know when it's coming so I can lay into him," I declared.

Bringing the ball up the court during the 2004-05 season with the Rockford Lightning. Am I looking back because Dales is calling a play or because he's calling me a moron?

50

The next night, the Stampede wore sweet camouflage uniforms, the sandy-beige kind that soldiers serving in Iraq and Afghanistan wear. Seeing one of the Idaho players come at you during the game in this uniform was pretty impressive and it got me to thinking about America's wars. In fact, the whole night, which the Stampede organization had made into an "Idaho cares" tribute to the U.S. military, got me to thinking about how rare it was for a single person affiliated with the CBA to even as much as bring up the Afghanistan or Iraq wars. This was rather remarkable when you consider that we were young, active men who spent considerable time together traveling around.

Not that we didn't think about the military privately. How could you not? I mean the Taliban kills girls for the simple act of going to school. It's just that in the CBA we didn't talk about it much.

Truth be told, though, I'd struggled for some time with the question of whether or not I should join the military. Only, *really* figuring it out did not come easy. I know the military stands between civilians and some really nasty folks, but the WMD Iraq war drum did seem a little odd, and I reckoned that I didn't want to find myself on the streets of Baghdad with an M-4 in hand trying to determine whether the person coming toward me wanted to shake my hand or kill me. At the same time, I didn't want to rationalize myself into some tired, anti-American stupor that left me incapable of making a stand.

While playing in Estonia, I'd told myself that if they found WMD, I'd sign up, and I got to thinking about joining the military enough that in the summer of '03 that I drove to Louisville to go through a bunch of preliminary physical tests that the Air National Guard puts you through if you're interested in Pararescue (with the mission to save downed pilots and others in hostile areas, Pararescuemen are some of the military's highest trained soldiers). I figured that this type of service might suit me. I passed the physical tests but never heard back from the lead interviewer. Maybe he didn't like my answer when he asked me my motivation. I started in on Pat Tillman, meaning to say something about how he seemed like "an ideal worthy of everything in my enthusiastic admiration, yet consummated and expressed in a human being," which is what F. Scott Fitzgerald said about World War I hero Hobey Baker. Only I think I mostly stumbled through it.[65] Bungling this, though, probably didn't concern the guy much. He might've, however, been concerned when I told him that I would soon be married. Maybe he did a little research and saw that I'd had my knees and right elbow worked on. Whatever it was, he didn't contact me again. A bit spooked by how much time away from the family the job involved, I didn't follow-up. Rather than joining the military, I'd returned to the underbelly.

On this "Idaho Cares" night in Boise, as had been the case the night before, the crowd was pretty large. Around three thousand energetic fans attended, and a local NBC affiliate televised the game, giving it a heightened sense of importance. As far as CBA games go, it all made for a pretty sweet atmosphere. Unfortunately, we lost yet again, and it was not even close. At one point, Ronnie virtually stopped running the wing, opting instead to call for the ball in the backcourt so he could walk it up.

At times, when we had the ball on our end but Ronnie wasn't involved in the action, he would actually come over to the sideline to talk with Dales about what had gone wrong or who had messed up. Marshall Phillips finally told him to shut up and get back on defense. But it didn't help all that much.

In his post-game locker room speech Dales seemed surprisingly mellow. He complimented us for fighting back to win the fourth and then went through the stats. When he got to Sydney's line, he told him he thought he played well and had good energy. Then he said, "And you can tell your mom you blocked a murderer's shot."

Someone told Dales that the block he was referring to actually came on a Sam Clancy shot, not one of Williams's.

"Oh, well, you can tell your mom you blocked the shot of a former NBA second-round draft choice—which was a gift of a pick," Dales said.

I originally had figured if Dales got on me after the game, I'd give him a piece of my mind. But he barely said boo to me all night, and by the time the game ended, I'd changed my mind about laying into him anyway. It happened at the free-throw line. As some guy from Idaho went through his routine and shot, I got to thinking about the little one floating around in my wife's uterus. I asked myself what I'd expect out of the little one in such a situation, and I figured I'd tell her not to sink to that level. It sounds cheesy and sentimental, but this really was how I changed my plan. Sure, it'd have felt good to lay into Dales, but he already knew how I felt about his antics—ripping into him wouldn't have the same effect. I'd already done it. Plus, it'd be too late anyway. As Dales would put it, "Who cares? The decision's been rendered."

My mission had been to try and see one last season through, despite its inevitable trials and tribulations. If I got cut, I planned on accepting it and moving on.

That night a bunch of fellows went out on the town and brought Keith with them. Given what we knew about Keith by that point, this wasn't a good idea, especially since everyone had to get up the next morning at 5:30 a.m. for a flight home. Sure enough, things went poorly.

Early the next morning, a riled-up Boss Closs came down to the hotel lobby where most of the guys and Dales were already munching on a continental breakfast. The Boss carried a mean, nasty look as he walked toward the yogurt and muffins on the counter; his unbraided hair was 'froed out, and his lips were pursed. Syd, sitting at a table, smiled and chuckled as Keith walked by. Closs caught sight of him out of the corner of his eye. Piling muffins on a plate, he asked Syd, "What the fuck you laughing about? You don't know shit. Don't be getting stuff misconstrued and misunderstood, fuck."

He wasn't screaming, but he was loud. Fortunately, only a few patrons besides us were in the eating area of the lobby this early in the morning. After his statement, guys just laughed under their breath and looked around at each other. Then Closs stalked out of the eating area, looking like a man on some sort of mission.

Eager to get the heck out of Boise, right about then I headed for one of the two passenger-vans out front, which were waiting to take us to the airport. As I walked through the modest lobby of the hotel, I could hear Keith starting to talk smack about somebody else—only seemingly to himself. I couldn't make out what exactly he was saying, but you could tell he was fired up. Other players trickled out of the hotel and into the vans. Some were pointing back inside, shaking their heads and laughing. Apparently, Keith was in the lobby giving it to Dales, telling him he didn't want to hear any of his crap and that he was pissed off. I guess he laid into Livan a bit, too. About what, though, I don't know. Keith finally came out of the hotel to get into a van.

As soon as he shut the door, he started talking loudly about Daleo: "That stupid motherfucker, I'll whoop his ass. That little bitch, afraid to say shit to Ronnie. Fuck him. He can suck my dick. I want to go home to South Central L.A. where I have a mom and four kids who love me. They love me, and I love them. I'm homesick. I'm tired of this shit. Fuck him. He can suck my..." He even suggested Dales use whipped cream, and Closs offered information on the size of his personal endowment, which made you think the equivalent of:

Is that even possible? Should someone call the Guinness Book of World Records? It's too bad he drinks. He should be in the League. This is why he isn't. You're Irish. Accept it.

After a few minutes of Keith's monologue, Trainer Brad took advantage of a pause to thank the young lady who was driving us to the airport, and in so doing to apologize for Keith's outbursts. The move got Keith's attention, and he apologized for his language too. Then he laid his head on a suitcase and appeared to go to sleep.

He popped up about ten minutes later, though, just before we arrived at the airport, and started in on Daleo again, apparently forgetting about the poor lady driving the van: "That motherfucker, I'll whoop his ass. I don't give a fuck. I want to go home anyway; fuck him, afraid to stand up to one of his players. He's a bitch. And if he says one more thing about Jayson Williams's murder case, I'm gonna go off on that motherfucker."

Trying to calm him down, I said, "Keith, don't worry about that, just try to get to the NBA, keep blocking shots."

"Fuck that, I've been in the NBA. Fuck him. I'll go play in Italy for the mafia. I'm tired of his ass."

As we stepped out of the van, he continued, "I'm about to go off on a motherfucker in here, and it may or may not be the coach. Watch me."

We gathered our bags and Brad and I apologized again to the young lady. She didn't know, just like we didn't know, Keith's past. If she had, it would've at least helped her understand things better.

No matter, it was a pst that Keith would one day have to confront. He did just that a couple of years later. And he won. Each year since 2007 marks a new year of sobriety.

Inside the airport, we got in line to check in at the United counter. During the wait, Keith had time to stew. He was in front of our group while Dales and Ronnie stood nearer the back. Every now and then Keith would turn his head and say something loud like, "That motherfucker," or "I don't give a fuck." After a while, his boldness picked up. He said, somewhat loudly, "That weak motherfucker, afraid to stand up to one of his players who's fuckin' up the team 'cuz our coach is a bitch."

Finally, Dales acknowledged Keith by looking up ahead to him and asking, "What? What'd you say, Keith?"

Keith turned around and mocked, "What, Keith? What did you say? You heard me, Chris, you heard me loud and clear. You motherfuckers may be afraid to speak up to his ass, but I'm not. Look at you all standing there. Behind closed doors you'll say the same thing."

Brad tried to quiet him down and things settled for a moment.

A few more minutes went by and we still hadn't made it to the front of the line, giving the volatility a chance to rise again. I was hoping the people at United could speed things up so we could just get on the plane and get home with as little damage as possible. But sure enough, Keith got around to giving Dales another piece of his mind. He muttered a few things and then got louder and looked back at Dales and said, "Chris, you're fuckin' ignorant."

He started to spell it.

"I-G-N...," he began, only to stop and look upward, like he was thinking. "Or is it I-N-G, no, I was right the first fucking time, I-G-N..."

He didn't even try to finish. "You're fucking ignorant," he said instead.

Finally, it was Keith's turn to go up to the lady at the ticket counter. As he did, he looked back a time or two, muttering, "You stupid motherfucker . . . dumbfuck," or some other such thing.

Dales continued to spend most of this time standing next to Ronnie talking quietly. At one point, having gotten closer to the ticket counter, he turned to me and asked, "What is it? A federal offense?"

I guess he thought Keith would get arrested for trying to board a plane drunk.

Standing in front of the receptionist who was trying to check him in, Keith again turned and said something else profane at Dales. Losing her patience, the receptionist asked Keith—really, our group in general—"Are we going to have to get somebody? Where is the coach?"

Keith pointed backward and said something. She responded by asking Keith, "You're the coach?"

Keith said no and then for some reason decided to walk up to an entirely different ticket counter, this one manned by an older gentleman. In the meantime, Dales made no effort to acknowledge he was the coach. He seemed interested, mainly, in seeing if Keith would be arrested for a federal offense.

Fortunately, the older man whose counter Keith randomly approached managed to settle the Boss down. The guy looked like he had experience, like someone who wouldn't flap easily. He had those late middle-aged wrinkles that seemed to smile. Sure enough, I watched him skillfully coach Keith. Within minutes, Keith was answering questions calmly, checking his bags without incident, and generally chilling out. As Keith walked away, the elder Idahoan pointed at the Boss and gave him a friendly wink, as if to say, "Hey, I worked with you, now don't let me down on that plane."

Keith was disarmed. By the time he reached the gate for our flight, he was nearly back to ol' happy-go-lucky Keith. He sought Dales out for a conversation, and they walked back and forth in the terminal talking calmly. Then Keith came over and sat down near Livan and me. He started talking about how much he missed his four kids and how he wanted to make enough money to open a couple of day care centers in Los Angeles so kids today could learn the things that his generation hadn't.

He asked Livan and I what we thought was wrong with the team. The thing was, as loose as his cannon had been in the airport and as much as he might have had to drink the night before, we basically agreed with what he'd been saying. But Livan added, "He's the coach, it's his world, we're just livin' it."

"That leaves us with two options: make the best of it, or get a new job," I said.

Keith was right about our team, yet that was part of the challenge, to try and overcome it all, to survive and to win. At least that's what I told myself. But at that point it seemed like two things were clear for me: there'd be no championship and no CBA survival.

As I walked onto the plane I heard Dales talking on the phone to the 6'10" center Lawrence Nelson, telling him he intended to trade for him. It sounded like perhaps this time, Dales really would dump Keith.

51

All-Star break followed the Boise bedlam. Those not involved in the All-Star festivities in Gary were to reconvene in Rockford in a few days. I figured my goose would be cooked in the interim, but again I received no call. So I went back. There was always the thought that perhaps we could somehow right the ship again.

Straight away, we took a flight to Seattle and then embarked on a few hours of driving across the Cascade mountain range for a Friday-Saturday back-to-backer in Yakima. Once we'd landed in Seattle, the bulk of the drive to Yakima was along Interstate-90. Only this time, I was the one thinking about how, if I was driving, I could have just kept on going straight down I-90 back to Chicago and home.

In Yakima, Dales continued ripping his favorite targets, when not huddling with Ronnie and milking what appeared to be their renewed bond. Still, we won the first game 112-106 thanks to two clutch threes by Lubes and an incredible defensive performance by Closs. Officially, the Boss finished the game with nine blocks, but the scorekeeper must've been surfing the web or something during the game, because by my rough count, Closs redirected thirteen to fifteen shots. I'd never seen anything like it live. As if redirecting this many shots wasn't enough, he kept many of the attempts he altered in play, jump-starting a fast break for us. You couldn't help but get a little sad thinking about how if he could just stay sober, he could get back to the NBA. Still, it was fun to watch him play like this.

We faced Yakima again the next night and lost. At one point, late in the second half, I put my "Cunn Cross" on Cliff Hawkins, a rookie out of the University of Kentucky, and he bit hard—nearly flew to the other side of the lane. I don't think the rook had seen that cross. It was a move I'd learned from my brother growing up and one that I wouldn't see elsewhere much until I started watching and playing European ball. Some folks refer to the move nowadays as the "Croatian Cross." No matter what you call it, I'd made it my signature move and appreciated it when a guy would ask me to show it to him, like Marshall Phillips did once. Phillips told me that when he played in Europe—France, Germany, it didn't matter—an American player out there would end up talking to him about the Croatian cross-over and a white guy in the CBA who put it on folks. "They didn't even know your name, but they knew your cross," Phillips said. "You had a patented move." Having a move that guys wanted to emulate—guys who were good at hoops and who knew the game virtually inside and out—was a badge of honor.

That night, sleep didn't come easy, so I stopped by Marshall Phillips's and Sydney Holmes's room. Boss Closs was already there, playing *Wrestle-Mania III* on PlayStation.

As the night wore on, Livan Pyfrom stopped by, intrigued by what was the liveliest game of *Wrestle-Mania* I'd ever seen. Phillips would hop on the bed, with his controller in hand, and recreate the moves he was inflicting upon his opponent. He'd go airborne and deliver an elbow to the mattress just like his character on-screen. It was hilarious. When Syd or the Boss were about to deliver a blow, they would hop out of their chair and get to dancing and pressing the buttons. Guys would talk smack to each other just like the wrestlers on the game, "It's coming, it's coming! There you go, there you go!"

For hours we shot the breeze and played and just hung out. It's funny about the CBA: you never knew when you might find yourself deep in the American West, playing *Wrestle Mania III* on PlayStation until 4:00 a.m. with a motley crew of teammates, among them a do-everything forward from Atlanta who in high school had gotten ensnarled in gang life until basketball saved him; a half-Cherokee, half-black, seven-foot three-inch, freckle-faced blocking machine with a big heart and a big vice; and a seven-foot Bahamian who had nearly gotten called up to the Knicks only to see it fall through and within a few weeks find himself trapped in Canada.

It felt good hanging out early into that next morning, but not getting to bed until 4:00 a.m. did make the 6:00 a.m. wake-up call and the ride back across the Cascades to catch our flight out of Seattle more difficult. I tried to sleep on the bus ride, but didn't fare too well. And, with the time change, by the time we'd made it back to Rockford, we'd used up the entire day traveling. I was spent.

Not long after returning, Trainer Brad called. I could tell right away that this time the gig really was up. He broke the news as nicely as he could. He felt kind of bad about having to make the call.

I told him not to sweat it and that I'd enjoyed working with him and that now I only wished that he'd have been the one to coach me in my last game. I told you I can be kind of sentimental sometimes.

I got off the phone knowing—pretty much full well—that my final, glorious comeback season had ended and my professional basketball career was over. But I didn't know what to think about it all, at least right then. Like the screenwriter Charlie Kaufman put it in the film *Adaptation*, I didn't want the type of story where "people don't change, they don't have any epiphanies. They struggle and are frustrated and nothing is resolved."[67] There had to be some meaning to it all, some purpose to the whole thing. I needed more distance from the underbelly to let it all digest.

Eventually, I came to appreciate some things. I figured at the bare minimum, at least the grappling was admirable.

I also found some comfort, as odd as it might seem, in recognizing that the move by Dales to drop me and then bring in Cordell Henry to replace me made some sense. You can certainly argue that Cordell Henry played basketball better than I did for the Lightning. All the crap from Dales aside, this was a big part of the problem, really: if I wanted to play professional basketball, I needed to be better at basketball. In that way, the CBA did its ruthless, competitive job.

Still, I wanted some grand theory to tie it all together, to make sense of all of it, and not just the hoops. Maybe I was overreaching.

Rather than basking in a glow of enlightenment, soon after getting canned, I started feeling exhausted. My nasals flared up, and I just felt worn out. Unable to figure it out, I kept telling myself I wasn't depressed and that getting sacked counted as a positive in the whole scheme of things. But I was lying around the apartment a bunch sleeping and generally feeling dog tired.

Finally, after a few weeks, I made a call on a doctor. She diagnosed me with Epstein Barr, otherwise known as mononucleosis. I imagine the bug had found my immune system broken down somewhere on that bus ride back across the Cascades.

It took a few weeks, but by and by my body started to get a better handle on beating back the Barr and I settled into my new life again, appreciating some semblance of normalcy. But that doesn't mean that I didn't occasionally check up on Lightning scores.

Indeed, just before the end-of-season transaction deadline arrived, I noticed that a roster spot opened with the Lightning because of an injury. I thought about putting a call in to Trainer Brad but instead actually decided to send Dales an email letting him know of my readiness. I know it's crazy. You don't need to tell me. I still had this notion that I'd do what I could to finish the season and go for that championship.

Just as crazy, perhaps, Brad called a couple of days later and told me to be ready. In the next twenty-four hours, apparently, Dales intended to bring in either me or forward Jermaine Williams, who'd gotten axed by then too.

That started me in on envisioning a championship again. But Brad didn't call back.

Now and again I would track the Lightning's playoff progress online. The squad ended up losing in the CBA Finals to Sioux Falls, three games to one. You knew it had to irk Dales mightily to lose to Joerger again.

On February 1, before the playoffs started, Dales had let Closs go, too. "We wish Keith the best of luck in his future endeavors but he is no longer a member of the Lightning. My team has to project a positive image on the Rockford community both on and off the floor. Keith has made some choices and I feel that it is the best interest of the team and the organization to let him go. Sometimes tough decisions are easy," Daleo waxed philosophically.[68]

A few weeks later, the former high school phenom Jackie Butler and swingman Mark Jones of the Storm got called up to the NBA.

As the months wore on and the next basketball season arrived, I actually started harboring visions of somehow popping in for the last few weeks of the season to help with a championship run, even with my adjunct gigs teaching history at local colleges. I thought maybe that was the way to do it, rather than trying to start at the beginning of the season. I could let all the insanity work itself out and then swoop in down the stretch. I knew it was unrealistic but I'd think about it now and again anyway.

Now, don't get me wrong, I loved the way things were rolling along with my wife and our little one, and I liked teaching history. And I could feel that things were changing as far as my need to work the hoops out of my system. But I still couldn't completely shake it. I still wanted a run.

I started to really feel it after we went to a dinner party and this couple with a bunch of advanced degrees started in on the movie *Crash*. The lady, kind of affected-like, said, "More than race, it was about class." I felt like puking. Nothing against the film—I don't think I've even seen the whole thing—it's just that people never said stuff like that in the CBA. She went on and on about how profound the movie was, but did so in a way that made me want to put on Tarzan gear and run out to the wild and beat a drum or swing from a tree—or go play in the CBA.

Oddly enough, right about this time, the 2005-06 CBA season's transaction deadline approached. And a couple of weeks prior, one of the Lightning point guards had gone down with an injury. I still kept track of such things online, and—I shouldn't even admit this—I freaking called Dales and told him if he needed a point guard, he could count me ready. As I say, somehow I'd convinced myself that I could pop in and out of Rockford and Chicago for a few weeks and take care of my teaching duties, especially with spring break coming up, while hooping in CBA games at night. Dales acted as nicely as he could when I called him, and he mentioned that he'd tried to get a hold of me earlier that season before training camp. Boy was I lucky to miss that call. I told him I'd been training, and he said that something might work out and that he'd call in a few days. I didn't hear back from him the rest of the season.

But a couple of months later, Daleo called unexpectedly and asked, "Hey, you want to go to China for a couple weeks in June to play?"

He told me the trip "is what it is" and that the previous year, the players had gone on the trip thinking they'd get looked at by professional scouts and agents overseas, but "nobody's getting a job out of this thing. You got to take it for what it is, a trip to China. You try to stay away from the food, eat a bunch of rice, get some massages, play some ball, and then at the end you get four hours of shopping in Shanghai where you can get anything for nothing. I bought more samurai swords and DVDs and silk robes and pearls and dresses than my family knows what to do with. You just pack light, buy a suitcase there for nothing, and then bring back a load of stuff. I've been going on this trip for three years, and now Christmas at the Daleos' house is in June. So it is what it is. Don't take it for anything more than what it is, just play some ball. Like guys last year were complaining about playing time, they were getting drunk, getting in fights, it was a nightmare. Just play some ball and get a bunch of stuff. They have more stuff than you can imagine, and for nothing. And that's it."

I knew he bought gifts for his family. Let's go play some ball, you crazy sonuvabitch.

52

I n June 2006, I arrived in the new and expanding Shanghai-Pudong Airport with about twenty other American basketball players. Most of us had played in low-level pro leagues across the globe, but not all of us had played professionally. One guy had gone to work at a factory after playing college ball; another, Jeff Riggs, a good buddy of mine and former Montana State hooper, who Dales had agreed to reserve a spot for on the trip, ran delis in Montana. I had to give Dales some credit for helping to get my buddy a spot on the trip.

Anil Vaswani was the American-based sports agent who had put the trip together with a Chinese agency, which organized our transportation, lodging, meals, and games in the People's Republic of China. The Chinese point person for the trip was a fellow named Mr. Weng (you say it like "Wong").

Mr. Weng and a couple of his female assistants met us at the airport and directed us to a bus that was made for people without long legs. As the bus pulled away, Mr. Weng stood in front of us near the driver and grabbed a microphone—apparently a feature of Chinese buses—to welcome us to China.

Upon passing hundreds of tall condo buildings, we stopped at Shanghai's Xin Min Hotel, where we had a team meeting. Daleo told everyone to use their money smartly: "Whether it's a lady, DVDs, or Palm Pilots—bargain everything." Yet again, he mentioned the goofball player who supposedly came on the China trip previously and tried to bring a dog home at the end of it. And he told us not to ruin it for other players by doing things like paying 400 yuan for extracurriculars, which another player had done and thereby raised the price of Chinese hookers for other players, which made them mad. Dales made it clear he didn't feel like dealing with players who were mad at each other for causing extracurricular inflation.

Alright. Don't bring a dog home and don't inflate the price of Chinese hookers. I can do this.

He encouraged us not to gripe about playing time and not to do anything stupid, like the two guys who got in a fight on the court the previous year. "If you're gonna gripe about playing time, just stay on the bus. I'm not fightin' with you, I'm just not," Dales said. Regarding the fighters, he threw up his hands: "They're not back. Because the sponsor doesn't want that, and then we lose sponsors, and then we have no trip . . . I mean, come on. People do that. In front of 3,500 people, get in a fight. What're they thinking? But people do stupid things. People are retarded."

Agent Anil stressed that for the people who lived in the places we planned to play in, this was a big deal. He said even the "small cities" we'd visit could have a million or more people, and the fans "will think you're NBA superstars."

Did they tell them that?

Anil also said, "For a lot of the people in these towns, this will be the best basketball they'll ever see firsthand." And he claimed that if they liked you, they'd do anything for you. "Like, you say you like a shirt or something, the next day they'll show up at your hotel with a new one for you. It's kind of like idol worship." (A Chinese man at the airport had already asked if we played in the NBA. He barely spoke English and asked so excitedly that I didn't want to let him down, so I told him we did. It was kind of a rotten thing to say, but you should've seen how excited he was.)

"This will be the biggest thing of the year for people in some of the villages we'll play in," Daleo interjected. "You step off the bus, you'll get mobbed. You'll sign a million autographs, and the place will be packed, 3,500 to 4,000, and filled with smoke. They smoke like fiends out here."

As the meeting wound down, one of the players asked what would happen if a scout for a Chinese team or some other team watched and decided they wanted to sign one of us. Anil stepped in and said they'd talk with whoever showed interest and see what could be arranged. Then Anil told us he'd been in the business for fifteen to seventeen years and that if you're good enough, someone will find you. "You don't know how many times one of us gets a call on a guy," Anil started to say. But right about then Daleo cut in to tell us that shortly after the trip last year he'd gotten a call on a player, "And I told them he was a bum. I wouldn't take him to the grocery market. Click."

Anil also informed us of the plan to stage a dunk play for each team at the start of each game and at the start of each half, because the Chinese love dunks. "But don't get me wrong, be competitive," Dales said. "It's a fine line between being entertaining and wanting to win."

Daleo warned us to be careful about what we ate, "because you don't want to be on the bus having to 'go' and we stop at some gas station, some CITGO, that has a hole in the floor for a shitter and no toilet paper." And from that he somehow transitioned into telling us, yet again, of his intention to save nearly all his yuan—only he called the Chinese currency yen—for the Shanghai shopping trip at the end of the journey. "If you're smart with your money you can buy silk robes, pajamas, samurai swords...I've bought more pearls for my wife than she knows what to do with. She's chokin' on them. She can't take it," he said. "Two weeks of bullshit, for four hours in Shanghai." This became his mantra for the trip: "Two weeks of bullshit, for four hours in Shanghai."

On day two, we played in Wuanjing, which looked like a virtually brand new city, in a newly constructed gym that had been financed by the government and seated some 3,000 people. Over the course of the trip we'd play in a few gyms that had a box-like feel—they were drab and workmanlike, reminiscent of the Cold War era. But this gym in Wuanjing was newer and more open and airy and colorful.

That night, an eager and near-capacity crowd of a few thousand fans showed up. The place was energized, and it made me feel springy. It'd been over a year since I'd played in an organized contest like this, and when the center-jump took place to tip things off, I felt how I imagine an animal feels upon getting released from a cage. I went buck wild: I drove to the rack with abandon, dribbled between my legs and behind my back in traffic, and when in doubt looked to put a little mustard on plays. The crowd loved it, and I tell you, my legs had bounce, and my blood was flowing nice and easy. I'd been given jersey number fifteen, but, as far as I was concerned, I was wearing Rossetti's forty-three. Before the game had ended, I'd poured in thirty-seven points and hit a driving lay-up to tie the score with only seconds remaining. But this guy, who had majored in geriatrics at Weber State only to encounter a tough job market that had forced him to resort to factory work and who hadn't played organized hoops in years, nailed a three-pointer at the buzzer to win it for the opposition.

Later that evening, at a coffee shop on the first floor of our hotel, a group of guys plugged their laptops into some kind of adaptor and tapped into a free wireless Internet connection. After a bit, Dales made it to down to the coffee shop and took a seat. It didn't take long for him to join a conversation Anil and I were having, about what types of overseas jobs Anil could get for players. I was asking Anil partly out of general interest, and, yes, I was also digging around to see if there was a possible gig out there for me and my family. Anil, who couldn't have been much more than forty years old, if that, claimed he didn't like to deal with lower-level jobs anymore because he was getting "too old" for that type of thing. This didn't bode well for me. In any event, we talked about the quality of jobs in various countries and which countries took guards and that type of general thing. He considered Ireland and Iceland some of the lowest-level gigs out there.

"Do you want to play?" he asked me.

"Well, it'd have to be the right gig," I said.

This is when Dales decided to chime in. "Anil, he'd play for anything, anywhere. Ireland, any of those gigs," he said.

That wasn't true anymore, but Dales thought it was.

By and by, a group of players, fresh off of combing the streets for some Chinese satisfaction, took a seat at a table in front of me. By then most everybody else had cleared out. After rehashing how much it cost to get a hooker, apparently fifty yuan, and how long it takes to explain that you want head rather than sex, these fellows got around to talking politics. One of them asked about Chinese money and the gold standard: "Doesn't all the money need to get backed by gold?"

"Yeah, but minus the deficit, which is trillions of dollars, but we're never gonna pay that shit back," someone offered.

Another guy said, "Man, Bush is a gangster n*****. Bush is my n*****. He's a cold hearted gangster n*****. I'm gonna get a t-shirt that says 'Bush Is My N*****.' He's my n*****. All he talks about is war and money. America and the other people slumped this n*****. Where they at right now? Afghanistan or something, Iraq? They got the n***** in Iraq, second to Bin Laden, I don't know his name."

Then someone asked, "You don't think Bin Laden's teamin' with Bush?"

"His daddy and his older brother been building houses for the last twenty to twenty-five years. I'll say fifteen."

The conversation turned for a bit to an analysis of whether or not Bin Laden was hiding in the United States. At one point, the main skeptic of the "Bin Laden is in the United States" theory asked me if I thought Bin Laden was in Connecticut. I suggested it wasn't likely. In turn, the main supporter of the theory said, "Bin Laden and Bush, they're in it together. It's just like Game and 50 cent. That shit ain't real. They're all in the game. You really think they're beefin? Come on Carson, they're in it together."

Well, at least someone mentioned Iraq and Afghanistan.

About a week into our trip, I interviewed Mr. Weng up in his hotel room. I'd told him that I was writing a dissertation on the history of U.S. Olympic basketball, and that I'd like to talk to him about China and sports over the past several decades. His two assistants, Susan and Rose, joined us, although I'm not sure why, seeing as, other than telling me how much Mr. Weng knew about history, they mainly just observed as Mr. Weng and I talked and ate peanuts and each drank a shot of Jack, which Mr. Weng had poured in preparation for my visit.

After talking about his life and Chinese history and declaring his support for one-party Communist-style politics in China, he asked me if I wanted to listen to him recite poetry by Li Bai. "One time I recited poetry for Rose for one and a half hours," he told me. Rose just shook her head up and down and smiled.

"Have you heard of him?" Weng asked.

He seemed shocked to hear I had not. He said that Li Bai was "the Shakespeare of China." Then he tilted his head up and to the side a little and all of a sudden was reciting a Li Bai poem about a mountain. Before I knew it he was rolling. He made his voice as pleasant-sounding as he could, and he kind of looked out beyond us as he recited, almost as if he was trying to gaze up at the sky. When he finished, I asked him the poem's meaning.

"It is about a man, you see, who did not like his master or boss and of his yearning to get out from under his boss's control." He thought about it for a moment and laughed, "You see, even Li Bai loved freedom."

53

Early in the trip, before the first week was out, I already missed my family something terrible, couldn't wait to get back home. I know it sounds cheesy and everything, but it's the truth.

Upon reaching Xuzhou, some ten days into the trip, we stopped at a restaurant for a "Spanish Barbecue." The people greeted us when we arrived with big signs. One of them read: "Warmly Embrace the Basketball Stars From the U.S.A." On it were pictures of Vince Carter and Dwyane Wade.

In Xuzhou, even though our hotel was only a quarter-mile from the gym, we bussed to our game because Mr. Weng worried that the crowd would mob us for autographs if we went by foot. Sure enough, as we pulled up to the gym, multitudes were milling about in anticipation of the game.

As we looked out from the bus at the people gathering in front of the stadium, Dales said, referring to us, "NBA All-Stars. Here they are."

About then, a car moved in the way of the bus, prompting Dales to shout, "The government wants you to move your car."

He got a kick out of saying stuff like that in China. During the games he'd get in a ref's ear during a stop in the action, all serious-like, and tell him, "The government wants gray to win. Mr. Weng and the government said gray must win."

All told, probably about 3,500 to 4,000 eager spectators attended this game. And I tell you they really did treat us like rock stars. All trip long, in fact, we were met with smiles and open arms and treated grandly.

Still, Mao's Revenge hit me about midway through the journey. The night after it struck we had a game, and during the warm-up the need to take a pre-game bathroom break arose. My buddy Riggs had taken to carrying wipes around with him, so I was able to borrow some from him—Chinese bathrooms commonly had no toilet paper. But, even though I had wipes, I still had to squat over a hole in the ground, because just about every public restroom I came across on the trip had holes in the ground rather than toilets—and no divider stalls to give you privacy between one hole and the next. When you combined this with the lack of toilet paper, it was a tough scenario. I think the absence of toilet paper was the worst of all. Without it—if you didn't have a buddy with enough wherewithal to bring wipes—you were left with two options: the chuck and go, inconceivable, or the bare hand wipe, even less so. Compounding matters, the bathrooms didn't have soap. Apparently, after a hand wipe a simple hand rinse was supposed to suffice.

They've had thousands of years to get the bathroom right and this is what they've got? Where's the U.N.?

One player, I kid you not, had demanded a ride back to the hotel during a pre-game warm-up just so he could use a bathroom with basic amenities, like a toilet. The Chinese managers at this gym, who were quite nice and rather accommodating, as were the Chinese throughout the whole trip, not only got him to the hotel and back, they gave him a police escort along the way.

Earlier in the day I'd tried to ask our Chinese host Rose for tissue paper, only she didn't understand me at first. She kept mispronouncing "tissue," thinking I was saying t-shirt or something. Finally I said "toilet," slow-like, and then she actually imitated the wiping motion to show me that she understood.

"Oh, the guys tell me I have to go 'Big Doo Doo' or 'shit,'" she said. "If you just said, 'I need to go Big Doo Doo' or 'shit,' I would have known."

In the trip's final week, Daleo started expressing his mantra— "Two weeks of bullshit for four hours in Shanghai"—with even more regularity. Meanwhile, the cities started to run together, and sleep deprivation increased as Mao's revenge continued to wreak havoc on virtually everybody.

At one point, we took a plane ride on China Eastern Airlines to Nanching. Landing there, while functioning on virtually no sleep, we stepped onto yet another bus for a ride through beautiful countryside. Rolling mountains peppered with pine trees were tucked beyond picturesque rice fields, upon which we could see workers harvesting rice with their bare hands in the punishing heat.

As striking as the terrain was, the bus ride ended up taking longer than anticipated, and the driver honked and swerved, too. With weariness and plumbing problems plaguing us, before long rumblings of discontent started to emerge in the back of the bus.

When the bus stopped and pulled up to a building, we thought we'd finally arrived at our lodgings. Instead, we were just making a stop at a Communist-run coat factory that was apparently sponsoring some part of our visit. Personnel representing the factory welcomed us and showed us around and gave us each a free coat. We tried to communicate as best we could but mostly we got by with hand gestures. The visit was both unexpected and a little odd.

When we got back on the bus, we all figured, considering how long we'd been traveling, that we'd go straight to a nearby hotel. Instead, we stopped off at the gym in which we'd be playing that night's game so that a couple of our bigger guys could go inside and jump up and yank on the gym's rims to make sure that the backboards could withstand their size and strength (we'd shattered two backboards on the trip already). As we waited for the volunteers to finish hanging from the rims, Chinese people came off the street and walked over to our bus to look in. The way they gawked, it didn't seem like they'd ever seen an American before.

By the time we pulled away from the gym, we'd become increasingly restless, tired of traveling, and ready to sleep. Really, for several hours now, considerable fatigue had been working away on us. But rather than a short drive to a hotel, we found ourselves back in the countryside. Right about when we saw the Chinese oxen again, the rumblings began anew. Finally, after about twenty minutes, a guy named Barton yelled from the back of the bus, "Where the fuck are we going? ... This is bullshit!"

Someone else shouted, "What the fuck is going on? We aren't getting paid enough for this shit." Really, we weren't getting paid at all. Minutes later, with no city in sight and the ride seemingly endless, I shouted, only half-jokingly, "Mr. Weng, you torture us."

"Why don't you tell us something—shit, man, tell us anything. You never tell us shit," a player named Jordan hollered from the back.

But between Anil, Dales, and Weng, nobody said anything. This prompted another player in the back of the bus to use a Chris Tucker-type voice as he frantically declared, "I can't take this shit no more, man!"

We nearly fell out with that one.

All the while, the bus driver continued to swerve about and honk his stupid freaking horn every time he came up behind another vehicle.

It was getting insanely comical. You could only laugh. No one was eating anymore, our stomachs were ravaged, and exhaustion reigned. Mutiny loomed.

Then we made it to our resort hotel.

It was going to take a lot for Mr. Weng to bring us back from the brink, but he delivered. As we stepped off the bus at the mountainside resort, women wearing red silk dresses were waiting for us with bouquets of flowers.

Each of us received keys to our own hotel room and when we got to the elevator, a woman in a silk dress was there to press the elevator button for us. When the elevator doors opened on the fourth floor, two women appeared to escort us to our rooms.

The newly constructed rooms had actual toilets, separate showers, toilet paper, and dapper linens. On the televisions we soon discovered that we could even tune into the overtime session of Game Five of the NBA Finals, between the Heat and the Mavericks. And we saw out our windows a massive water slide and pools throughout the grounds.

It was all splendid except that, somehow, Dales ended up meandering into my room as I watched the Finals with Riggs. Dales told us how much he liked James Posey's versatility but he didn't like Avery Johnson because he figured he went behind Don Nelson's back to get the Mavericks' head coaching job. "Who wants to be a consultant, when you could be the head man?" he said of the raw deal he thought Nelson received. Dales also kept laughing at Jason Williams's defense on the pick-and-roll and asked over and over again, "Why is Gary Payton playing? What is he doing?"

We only had an hour or two before departing for our own game, but we were coming back to the resort after it, which fired us up, as did the anxious crowd in Nanching. As we got ready for the game in our locker room, throngs of fans flocked to the windows just to get glimpses of us. Through the bars of an open window, excited kids reached their hands in to give us five. We had to go into little windowless side rooms in the locker room area so we could change in privacy.

Places other than Nanching also made it clear that the Chinese love their hoops. We'd drive by a park and it'd be filled with hoopers or I'd step out of my hotel—a hotel that lacked an internet connection or the ability to make calls to America—and find myself in a working-class, dusty, and cash-strapped city, only to be shocked to find And-One mix tapes at a slipshod video store across the street. Or consider the scene during halftime of one of our games, when street-ballers were pulled from the crowd and asked to perform funky dribble moves. The fans dug this, and in watching the street-ballers I got the impression that they'd watched the mix tapes I'd seen for sale, that American ball players had spoken to them just like Sherman Douglas had spoken to me, that they wanted to express themselves, just like they'd seen us express ourselves.

As re-charged as we were by the resort and the fans, the Nanching gym nearly drained us because of its stifling heat. It was so hot that by the second quarter little water circles from condensation started to form on the floor. As the game progressed, the floor became wetter and wetter until, by the third quarter, it looked like we were carrying out an ice skating exhibition as much as a basketball game. Several players hit the deck trying to cut or simply jump straight up. It got so ridiculous that some of the players asked Dales to call the game. He responded by saying, "We finish the game."

Throughout much of the contest, he would look down the bench and say, "Two weeks of bullshit for four hours in Shanghai."

Eager Chinese fans looking in on the American hoopers as they prepare for the upcoming game. You might notice I look a little weathered, a bit like the basketball on Underbelly's cover.

Within hours, all was good again. We were back at the resort, getting directed to a staggering array of natural hot springs. Women patiently stood by until you were finished soaking, ready to provide you with fresh, plush-white towels. The ratio at the place seemed like two workers for every one guest.

One hot tub we lounged in featured thousands of Chinese kissing fish that naturally exfoliated our skin. The fish would start around the toes and ankles and work their way up your leg, ever so lightly kissing your skin as they sloughed off the outermost epidermal layer. After that it was on to a hot spring with a large, outdoor flat screen hanging above, on which we could watch the World Cup.

When we'd had our fill of the hot springs, a group of us players walked back to the locker room. There male attendants furnished us with yellow silk robes and silk shorts. Comfortable in our robes, we headed upstairs to relax in the lounge, which had about fifty La-Z-Boy-type chairs lined up in rows of ten or so, facing big-screen televisions. When we settled into the chairs, female attendants brought out pillows for us.

As we lounged and watched World Cup action on the big-screens, we didn't care that none of the World Cup players probably scored a goal and a bunch of stretchers were probably brought out after players flopped on the ground writhing in pain as if a sniper had just shot them in the leg. Women were serving us free fruit and beverages, and for about thirty-five Yuan, or $4, you could get a forty-minute foot massage. It was so buckets that the near-mutiny earlier in the day seemed like old news already.

We had to get up in a few hours to get on the road for another game, but that didn't matter either. We sat there relaxed, shooting the breeze, figuring that back at home people wouldn't believe us if we told them. But it's true. It was in Nanching, when we were kings.

In Nanching, they treated us like kings.

54

One of our last games took place in another brand new gym; in fact it was the first game ever played there, and in front of a packed house no less. My team won the affair on a late three-pointer, giving the teams I was on during the trip a 4-4 record (the two rosters were changed around throughout the week). In the third quarter we'd lost the lead, and Dales had started making a bunch of noise. After telling him I didn't want to hear it, he threw a towel at me, so I called him a bitch.

Maybe Barton, one of those guys that played fiercely, was right. After getting all riled up and barking at guys during one game earlier in the trip, he thought maybe he needed to cool it a bit. "This really doesn't matter, at all. No paper is gonna write about this. Nobody's gonna remember this," he said. But he really only had one gear.

When the buzzer sounded on this game, Dales nodded and said the equivalent of "good win," and we gave each other five. No matter how many people remembered this game, or what we thought of each other, right then we both felt good about competing hard and winning.

Yet times had changed. I knew it was time to move on. It had taken a lot to work my high-level playing days out of me, the CBA and then some—the full underbelly and more. I'd had a good run, but I needed to get back to my family. We were goin' on a bear hunt; we were gonna catch the big one. It was going to be a beautiful day. The type of day, I'd learned, that—hoops or no hoops—actually made you feel like a man.

Not that fatherhood's all Central Park strolls. In fact, I suppose it's a bit like hoops, but with the potential for even more. It takes effort and discipline and yet you've got to be creative and free with it, so your kids can stretch out and you can too. Some days can be tougher than others, but if you're lucky, on your tougher days, your partner will give you as many timeouts as you get in a CBA game. No matter what, it can be whole and harmonious and radiant.

Sometimes while chasing dreams, whether you've completely caught 'em or not, new ones emerge that are bigger and fuller. When you're eight-years-old, you don't dream much about being a provider, no matter what your job is. When you're twelve, you don't think much about what you need to do to help your future children grow into ethical adults, ones who can empathize with others and apply themselves and manage their emotions. And when you're fifteen, you don't spend much time hoping you can be as good a partner to your future wife as she is to you. That's not flashy.

And when you're in college, you don't really know how powerful it can be to be there for a night like the one I had a couple of years after the China trip, when my daughter, Caroline, was feeling anxious as she lay in bed trying to fall asleep. She was only three, and, having heard her crying a bit, I'd come in to check on her. Upon asking her what was wrong, she asked me, "Dad, what happens when you die?"

Having children can give you a sense of how vulnerable we all are, of how short life is, and of what's really important. But I didn't know that something like this could be weighing on *her* mind already.

Trying to put her at ease, I told her how much her mom and I cared about her, but I could see her thinking about matters and I could sense the nervousness in her voice when she said, "Daddy, I don't want to die."

At that, I hugged her tight and tried to let her know that it'll be alright, that she'll always be loved, that she'll always have people there for her, helping her when she falls and cheering for her when she rises. And that we all live on after death. I tried to let her know, as best I could, that love is not a word but an enduring reality, and that no matter where she is she can always find it at home.

Before I returned home from China, something kind of magical happened in the city of Sihang. With humidity blanketing the air and the temperature surpassing 100 degrees, I decided to take advantage of a few hours in the afternoon by walking around the city and hunting up an internet café. The internet cafes we'd seen to that point were usually crammed with over a hundred computers, all lined up in neat rows and teeming with young Chinese people, most of whom would play video games for about two yuan an hour, or about twenty-five paltry American cents.

Walking out on Sihang's streets, I noticed that it was grittier and dirtier and less developed than most any of the other cities we'd visited.

Before long I was overheating and coming up empty in my search, when I spotted a Chinese student who looked about college age walking around with some buddies. I asked him for directions to an internet café. He spoke English pretty well and he and his pals agreed to walk me over to one they knew of. But when we got there, it was full. So we went to another. It was packed too.

On the way to the second one, we had passed by my new buddy's school. It had a full-length basketball court in a courtyard beneath its four-story-tall main building, which housed students as well as classrooms. My guide said he lived at the school and studied physics there.

He's studying science and math. We're throwing a leather ball at a rim.

By then he and his friends knew I played basketball, and they told me how they wanted me to play a game with them in the courtyard. One of them, an avid hoops fan, even ran home to change into his basketball gear. He came back wearing a Mike Bibby jersey. I imagine it crossed my mind to tell the guy that I'd once been runner-up to Mike Bibby for Pac-10 Freshman-of-the-Year, only to figure the heck with it because it'd be hard to explain.

Although the heat was sapping us and the search for an internet café was a bust thus far, my guides didn't seem annoyed, just happy to help. And, as it happened, in walking to a third café, we passed by my guide's school again, and this time we ended up going into the courtyard to shoot some baskets. Students had already begun converging on the court, hoping to play with us, while other students started to line up on the balconies overlooking it, wondering about the American who had just wandered in.

We started shooting baskets at one end of the court, while on the other end a stern-looking man in a military uniform was leading a group of students, clad in military garb as well, in drill exercises. As he shouted out directions I snuck up behind him and gave him bunny ears. The young drillers could see me do it but their instructor could not, and they smiled while still trying to keep their step. The students who were looking down from the balcony got a kick out of it too.

When the students finished drilling, they came over to watch us play. One of them even took off his camouflage military shirt and joined the action.

It was a somewhat chaotic, ad-lib style of ball. Guys crashed in for rebounds, tossed around wild passes, and chucked up shots. The skills needed work, but the passion was there. And even though the heat continued its relentless assault, we kept on playing, free and easy.

The student spectators standing alongside the court, those looking over the balconies, and the young military drillers sitting on the sideline all enjoyed watching. If someone hit a deep one, they'd cheer, if someone made a fancy move, they'd ooh and ahh.

Oh, we danced on that court that afternoon, unencumbered by things, like the race to get ahead, or politics, or how short life seems the older you get. We might not have known each other, but we were speaking to each other as if we did. We were playing ball.

It made you feel connected, and it made you think of people like Paul Rossetti. Oh, my, if Paul could've dunked for them. They'd have erupted. It also made me think of Paul's mother, and the letter she wrote me when I was at Purdue. Her only son had been dead for almost a decade by then, but you could tell the pain of losing him hadn't left her for a second. Still, she said she'd written because she wanted to thank me for helping to keep her son's spirit alive through basketball.

We all face hard times. Some people, like Paul's family, face really hard times. There's no easy answer. It's just hard, and it can strike fear in your heart.

And we live in an age in which we're told spooky things, like the universe is expanding rapidly, and yet at some point it might start contracting in on us. That the sun could implode and we could be smashed into each other, millions upon millions fused into one, only to surge forward again with spectacular force, in individual and yet interconnected parts.

But scientists don't have all the answers. Mystery remains. Science can't tell us why music stirs the soul, and it can't tell us why we feel a natural desire to dance to the beat. Einstein recognized this, and yet for him science offered a quixotic way to get close to life's mysteries, to brush up against the whiskers of God. Some guys, like me and Marshall Phillips and Paul Rossetti and Gary McQuay, haven't had the smarts to use science to do that. But, just like these students in China, we've found a way to do that with basketball.

We all search for a grand theory to unify things. Scientists tell us nowadays that perhaps the answer lies with string theory, which says that there is quantum symmetry—a string—connecting all things. It's hard stuff to wrap your head around, and it hasn't explained everything. But when you're playing ball in Ogden Dunes, Indiana, with your dad and your brother and your buddies, or you're in Rockford, Illinois, playing with your teammates and the flow gets good and you all get to moving in unison and it feels like you've actually got the ball on a string, you can sense interconnectedness. And when you're in China, playing hoops with a bunch of strangers, you can feel this too. Just like I can feel it when I think back to my Boilermaker days, when I threw an alley-oop to Gary McQuay in Madison Square Garden, when he was healthy and spry, the epitome of possibility. And I can feel it when I envision Paul Rossetti going up for a dunk, rising through the air with powerful grace, ceaselessly into the future.

When me and my new Chinese friends finally finished, I went down to the other end of the court, where the rim seemed an inch or two short, just short enough to make me think about dunking. As I lined things up, the spectators nudged each other, taking notice. I charged at the rim, elevated, and threw it home.

Ogden Dunes' annual Paul Rossetti Basketball Classic. Notice the Bishop Noll high school jersey, Rossetti's forty-three, hanging from the bucket.

WHERE THE CHARACTERS FROM
UNDERBELLY HOOPS HAVE ENDED UP...

Keith Closs: Attends AA meetings regularly. As noted, each year since 2007 marks another year of sobriety. Married and living in southern California, the Boss recently played in the little-known West Coast Basketball League, and with his life back on track hopes to play in China or Australia in the coming years. He recently told *Sports Illustrated's* Jon Wertheim, "I was sloshing my way through life in a drunken stupor, I got my ass kicked and I was lucky enough to see what I was doing to myself before it was too late. I look at it that way and life is good, man."

Marshall Phillips: Hung up the sneakers for good in 2009. He lives in Atlanta with his wife and daughters. He runs Atlanta Technical Support, a computer repair, networking, and sales business. Phillips first met his father after a CBA game in Grand Rapids. He also learned that day that he had more than a dozen half-brothers and sisters. He knew all too well that there were too many CBA players without Dads, and he recognized that there were too many CBA players who had kids but weren't being Dads. He's doing his part to break that cycle.

Ronnie "Rockford" Fields: Fields last played for Dales in the CBA in Minot, South Dakota, where he and Dales, in 2008, were CBA runner-ups yet again. Continuing the life of a basketball nomad, in 2011 he played in the Dominican Republic and Puerto Rico. In a recent interview, he said being spiritual plays a bigger role in his life now. And in 2009 Fields told *Sports Illustrated*, "People can't say 'This kid dropped out and hung on the street corner and gave up on life.' I pushed through the situation. I owned up to the things I did and became a better person, player, and father—those things are more important to me than playing professional basketball."

Brant "the Baffler Bailey": For the 2009-10 season, Bailey played basketball for the Dusseldorf Giants of the German Bundesliga. The team spent big on advertising. It even had a salad dressing named after the Baffler. But in 2010 the financially-strapped squad folded. Despite being several years past thirty, the Baffler hasn't yet retired. He played in Finland during the 2011-12 season.

Teddy Dupay: Teddy stopped playing professional basketball in 2005. He lives in the Tampa, FL, area, where he works for an investment fund. In 2009, facing three first-degree felony charges for an attack on his then girlfriend, Dupay pled guilty to a lesser-degree felony count of aggravated assault, as well as to misdemeanor counts of threat against life or property and intoxication. He was sentenced to 30 days in jail, three years' probation, $800 in fines, 100 hours of community service and ordered to undergo domestic violence and anger-management counseling. In 2010, Teddy said he and the woman involved were still in love, but her voice mails and text messages to him went unanswered because of a restraining order.

Inspired by a poll that came out after Barack Obama's presidential victory, which suggested that a lot of Americans were more concerned with legalizing marijuana than the economy or the war in Afghanistan, Dupay started S'Boalnation, a subscription-based website intended to promote the legalization of pot. Some called it a scam. The site does not seem operational any longer. In late 2011, Dupay was a spokesperson and salesman for a health company that says it sells a batch of health products that can change your life.

About his still-standing Florida high school total points record, Dupay recently told the *Huffington Post*, "It'll never be broken . . . unless they add a 5-point line."

Brian Lubeck: After playing professional ball all over the world for eight years, Lubeck retired in 2010. He's engaged and working in real estate in Kentucky.

Jamario Moon: In 2008, Moon was named to the NBA's second-team All-Rookie squad. He participated in the NBA's All-Star Weekend Slam Dunk Contest that year, finishing third. He signed a three-year $8.92 million contract in 2009, and last played for the L.A. Clippers.

Chris "Dales" Daleo: Daleo last coached in the CBA in 2008, when he and Fields lost in the championship again. He lives in the Rockord, IL area with his family, where he is the director of operations for the Rockford RiverHawks minor league baseball team.

Dave Joerger (Dales's nemesis): Joerger was recently a finalist for the Houston Rockets head coaching job. He is the head assistant coach for the NBA's Memphis Grizzlies.

Carson Cunningham: Lives in his hometown with his wife and three kids, teaches history at DePaul University and coaches high school basketball where it's played best, in the state Indiana.

REFERENCES & NOTES

1 *Rockford Register Star*, 16 March 2006.

2 Kevin Conley, "Have I Got A League For You! New CBA owner Isiah Thomas is selling a high-scoring, high-quality brand of minor league hoops, but is NBA commissioner David Stern buying?" *Sports Illustrated* 7 February 2000 [on-line] http://www.sportsillustrated.cnn.com/vault/article/magazine/MAG1141 542/index.htm: accessed 12 December 2011.

3 *Rocky Mountain News*, 19 September 1999.

4 Christian Red and T.J. Quinn Daily, "Menace Behind the Smile. CBA Owners: Isiah nasty, incompetent behind closed doors," 5 February 2006 [on-line] http://www.nydailynews.com/archives/sports/2006/02/05/2006-02-05_menace_behind_the_smile__cba.html: accessed 26 January 2011.

5 "Investors Acquire Rights to Continental Basketball Association, Will Relaunch League in Familiar Cities and New Markets in 2001," *Business Wire*; 9 August 2001, accessed 6 July 2005, http://www.highbeam.com/library/docfree.asp?DOCID=1G1:7707773 7&num=76&ctrlInfo=Round13%3AProd%3ASR%3AResult&ao=&Fre ePremium=BOTH

6 Creatine is an organic acid that helps provide energy to muscles. It's taken to help with strength-building.

7 Mike Eisenbath, "Florida Gunner Shoots Down Records," 13 December 1997, *St. Louis Post-Dispatch*, pg. 16)

8 John Gustafson, "ESPN the Magazine: The Exile," 1 April 2002, ESPNMAG.com [on-line] http://espn.go.com/magazine/vol5no07dupay.html: accessed 15 July 2006.

9 David Dorsey, "DuPay[is "Dupay" in main text--confirm cap "P" here?] Signs Deal With Rockford," Most Valuable Network [on-line] http://independent.mostvaluablenetwork.com/2004/11/05/: accessed 7 July 2006.Story originally published by news-press.com on 28 October 2004.

10 Quoted in Michael Mandelbaum, "The Meaning of Sports: Why Americans Watch Baseball, Football, and Basketball and What They See When They Do" (New York: Public Affairs, 2004), 248.

11 Documentary, *Hardwood Dreams*, *Volume I.*

12 Stais Boseman, *Hardwood Dreams, Volume II.*

13 Jim Boylen and Stais Boseman, *Hardwood Dreams Volume II.*

14 Stais Boseman, *Hardwood Dreams Volume II.*

15 Knight-Ridder, *Tribune News Service*, 7 June 1997.

16 *Minnesota Star-Tribune*, 13 November 1997.

17 Ibid.

18 [on-line] http://www.msnbc.msn.com/id/6257773/: accessed 23 October 2004.

19 Quoted in John Simmons, "Improbable Dreams," *U.S. News & World Report*, 24 March 1997.

20 Ibid.

21 Jim Souhan, "Article Title," *Minneapolis Star Tribune*, 13 November 1997.

22 "Article title," *Chicago Sun-Times*, 1 July 1994.

23 Interview with Ronnie Fields, conducted by author, 5 December 2004.

24 *The Record*, 3 March 1996.

25 *Chicago Sun-Times*, 3 March 1996.

26 Quoted in the *St. Louis Post-Dispatch*, 20 October 1996, story originally written by Bonnie DeSimmone of the *Chicago Tribune*.

27 *Star Tribune*, 13 November 1997.

28 Interview with Ronnie Fields, conducted by author, 5 December 2004.

29 *Star Tribune*, 13 November 1997, Jim Souhan.

30 Ibid.

31 16 January 2005, interview with Trainer Brad by author.

32 *USA Today*, 16 July 2002.

33 "Dupay Gambling Charges Illuminated,"17 July 2002, StaffGatorBait.net, http://www.rivals.com/content.asp?cid=111714.

34 *USA Today*, 16 July 2002.

35 Ibid.

36 "Dupay Gambling Charges Illuminated,"17 July 2002, StaffGatorBait.net, http://www.rivals.com/content.asp?cid=111714

37 *National Post*, 30 October 2007.

38 *The Post-Tribune*, 11 July 2007. Doug Smith, "Hoops Hobo Moon Gets His NBA Shot," TheStar.com, 15 September 2007 [online] http://www.thestar.com/Sports/article/256918: accessed 7 December 2007.

39 Ibid.

40 Paul Jay, "Shoot the J From Nowhere," *CBCNews*, 26 November 2007 [online] http://www.cbc.ca/sports/nba/jay/2007/11/from_out_of_nowhere.html: accessed 7 December 2007.

41 "Butler's Service Pleases Knicks Coach," *Star Tribune*, 11 December 2005.

42 "2004 Draft," SI.com [on-line] http://sportsillustrated.cnn.com/basketball/nba/2004/draft/players/18953.html

43 *Star Tribune*, "Butler Determined, Despite His Regrets; Wolf wishes he had chosen college," Kent Younblood, 9 October 2004.

44 *The Columbian*, 25 July 1997.

45 Charley Rosen, "True Tales From the Camp Fires," ESPN.com [on-line] http://espn.go.com/page2/s/rosen/021009.html: 14 December 2007.

46 *Daily News*, 7 October 1997.

47 Ibid., 1 November 1997.

48 Ibid., 8 January 1998.

49 Ibid., 12 October 1999.

50 *Orange County Register*, 20 January 2000.

51 *Daily News*, 25 January 2000.

52 Ibid., 6 February 2000.

53 ESPN somehow acquired videotape of the brawl, but the network could not conclusively confirm that the tall, light-skinned, skinny guy getting pummeled was in fact Keith Closs. What most could agree upon was the brawl's outcome. As *Daily News* writer Randy Hill put it, Closs "was not exactly declared the fight's victor." Ibid., 19 April 2000.

54 "Outtakes: Steve Francis (uncut)," Dan Patrick Outtakes [on-line] http://espn.go.com/talent/danpatrick/s/ 2001/0417/1174369.html: accessed 7 July 2006.

55 *Daily News,* 15 December 2000.

56 Mark Twain, *Adventures of Huckleberry Finn* (New York: Pocket Books, 2004), 173.

57 Section based on author's phone interview with Marshall Phillips, Summer 2011.

58 "Clippers Beat SuperSonics 103-92," 13 January 2005, *AP Online* [on-line] http://www.highbeam.com/doc/1G1-126975374.html: accessed 5 March 2008. "Clippers Sign Darrick Martin for 10 Days," 5 January 2005, *AP Online* [on-line] http://www.highbeam.com/doc/1P1-103994260.html: accessed 5 March 2008.

59 *Rockford Register Star*, 8 April 2002. Ibid., 22 January 2004.

60 Mark Urban, "NBA: Suns to sign Huffman Petoskey grad to get his shot in the NBA," *Traverse City Record Eagle*, 23 September 2003.

61 Ken Palmer, *The Flint Journal First Edition*, "Slam Dunk or Slammer? CBA Player Ends Up at Cop Shop," 31 December 2004. Palmer got part of the story wrong. He claimed that Lightning players had left Closs at the police station.

62 *Seattle Post-Intelligencer,* 20 March 2002.

63 Ibid.

64 *The Record*, 16 January 2005.

65 Emil R. Salvini, *Hobey Baker: American Legend* (Princeton: The Hobey Baker Foundation, 2005), 49.

66 Glenn Hibdon, "The Long Road Back," *Tulsa World*, 12 February 2008 [on-line] http://www.tulsaworld.com/sportsextra/article.aspx?articleID=2008021 2_2_B1_ONWor42741: accessed 7 July 2011.

67 Charlie Kaufman and Donald Kaufman, adopted from the book *The Orchid Thief*, by Susan Orlean, Adaptation, [on-line] http://www.beingcharliekaufman.com/adaptation.pdf: accessed fifteen July 2006.

68 Tracy S. Graven, "Player News & Movement - Tuesday, February 1st ," *HoopsWorld* [on-line] http://www.hoopsworld.com/cgi-bin/news/exec/view.cgi?archive=42&num=11404&printer=1: accessed 16 July 2006.

VIDEOS

Online video clips of *Underbelly* characters:

Ronnie Fields
http://www.youtube.com/watch?v=g_gNNVZc4w4&feature=fvsr

Keith Closs
http://www.youtube.com/watch?v=lbsVZ59_ET4

Stais Boseman
http://www.myspace.com/video/vid/8444793

Digger Phelps
http://www.youtube.com/watch?v=WcM7kScI0-g

Carson Cunningham
http://www.youtube.com/watch?v=FwVzLCchxwE

ABOUT THE AUTHOR

Hailing from basketball's epicenter, the great state of Indiana, Carson Cunningham memorized Georgetown's starting five in Kindergarten. Over the next twelve years or so, he played all the time with his buddies, stopping occasionally--oftentimes only because his parents forced him to--to read the books and magazines and newspapers laying around his house. Before he knew it, he'd become an all-state player in Indiana, a runner-up for PAC-10 Freshman of the Year honors, and then, after transferring to Purdue, a two-time Academic All-American. From there, came a journey into basketball's professional underbelly, which consisted of all or parts of three seasons in the CBA and stints playing in Australia and Estonia.

Cunningham is the author of American Hoops: U.S. Men's Olympic Basketball from Berlin to Beijing, which offers a dynamic portrait of the global age through basketball, and of Before the Curse: The Chicago Cubs' Glory Years, 1870-1945. In 2006, he earned a Ph.D. in history from Purdue University, and is on track to complete an MBA in DePaul University's Kellstadt Graduate School of Business. He teaches history at DePaul and lives and coaches where basketball thrives: Indiana. His wife Christy and his three children are his seashells and balloons.

Made in the USA
San Bernardino, CA
01 February 2013